Just a Phrase I'm Going Through

'David Crystal loves and appreciates every word he speaks, and every word written in this book helps us to understand someone who is not just a great linguist, but a true champion and lover of language.'

Benjamin Zephaniah

'David Crystal's writings on linguistics never fail to be readable and full of fascination for the general reader. I enjoyed this very much: it is a clear and modest account of a good and useful life.'

Philip Pullman

Kidnapping, attempted assassination, espionage . . . not the answers you'd expect to the question 'what happens when you become a linguist?'

But now, reflecting on a long and hugely successful career at the forefront of the field of English language and linguistics, David Crystal answers this question and offers us a special look behind the scenes at the adventures, rewards, challenges and pitfalls of his life in language.

Both an autobiography and a highly accessible introduction to the field of linguistics, *Just a Phrase I'm Going Through* illuminates and entertains us with its many insights into the ever-fascinating subject of language.

David Crystal is synonymous with language, both as a great populariser and linguistic pioneer, and his contribution to the field is unparalleled. This is a book not just for students and teachers but for all lovers of language.

David Crystal received an OBE for services to the English language in 1995, and was made a Fellow of the British Academy (FBA) in 2000. He is Patron of the International Association of Teachers of English as a Foreign Language (IATEFL) and the Association for Language Learning (ALL). Having published over 100 books, covering a diversity of language topics, his most recent publications include *Txtng: The Gr8 Db8* (2008) and *Think on my Words: Exploring Shakespeare's Language* (2008). He has been a freelance writer, lecturer and broadcaster since 1984 and continues his work with language from his home in Holyhead, North Wales.

'David Crystal, the UK's Linguist-at-Large, starts his autobiography *Just a Phrase I'm Going Through* right off in Chapter 1 by summing up what it means to be a linguist. He does such a good job that every linguist in the world will go yessing through this chapter, and copy it on the sly to pass out to their students who ask what linguistics is really all about.'

John Lawler, *University of Michigan, Ann Arbor, USA*

'Crystal's story-telling and wit skills continuously reveal the magic of encountering and investigating the ever-new kaleidoscope of language.'

Paola Vettorel, *University of Verona, Italy*

'Academic researcher, editor, broadcaster, lecturer, consultant, and now language autobiographer, David Crystal is simply a unique phenomenon who is constantly breaking new ground. The book is a delight to read. It's beautifully written, witty, entertaining and profoundly reflective on matters of language and life. If anyone needs persuading how and why language is central to our lives and can be both serious and fun, it is here.'

Ronald Carter, *University of Nottingham, UK*

'David Crystal has a magic narrative touch. In this captivating professional autobiography he intertwines linguistic insights with his own personal and professional story, demonstrating what he has always told us so eloquently: that neither life nor language can be understood without the other.'

Guy Cook, *The Open University, UK*

'An engaging, can't-put-it-down hybrid of autobiography, suspense, humour, scientific writing, narrative, and even a bit of trivia. As an introductory linguistics text or leisure reading selection, it addresses the kinds of language-based questions that emerge literally everywhere and that pique the curiosity of linguists and non-linguists alike – transmitted to us through the wonderful wit, style, and personal perspective of David Crystal.'

Susan Strauss, *Pennsylvania State University, USA*

Just a Phrase I'm Going Through

My Life in Language

David Crystal

LONDON AND NEW YORK

First published 2009 by Routledge
2 Park Square, Milton Park, Abingdon, Oxon OX14 4RN

Simultaneously published in the USA and Canada
by Routledge
270 Madison Ave, New York, NY 10016

Routledge is an imprint of the Taylor & Francis Group, an informa business

Typeset in Joanna and Scala Sans by
RefineCatch Limited, Bungay, Suffolk
Printed and bound in Great Britain by
MPG Books Group, UK

British Library Cataloguing in Publication Data
A catalogue record for this book is available from the British Library

Library of Congress Cataloging-in-Publication Data
Crystal, David, 1941–
Just a phrase I'm going through : my life in language / David Crystal.
p. cm.
Includes index.
1. Crystal, David, 1941– 2. Linguists—Great Britain—Biography. 3. Linguistics—Great Britain—History—20th century. 4. Scholars— Great Britain—Biography. 5. Lexicographers—Great Britain— Biography. I. Title. II. Title: My life in language.
P85.C79C79 2009
410.92—dc22
[B]
2008047318

ISBN 10: 0–415–48575–4 (hbk)
ISBN 10: 0–415–48574–6 (pbk)
ISBN 10: 0–203–87849–3 (ebk)

ISBN 13: 978–0–415–48575–3 (hbk)
ISBN 13: 978–0–415–48574–6 (pbk)
ISBN 13: 978–0–203–87849–1 (ebk)

Contents

List of illustrations

Note: all illustrations appear in a colour plate section between pp. 148 and 149.

List of panels

Prologue

The invitation seemed harmless enough, and not so different from dozens which had arrived before it. It was early 1981. I received a phone call from Sister Marie de Montfort, the head of the speech therapy course at Trinity College, Dublin. Would I be willing to come over and give a public lecture on the subject of language handicap? They were in the early stages of developing their new degree course, so they were, and they'd been thinking it might be good to put on some talks of general interest, indeed, and as I'd written a few books about the subject, well, sure, it might bring in some of the public, as well as the students, which wouldn't be bad . . . and apart from anything else, it was ages since we'd last met, and wouldn't it be a chance to see how the new course was getting on, well now, wouldn't it? Would I think about it, at least?

A visit to Dublin is always a treat. I am half Irish myself. And it was true that I hadn't seen Sister Marie for several years. She'd been part of a postgraduate group I'd helped to teach just after I joined the linguistics department at Reading University. The liveliest nun I'd ever had the good fortune to meet. Twinkling eyes, great presence, a lovely sense of humour. I'd got to know her quite well, through shared professional and religious interests, and she was the best of company. I'd once carried out some external examining for her department, and rediscovered Dublin in the process. Then, as is often the way, there'd been a lull, and several years had passed. It would be a real pleasure to see her – and Trinity – again. I thought about it, seeing as she'd asked, for two seconds, and fixed the date and place on the spot.

Time passed. Hilary (my wife) and I made travel plans. More time passed. We were sent the details of the venue. Then, on 25 March, just a week before, we opened the daily newspaper. 'Lecturer shot at Dublin university,' said the headline. At Trinity College. Giving a public lecture. In the arts building. In a lecture room. In the same lecture room that I was scheduled to talk in exactly one week later.

Could it have been the IRA? The Northern Ireland troubles had been building up, since the early 1970s, and southern Ireland was feeling some of the effects. The lecturer who had been attacked was a businessman, and not known for his political views. He hadn't been killed, but was seriously wounded in the legs. Nobody knew if this was a one-off incident, or the start of a new campaign, or something completely unrelated. Hilary and I looked at each other. Of course it was a new campaign. And wouldn't they be just looking out for another easy target? A fresh, pink lecturer from a British university? My talk had been given plenty of advance publicity. They knew I was coming. The marksman was probably already chosen. We could see the headlines. We could hear the screams. We——

pulled ourselves together, and decided to get some advice. When I got to work the next day I rang up the Vice-Chancellor. The VC's secretary said he wasn't in yet, but she could give him a message. I explained the problem. She didn't seem at all concerned. A routine lecturing risk, she probably thought, remembering the student riots of '68. I waited a couple of hours, then tried again. There must have been something in my voice – the total lack of quiver, perhaps – which impressed her. She put me straight through.

I described the situation, and – to be fair – the VC was impressed. He had read the newspaper report, and, no, he hadn't realized I was going there next week. He didn't think there was any likelihood of the same thing happening again, but still, academic joke, he didn't want to lose a lecturer (this was a few years before the era of university cuts, you appreciate, when such remarks would no longer be funny), so he would phone his opposite number in Dublin. Half an hour later, he called me back. His tone was too jocular to be totally convincing. I could sense a 'but' in the offing. He had discussed the matter with the people at Trinity, and they felt there was no reason whatsoever for the visit not to take place. (Too many negatives in that sentence, I thought, but they did at least seem to be cancelling each other out.) They were very much looking forward to it. All should be well. No, all *would* be well. But – ah, there it was – to be on the safe side, they would make some special security arrangements. The Irish Special Branch would be informed.

'You're not going to Dublin, are you?' asked my mother. 'Not after that shooting?' And that was the way the week went. The news travelled at speed around the university. Everyone seemed to be concerned. Departmental colleagues asked me whether I was sure about this. Lecturers I hardly knew stopped me in corridors and commiserated – almost as if I'd been shot already. A student asked if I'd marked his essay yet. We appreciated the concern, but it didn't do much for our frame of mind. Fortunately the children weren't old enough to be aware of current affairs, so we had no problems there.

We spent the week rationalizing. We were committed. We couldn't back out now. It wouldn't be professional. A large audience was expected. The IRA wouldn't be so stupid. They'd know there would be extra security. Besides, my mother's family came from County Wexford. *And* I was born in Lisburn, in the north. *And* I was Catholic. *And* we were going to be looked after by a nun.

That clinched it.

We flew out from Heathrow, and arrived at Trinity in time for lunch. Wonderful place, Trinity. An academic oasis in the very centre of Dublin. The glorious Book of Kells nearby, to keep you humble. Guinness, to restore your pride. Slightly fortified, we walked over to the lecture hall with Sister Marie. It was a fine, sunny afternoon. As we approached the foyer of the lecture block, our pace slowed. We looked around for the extra security. There was the normal bustle of students and staff milling around, searching for venues, waiting for things to happen. Nothing special was happening. It seemed to be a perfectly normal day.

There was a porter on duty at the entrance. Sister Marie went up to him, looked about her, stood sideways on to him, and through the corner of her mouth asked him surreptitiously whether he knew anything about the 'special arrangements' for the 'visiting lecturer'. Her head jerked briefly in my direction. She seemed to be thoroughly enjoying her new role as undercover agent. The porter looked at me, then back at Sister. He obviously had no idea what was going on. Then there was one of those marvellous Irish conversations, as Sister seized the initiative.

'There's supposed to be a Special Branch man here. Have you seen anything of him?'

'I have not, Sister. But would he be in uniform, now?'

'Ah sure, not at all, he'd be in plain clothes.'

'Plain clothes, is it? So what would they be like, Sister, would ye say?'

'Sure, they'd be just plain. Like what anybody might be wearing. It's to show he's in the Special Branch, don't you see.'

'Well, I'll keep me eyes open, Sister, and if I sees anyone in plain clothes uniform, I'll tell ye straight.'

We moved on towards the lecture room. You couldn't miss which one it was, because just outside was a small book exhibition, arranged by a publisher who specialized in books on speech pathology, and who'd handled some of my work. The rep was standing at the side, handing out publicity material. We went up, introduced ourselves, and chatted for a moment. He was very sorry that he wouldn't be able to hear the lecture, he said, as he had to stay with the books, in case anyone pinched them. But if things were quiet, he'd try and pop in, every now and then, that's if I didn't mind. Not at all, I said, and followed Sister Marie in.

The room had one of those close-fitting, fire-proof double doors – the sort where one panel rests heavily over the edge of the other, so that if you push the wrong one, nothing happens for a moment, until you push harder. Then it springs open – and closes behind you with a crash. I trapped my thumb in it. A bad sign.

I looked around the room. It was almost full, about a hundred or so, all charming, young, female, smiling speech-therapy students, notebooks at the ready. Then, a double-take. Not all. At the back, opposite the door, a burly figure, balding, male, with no notebook, and very definitely not smiling, or charming. 'Ah,' said Sister Marie happily, when she saw him, 'That'll be the Special Branch.' Good to see him blending into the background, I thought, in his plain clothes. And I got the feeling that everyone *was* glad to see him there, actually, the events of the previous week being an unmentioned commentary throughout the day.

It was time to start. I began the lecture, talking about the relevance of linguistics to speech therapy, and all went well – until about twenty minutes in, when the publisher's rep, bored with nothing to do, and taking advantage of the fact that nobody was around outside except the porter, decided it was safe after all to come in and listen for a bit. He pushed at the door, but misjudged it, and went for the wrong side. When he let it go, there was an explosive bang. Nobody was expecting it. The suppressed anxiety in everyone's mind rushed to the surface. Heads whipped round expecting the worst. Some of the students ducked under their desks. One let out a scream. The Special Branch man went for his gun. I promptly disappeared down behind the lectern.

When I cautiously peered over the top, the poor publisher's rep stood framed in the doorway, highly embarrassed at all the commotion, and obviously trying to work out why somebody in the audience for a lecture on speech therapy should be pointing a gun at him. He spluttered an apology. Everyone eventually regained their composure, laughing a bit self-consciously, and I carried on. But of course, a few minutes later, the rep, wanting to check that all his books were still there outside, decided to leave. He was going to be so quiet, he told me afterwards, nobody would even know he was moving. Only he forgot the door. There was another loud bang. Down went the audience. Twitch went the policeman. Scream went the students. I saw the back of the lectern again.

And I remember thinking, as I went down for the second time: There must be easier ways of earning a living! Then, asking whoever might have been listening in to my thoughts: 'What on earth is going on? How have I ended up here?'

Chapter 1
Being a linguist

How, indeed? How did I get to be a linguist, a linguistics person, a linguistician, a language geek? How does anybody? And what does 'being a linguist' mean, anyway? There's a problem here. The biographical bit will have to wait a chapter. Bear with me, while I go on about my subject for a bit.

It's not as if it's the most obvious label for a way of earning a living, after all. Indeed, it's a succulent irony that the very name of the profession which has come to be known as 'the science of language' is itself ambiguous.

> 'What do you do?'
> 'I'm a linguist.'
> 'Ah. And how many languages do you speak?'
> 'Do you mean really fluently?'
> 'Of course.'
> 'Just one.'
> 'But you said you were a linguist!'

So I am, I am, but not in that sense. I would love to be fluent in many languages. As it happens, I *can* 'get by' in a number, but there's a world of difference between 'getting by' and 'being fluent'. Ordering a gin and tonic, or asking the way, is one thing. Carrying on a proper conversation about the local political scene is very much another. It's the vocabulary that's the killer. Getting a grasp of the basic grammar of a language, and learning to pronounce the sounds accurately, need not take too long. But vocabulary is the Everest of language. Memorizing the tens of thousands of words you need in order to hold your own in long conversations on variegated topics takes time, lots of it, and – unless you happen to have been brought up bilingual – a level of motivation and opportunity which is usually missing in Britain for all but a very lucky or very gifted few. How the multi-tongued record-holders of the past managed it is beyond me. Take the great Harold Williams, who died in 1928. He was a journalist – the foreign editor of *The Times* – said to have spoken fifty-eight languages fluently. He was apparently able to talk to all the delegates attending the League of Nations in their own language. Nobody else came anywhere near him. Fifty-eight languages! I wonder he ever managed to do anything else.

Being a linguist, in my sense of the word, evidently doesn't mean that you've managed to learn lots of foreign languages. But it does mean that you're interested in them. All 6,000 or so of them. All languages that have ever been or ever could be. No, 'interested' is too mild. When you dip your toe into linguistics, you end up being enthralled, captivated, obsessed by languages. Because they are all around you (increasingly so, in an escalatingly multicultural world), their sounds, words, and sentences keep thrusting themselves on to your attention. You are surrounded by an ever-playing linguistic orchestra. You cannot avoid listening, analysing, reflecting, comparing, contrasting, making notes. You delight in the diversity of the very sound of language. The pleasure must compare with that of a botanist in a garden full of the brightest flowers. Or of a bibliophile surrounded by antiquarian bookshops in a heaven like Hay-on-Wye. Except that you don't have to travel so far to enjoy the diversity of language. You just have to walk down the street, or go into a shop. You don't even have to leave home. On television every day there are more accents and dialects than Horatio would ever have dreamed of in his philosophy, and they are all calling out, 'I am interesting. Study me.'

And so you do. If you're a linguist. That's what linguists, in my sense, do. They revel in the variety of local accents and dialects. They are fascinated by the phenomenon of daily language change. They bathe happily in a warm sea of foreign tongues, and the more esoteric the better. They explore the upper orifices of the body to work out their phonetic capabilities. They marvel, along with everyone else, at the self-assuredness of the language-learning child, then try to understand how on earth such ability emerges so quickly, and what has gone wrong when it doesn't. They puzzle over how language must be represented in the brain. They try to work out what all languages have in common, to capture the essential identity within the very notion of 'language'. They speculate about the linguistic past, along with historians and archaeologists, and ruminate – especially after a glass or two – over how languages must have originated. After a third glass, they can develop opinions about what might be going on in the way non-human animals communicate, or even extraterrestrials. They do not lack experience in such matters. Linguists were brought in to advise on the alien speech-forms in *Star Wars*. And arising out of *Star Trek*, there is a grammar and dictionary of Klingon.

There are certain quotations which all linguists use to show that they are literate human beings – most of them from Lewis Carroll. An instance comes to mind now. In *Through the Looking Glass* (Chapter 6), Alice meets one of the most hard-boiled linguists ever, who points out that there are 364 days of the year when people might get un-birthday presents.

> 'Certainly,' said Alice.
>
> 'And only *one* for birthday presents you know. There's glory for you!'
>
> 'I don't know what you mean by "glory",' Alice said.
>
> Humpty Dumpty smiled contemptuously. 'Of course you don't – till I tell you. It means "there's a nice knock-down argument for you!" '
>
> 'But "glory" doesn't mean "a nice knock-down argument",' Alice objected.
>
> 'When *I* use a word,' Humpty Dumpty said, in rather a scornful tone, 'it means just what I choose it to mean – neither more nor less.'
>
> 'The question is,' said Alice, 'whether you *can* make a word mean so many different things.'
>
> 'The question is,' said Humpty Dumpty, 'which is to be master – that's all.'

Master of Words. It sounds like a degree. And Humpty certainly claims to have his MW. As he goes on to say:

> 'They've a temper, some of them – particularly verbs: they're the proudest – adjectives you can do anything with, but not verbs – however, *I* can manage the whole lot of them!'

Managing the whole lot of them. That's linguistics for you. And of course, not forgetting to tell the rest of the world what you discover when you become a word-manager. Because the things you find out are not just fascinating. They are also immensely useful to others.

But more of that later. What became plain to me, very early on in my close encounter with linguistics, is that being a wordmaster alters your behaviour, in the way you deal with words, sounds, and languages. To begin with, you discover you're not scared of them. And you find yourself going out of your way to try things out – enquiring about the time, when you don't really want to know, just to see if your pronunciation is intelligible, or if a sentence construction works. It's an indescribable thrill when you try out something in a new language for the first time, with foreigners who don't know you from Adam (or Eve), and realize that your freshly cooked mix of novel sounds does actually work as a tool of communication! There's also a different kind of thrill, when your interest takes you over and you end up the focus of attention. I went to a phonetics talk once, in which the speaker was discussing whether or not it's possible to make a sound by trilling the epiglottis (that's the flap which covers the windpipe when you're swallowing). Reflecting on the point, I tried it out repeatedly on a London underground station platform. I stopped when it dawned on me that everybody was avoiding eye contact, and nobody was standing near me any more.

You also find yourself asking people questions about the way *they* use language – such as what their name means, or why their house is so called, or where their accent comes from. You don't plan it. The questions just sort of pop out. A woman telephoned me once about a new deal for car insurance, and asked to speak to my wife, who wasn't in. I took the message, and asked who it was from. She said her name was Aniela such-and-such. It came across as 'ann – ye – la'. 'You'll have to spell that,' I said, which she readily did. I'd never heard the name before. I know I should have just said thankyou, and put the phone down. But linguists aren't made that way. 'That's an interesting name,' I remarked, adding – in case she thought it was a new kind of come-on – 'I study names.' Twenty minutes later, we ended the conversation, the car still uninsured, but both of us more knowledgeable.

Why twenty minutes? Five minutes to establish that she didn't know what Aniela meant, though she thought it was from her grandmother's side of the family, and *she* came from Poland, and she hoped one day to visit there, and so on and so on. Another five thumbing through various books on the origin of first names, with her holding on, until, yes, there it is, eventually finding it in Patrick Hanks and Flavia Hodges' excellent *Dictionary of First Names*. Of Polish origin, indeed – the Polish form of Angela, 'occasionally used in the English-speaking world'. I felt honoured: I had now met one of the occasions. But Aniela wanted to know more. What did *Angela* mean? Did it have anything to do with angels? That one I knew. *Angel* goes back to Greek *angelos*, which meant a messenger, I told her. She was delighted. She'd been a messenger in her first job, you see, and she thought this was highly significant. Then she wanted to know what her best friend's name meant, and her boss had an interesting name too . . . As I say, twenty minutes before she remembered there were other things in life than etymology, and that she'd better get on with them. She went back to insurance sales. I went back to – well, etymology, as it happens.

It's often like that. Conversations tend to grow unchecked, when the topic turns to language. I think it's because everyone has an interest in it. Everyone has a name, an accent, a favourite word, a pet linguistic hate. Everyone has a linguistic history, and thus a story to tell. When it comes to language, everyone's equal. Everyone's an expert. And, to be sure, everyone is, having spent much of the first five years of life learning how to talk, and (for those lucky enough to get to school) much of the next five learning how to read. You don't have to have special qualifications or go in for special training in order to sound off about your language or to play a word-game show, like those where you have to fill the blank in a sentence. You don't even have to phone a friend. You just have to use your own linguistic intuition. You want to hate a word? Invent a new one? Fill a blank? Just do it. Go on. 'Spick and ——'? 'They were green with ——'? You already know the answers (if you speak English). The associations are there, deep within your brain. You just need to bring them to the surface, and (if you happen to be on TV at the time) without panicking.

Most people enjoy my interest, when they're on the receiving end of language questions. And I enjoy theirs. A few tell me to mind my own business (which of course, if I take the observation literally, is what I *am* doing anyway). But most end up asking questions in return, and are pleased to learn that there are books or websites which can answer many of them. I sometimes think I should be asking for commission for acting as an unofficial publisher's rep. Mind you, conversations can be dangerous things, if you're a linguist. It's a danger which can affect anyone, but linguists are especially prone. Accommodation is lying in wait to get them.

Now, I appreciate that what I've just said looks like one of those weird sentences linguists sometimes dream up to make a Linguistic Point. (I'll be talking about another one later – Chomsky's 'Colourless green ideas sleep furiously'.) But it does make sense. By 'accommodation' I do not mean the place where you live. This is accommodation in the sense of 'adaptation' – a notion that was discovered by sociolinguists, a species of colourful linguist that formerly flourished well only in the shade, but is now regularly encountered in new cultivars in sunnier and more prominent positions. I think it was one of the great linguistic discoveries of the twentieth century.

Sociolinguists study what happens to language when it is put to use in society. And one of the things they noticed was that, when people talk to each other, something happens to the language they use. Imagine: I meet you, and we start talking. If we hit it off, and we start to enjoy one another's company, then one of the ways in which we unconsciously display this rapport is that our accents start to move towards each other. I begin to sound a bit like you, and you a bit like me. We 'accommodate' to each other. (If we don't hit it off, of course, then the opposite applies. I try to make myself sound as *different* from you as I can, and you from me.) It's not just accents. We start to share words, too, maybe bits of grammar. We even start looking a little like each other, adopting the same sort of facial expression or body posture. But accent is always the most noticeable thing, because it's there in everything we say. Everybody accommodates, to some extent, even if they don't realize they're doing it. It must be part of our evolutionary make-up, a way of showing a group who belongs to it. Some people, though – perhaps those with a good ear for accents, perhaps those with a specially sensitive personality – do it more noticeably than others. That's when it can get dangerous, and linguists are at risk more than most.

Linguists are professional accommodators, phonetic chameleons. My wife tells me that she can always tell who I'm talking to at the other end of the phone – or, at least, which part of the world they're from – by the accent I slip into. I accommodate within a few seconds, and (unless I remember to stop myself) totally. I have long learned to lie with the consequences. That is not a typo. I mean 'lie', not 'live'. I remember meeting a Scot at an arts conference a few years ago. He had a strong Glasgow accent. We were both involved in community arts centres, and in the meeting we both seemed to be in agreement about what needed to be done, if such centres were to survive in a world where successive British governments were rating the arts as a funding priority several levels below what was being allocated for waste disposal. We start to talk. Within seconds, I can sense my vowels turning into Billy Connolly. And I know it's only a matter of time until he asks the jugular question. Sure enough, he begins to stare at me:

'Are you from Glasgow?'

I now face a dilemma. Either I lie and say 'yes', in which case he asks 'Which part?' and I have to say 'I don't know', because I don't know Glasgow well – and then he hits me. Or I say 'no', in which case he asks 'What are you taking the piss out of my accent for, then?' – and *then* he hits me. Actually, I've been lucky, and never been hit. But I often get some funny looks. I did once try to explain the concept of accommodation to a taxi-driver in Sheffield who insisted that I was from Leeds, because he was from there and he 'recognized the accent' – but it took so long and he got so interested that he missed the turning and I missed the train. So I now just say something vague, like 'Oh it's a great place, Edinburgh / Manchester / Birmingham / Melbourne . . .', and hope that this is enough to prompt a conversation about something else, such as the traffic problems.

At other times, you find yourself becoming a catalyst for all kinds of strange linguistic behaviour. You find yourself playing with the words of a language, to see what kind of effects you can create. Some people are amused by the word-play. Others cannot bear its awfulness. But most end up intrigued, and find themselves joining in. For everybody, deep down, is interested in what makes languages tick, and what happens when people tock. 'Catalyst' reminds me of one such occasion which was so punful that it ended up as the opening example in my book *Language Play*. I didn't start it, mind. It wasn't me, Miss. But there we were, Hilary and I, and Kim and Wendy from across the road. They'd not long moved into the house, and their cat, Crumble, and ours, Splash (both now, sadly, ex-cats, RIP), had been seen approaching each other warily outside the house. One of the group (it doesn't matter who, but it wasn't me) described the event as a 'catfrontation'. The level of groan suggested that this was an excellent pun. Too good to be left to die in peace. It was time to stir the pot, to see what came out. 'Near catastrophe, if you ask me,' I said. More groans. And then the gold-dust. Within a minute, there was a 'catalogue' of disasters, I was accused (correctly) of being a 'catalyst', Splash was diagnosed with 'catarrh', remarks were made about 'catechisms', and so it went on, until everyone ran out of 'cat-' words. Later, Ed McLachlan added 'catatonic' when he did a brilliant cartoon for the book to illustrate the occasion. Some people with their heads screwed on write books based on this kind of word-play. Ever seen Peter Gammond and Peter Clayton's *101 Things*? A 'thing' in this context is a created being that looks a bit like an animated potato. 'Things ain't what they used to be' is illustrated on one page, and you see two of these mannikins, elderly and with sticks, having trouble getting around. 'These things are sent to try us' is shown on another, and you see an ugly-looker in the dock, commenting on the arrival of two bewigged beings into the court. There are ninety-nine more like that.

Linguistics, indeed, is what linguists do. But linguists can be as different from each other in their interests and personalities as the proverbial chalk is from cheese. So the subject needs a more judicious definition. 'The study of languages'? That's where it starts. But it doesn't stop there. Before too long we need to drop the -s. For the study of languages leads, inevitably, to the study of language. Language. Roll it round the tongue, and meditate on its meaning. A phenomenon, a behaviour, an ability, a faculty, a social fact. Something (no, 'thing' is wrong) which takes you above and beyond individual languages. Or maybe it should be below and within. It is such an abstract notion that writers try to pin it down with metaphors. And the metaphors are endless. My wife, Hilary, and I collected dozens when compiling *Words on Words*, a book of language quotations. Language has been called an instrument, a tool, an art, a symphony, a game, a city, a social force, a force for humanization. Roland Barthes called it a skin. Anthony Burgess 'a mouthful of air'. For Ralph Waldo Emerson it was both 'fossil poetry' and the 'archives of history'. For Max Müller 'the autobiography of the human mind'. For Martin Heidegger, it was 'the house of being'.

The simplest definition of linguistics that I know is to say that it is 'the science of language'. It sounds dull, put like that, a long way from games and symphonies. But it is dull-sounding only to those who have not experienced the thrill of scientific enquiry – the drama of not knowing. Ignorance is a tension that has to be resolved. If you are scientific in temperament, it isn't a rational matter. You just *have* to know, to find out. Or, at least, you have to push knowledge to its limits, to find out what is findoutable. And that means being disciplined and thorough and systematic and humble and objective and experimental and all the other things that make a good scientist. It is a frame of mind which manifests itself in the smallest enterprises. Science is not just for the million-dollar projects. It colours every enquiry, no matter how tiny. And every enquiry requires the same devotional energy, the same readiness to expend time.

LINGUIST AS DETECTIVE

I was planning the section on personal names for *The Cambridge Encyclopedia of the English Language*, and needed some interesting names. I skimmed through a history book to see what I could find. 'Franklin D. Roosevelt', there was one. The 'D.' stood for 'Delano'. Unusual. 'Harry S. Truman', there was another. And the 'S.' stood for——? The book didn't say. Careless editor, I muttered. I found another reference book. 'S.' again. And after three or four more books, still just 'S.' My linguistic nose started to twitch. Something Was Up. They couldn't all be careless.

The 'S.' saga began. It was time to look for primary sources. Somebody's biography, perhaps? A few clicks of a mouse now, and the question is answered; but in 1992 it meant a trek to the local library and a trawl through a catalogue. Yes, there were several biographies of Harry S. Truman. Now it was reading time.

Nothing in the first book, nor in the second. Then, in Margaret Truman's biography of her father, bingo. I discovered that the 'S.' stood for – well, everything and nothing. She explained how

Truman's grandfathers were called Solomon Young and Shippe Truman, commenting: 'Dad owed the middle initial in his name to both grandparents. To placate their touchy elders, his parents added an S, but studiously refrained from deciding whether it stood for Solomon or Shippe.'

In my book the report of this saga takes up just fifteen lines of a sidebar – a mere fifty words. Was it worth the effort? In all, it took about two full days of searching and reading. But I am as pleased with that result as with any lengthy article that might have taken a couple of days to write, for it has altered my understanding of language, in a small way. If you had asked me before, 'Must an initial in a person's name always stand for a name, and only one name?' I would have said 'Of course', as you would have. But not now. It proved to be an interesting exception. People are always doing unexpected things with language. It's just a question of their being master, that's all.

If you're a professional linguist, you're always on the lookout for unexpected developments, and you have to be prepared to spend time following up leads. Sometimes the leads don't take you anywhere. The 'S.' hunt might have been an awful waste of time, ending up with 'Simon' or 'Stanley' or some other unsurprising appellation. I know dead ends very well. I have a drawerful of them, chronicles of wasted time, which have never appeared in any of my books. But I don't throw them away. Never throw anything away. Today's dead end can be tomorrow's fresh pointer.

I love the sciences, and I love the arts too. It is the best of lives when you can deal in both, and linguistics lets you do just that. I can find myself working in the morning on a topic to do, say, with the anatomy and physiology of the vocal cords, and in the afternoon exploring the stylistic impact of an interesting word order in James Joyce. That's what makes linguistics really interesting for me, the way it cuts across the conventional boundaries. There are so many parallels between the sciences and the arts. Being a scientist is a way of looking at the world, just as being an artist is. Artists have often made use of scientific ways of thinking, in their creating process. And one of the most interesting developments in the twentieth century was the growing awareness that so many scientific discoveries come from the use of insights which are strikingly artistic in character. Peter Medawar even went so far as to call his famous book on the philosophy of science *The Art of the Soluble*. Certainly, being a linguist has brought me into contact with worlds I never dreamed I would enter when I started my degree course in English – acoustics, anatomy, medicine, education, psychology, sociology, anthropology, geography, mathematics, computer science, IT. All part of the professional world that linguists inhabit, as they explore the nature of language.

Language. The very word is like a bell . . . I put it on a mental pedestal and view it from different angles, to try to grasp its totality. All I see is a multiplicity of angles, models, options, possibilities . . . stories. I see it interacting with lives, and with my own life, in a profusion of ways, some predictable, some unnervingly unpredictable. I can feel how central it is to everything people do. 'House of being' is exactly right. But it is mind-numbingly difficult to hold on to this vision, or to communicate it to others in such a way that all its facets are visible. It is at once stable and changing, unified and diverse, personal and social. Once I was asked to give a lecture on linguistics to a group of Fine Arts students at Reading University. It was part of a series where specialists on different subjects would lecture, and afterwards the students would draw or paint what they heard. I have a print of one of the offerings (see plate 2.3). It is a large square of blues and yellows, divided up into sixty-four smaller squares, eight by eight, like a chessboard. When I first saw it, I thought, yes, my point about language having a regular structure has got across. But then I looked more carefully, and began to feel dizzy. The picture seemed to be full of geometrical symmetries, but when I tried to plot them, they faded into randomness. A diagonal series of distinctive squares fails to meet in the middle. Cubes approach each other and intersect, some shaped like an L, some like an X, some like no imaginable letter shape. Double perspectives are everywhere. Look at the picture in one way and you see steps; look at it another way and you see boxes. The picture has no obvious orientation: any side can be the top. Different observers see different things in it, and in showing it to others anyone can make you see what they want you to see. Look at that pattern. A camel, perhaps, or a weasel? Or like a whale. Very like a whale. I had talked a lot about variations and changes and exceptions and deviations and idiosyncrasies in my lecture. The students had caught the key point perfectly. The tension between regularity and irregularity, between convention and deviation. That is what exists at the heart of language.

The story of language, like the story of Dylan Thomas's childhood, has no beginning and no end. A television series was made once called *The Story of English*. But there is no 'story' of English, or of any language. Rather, there are many stories, many perspectives, many points of view. And it is the same with language as a whole. No 'introduction' to linguistics says all there is to say about language, or says it in the way in which it might best be said. Individual linguists can only report their own perspectives, and they are all different. Each one has a personal tale to tell. This is mine.

Chapter 2
A semilingual start

Linguists in my sense, I suspect, are made, not born. I doubt if I'd ever have become one if my curiosity about languages hadn't been roused very early on, by living in a bilingual community. That shouldn't be surprising. If we are all born, as Noam Chomsky first suggested, with parts of our brains ready for learning language, then surely we are going to end up as more sensitive language users if those parts are nurtured through being exposed to more than one of them. When I first encountered the way Chomsky talked about this innate ability, his 'language acquisition device', or LAD, I thought what a boring old metaphor that was. I still think so. If our brains are indeed wired for language, suggesting that, as humans, we're evolutionarily eager to start this business of talking as soon as possible, then we need a more dynamic image. Something like chicks in a nest, mouths perpetually open, waiting for worms. Gimme, gimme! Only with us, it's languages, not worms. And the more languages we manage to acquire, the more human they make us. As the French proverb goes: 'A man who knows two languages is worth two men.' Or the Slovakian: 'With each newly learned language you acquire a new soul.' At the very least, we have a MAD, not a LAD – a 'multilingual acquisition device'.

In my case, the bilingual community was Wales. I was brought up in Holyhead, a small town in the top left-hand corner of the country, on the isle of Anglesey. It grew up as a port town, with Dublin some sixty-five miles away to the west, and the mail-boats and railway line the backbone of the economy. All kinds of people would pass through, usually as quickly as possible. When the weather was bad, they were stuck. Jonathan Swift was one who wrote about his enforced stay, on 25 September 1727:

Lo here I sit at holy head
With muddy ale and mouldy bread
All Christian victuals stink of fish
I'm where my enemies would wish
Convict of lies is every sign,
The Inn has not one drop of wine
I'm fastened both by wind and tide
I see the ship at anchor ride
The Captain swears the sea's too rough
He has not passengers enough.
And thus the Dean is forced to stay
Till others come to help the pay.

People still get stuck, though there's plenty of wine in town now, and the bread's no longer mouldy. There's a Tesco, after all. Nor does it take the best part of a day to get across to Ireland. The fastest ferries can do the journey in an hour-and-a-half. You can leave Holyhead at seven o'clock and be in Dublin city centre soon after nine. Go by train in the other direction and in the same time you've only got as far as Crewe, with London still two hours away.

There's a close bond between Holyhead and Ireland, and it shows in the people. There are some 12,000 in the town, and a third of them are of Irish descent. Most would be descended from those who fled from Ireland in the days after the potato famine, in the 1840s, and who came across to Holyhead to find work. Some of them travelled to Liverpool, and then helped to build the railway line along the North Wales coast, a few years later; and when they got as far as Holyhead – as near to God's own country as you could be without getting your feet wet – they stayed. George Borrow met a crowd of Irish workers on the pier when he visited the town in 1854 (as recounted in *Wild Wales*, Chapter 41); they mistook him for an Irish priest, and wouldn't let him go until he'd given them a Latin blessing. You can actually see the oul' country from South Stack head on a clear day, with the tops of the Wicklow Mountains stretching like a black pencil line along the horizon. A Gaelic welcome (*Fáilte*) greets you on a café wall as you approach the main street. And the local Catholic church has one of the largest memberships to the west of Wrexham.

Some of the Murphys from County Wexford travelled over in those post-famine days, and one settled in Holyhead: Mary Murphy, a farmer's daughter. In 1906 she married Lewis Morris, a railway guard – and, judging by a solitary surviving photograph, not one you would mess with. Their daughter, Mary Agnes, was my mother.

The Irish were everywhere. Most of them got jobs on the boats, or on the railways. In those days, because of the Irish link, Holyhead was the most important station on the line from London Euston apart from Euston itself. The chief daily train was called the 'Irish Mail'. The incomers found a small population on Holy Island, almost entirely Welsh speaking. Over a century before, in his *Holyhead Journal*, Dean Swift had commented, during his enforced stay, 'I should be glad to talk with Farmers and Shopkeepers but none of them speak English. A Dog is better company than the Vicar.' Today, the Welsh element in the population is much reduced, and English is the language you will hear in most parts of the town. A third or more of the population is of English descent – many of them people from Manchester, Liverpool, and Birmingham who visit the area on holiday, because of the beaches, the scenery, the mountain-climbing, or the sailing, and who then buy a holiday home, or settle there after they retire. Holyhead is a cosmopolitan town, therefore, by no means as Welsh as a few miles east on the 'mainland' of Anglesey, where 60 per cent or more of the population of a village can be Welsh speakers. In Holyhead, the figure is less than 20 per cent. Imbalances of this kind can lead to complications when bilingual policies are introduced, as we shall see.

LINGUIST AS HISTORIAN

Holyhead is actually on Holy Island. An island off an island. Off yet another island, if you go as far as the English Channel. Why 'Holy'? It is named after Saint Cybi (pronounced '<u>cub</u>by'), a sixth-century abbot who founded a monastery at Holyhead. The island is called *Ynys Gybi* in Welsh. It means 'Cybi's island', though the point is not immediately clear without a gloss. What you need to know is that adjectives and other qualifying words follow the noun in Welsh, so that it's literally 'island Cybi'; then you have to appreciate that the first consonant of a word can change ('mutate') if it combines with another word that has feminine grammatical gender. The *C* of *Cybi* has changed to *G* because *ynys* (pronounced '<u>un</u>iss') is one of those feminine words. It's an unholy job looking words up in a dictionary, when they change their first letters like this, but that's language for you. Cybi's church is thought to have been located within the walls of a fort, erected as a coastguard defence during the late Roman period to protect the inhabitants from marauding Irishmen. There's no sign of the original church now, but some of the Roman walls are still there, with their characteristic herringbone stonework.

The isle is full of historical noises. There is an inescapable sense of time and place. Prehistoric standing stones are all around. To the south is a famous burial chamber, at Trefignaeth, dating from about 3000 BC. As a child, I lived in a flat on Stanley Street, whose back windows overlooked the Roman walls, and I was repeatedly told off for climbing on the corner towers, but it was just not possible to be a Roman soldier otherwise. Grown-ups never understand. They said it was dangerous, but Roman soldiers aren't supposed to be bothered about things like that.

A short walk up the hill, out of the town, and there was Holyhead Mountain, in all its natural glory, except for the huge gouge taken out of its north end – the quarry from which seven million tons of stone had been blasted in the mid-nineteenth century to construct the harbour breakwater – the longest in Europe at 1.86 miles (as every local lad knew). A regular weekend walk would be up this mountain – hardly a mountain, at only 710 feet, but the highest point in all Anglesey, and richly endowed with history. At the top, the site of a Roman lookout post. To get there you had to clamber over the remains of the walls of an Iron Age hill-fort. On the lower western slopes you could walk through an array of hut circles, the well-preserved remains of a village settlement from the third century AD, wisely placed beneath a ridge protecting it from the hostile south-westerlies. Just beyond was South Stack lighthouse, the stuff of picture postcards, a monument to nineteenth-century shipping.

It is the sort of place someone taking early retirement might easily retire to – but more of that later. For a young child, it was so easy to reach out and touch the history. In one of the hut circles there is a huge hearthstone, opposite the entrance, and, to the right, a stone mortar in the ground, in which grain would have been ground. You can sit there, rub the stone with your fingers, and just imagine. Years later, I used it as a backdrop for a television magazine programme; it provided the perfect setting for a discussion on the history of language. A keen sense of history is prerequisite for being a linguist. Mine came out of those hut circles.

When you live in a cosmopolitan place, language variation is in the very air. There are different accents and dialects all around you, if not different languages. Holyhead had the lot. You could hear snatches of Gaelic alongside Welsh and English. And Welsh English, Irish English, and English English. In such places, your ear is being perpetually tuned. You keep having to shift perspectives, recalibrate your auditory registers. You learn to accommodate very early on. You install a language checking device in your head, and make routine use of it. 'What did that mean?' 'Did I hear that right?' 'What did she say?' I remember sitting with a group of children, I think it must have been at a Sunday school. The lingua franca was English, but this particular teacher was (I later realized) using some Welsh as well. ' 'Nawr, plant,' she began. I had no problems in processing *'nawr*. I had heard that before. It was obviously 'now', said in a funny way. (My guess was right, though the reasoning was wrong. In fact, it is a shortened form of *yn awr*, literally 'in hour'.) But I didn't understand *plant*. I remember asking the boy who sat next to me what the teacher was calling us flowers for. He evidently knew more Welsh than I did. 'It's children, stupid.' I logged that one. Later, I would know it as the irregular plural of the noun *plentyn*, 'child'. But at the time, I learned it as just another meaning of the word *plant*. *Plant*$_1$, 'something that grows in the garden'. *Plant*$_2$, 'children'.

This is all normal behaviour. Something adults often forget, when they reflect on bilingualism, is that very young children don't know they speak two languages. The adults do, of course, and when the child experiments first with one language, then the other, they can identify the two immature tongues and call them by their different names. But to the young child, they're not different languages. They're just alternative ways of talking. From the infant perspective, you speak one way to the woman who lives in your house and another way to the man – or to the milkman, or next-door neighbour, or shopkeeper. Louis St Laurent, the Canadian prime minister, is recorded as saying, 'I didn't know at first that there were two languages in Canada. I just thought that there was one way to speak to my father and another to talk to my mother.' That's a standard reaction. The literature on children's language learning has many accounts of the way children mix up their different languages, early on, and only gradually sort them out. Especially interesting are the stories of the point in time, usually in the fourth year of life, when children wake up to the fact that they do have more than one language at their disposal, and that an adult doesn't necessarily understand as much as *they* do. Then they begin to appreciate the true power that comes with being bilingual. Language can become a strategy. In one study, a mother approaches her child at bed-time, speaking French, and the child affects not to understand, but runs to her daddy speaking German. No way is she going to bed. Another time the child actually replies to her mother at bedtime by saying, in German, 'I don't speak French.'

Thinking back, my preschool language balance in those days must have been about 90 per cent English and 10 per cent Welsh. The language of my home was English, and virtually all my relatives were from Ireland. After the Second World War we would cross the Irish Sea to visit them – an interminable journey, but with a farm at the other end, and rides in a pony and trap. This was Courtown, in County Wexford, which seemed to be full of uncles and cousins. Some spoke Gaelic to me, but by the time I realized that this is what had happened I'd forgotten it all, and had to learn it afresh from a book. The normal language there, as in Holyhead, was English. And so in Holyhead too, I spoke English – apart from when I visited Uncle Joe. Joe Williams. A warm, welcoming man, who could see only the best in everyone he spoke to. A man who ignored your faults, and exaggerated your achievements to the point where you began to believe them yourself. He made you feel good – is there any better epitaph? He had married my mother's cousin, Rita, and was as Welsh as the hills. They lived just round the corner. I was often there. It was a home from home. And from time to time he would speak Welsh to me. He called me *Dafydd y Garreg Wen*, 'David of the White Rock' – an allusion to a poignant traditional Welsh melody. He would tell me Welsh stories. But it was one-sided Welsh, for the most part. I didn't have much at my disposal to talk to him back. He would call me *machgen i*, 'my boy', but I couldn't use this back to him. Thus began my curiously asymmetrical relationship with the Welsh language, of which more later.

At home there was my mother and my grandmother. I was born in 1941, and – like Dylan Thomas a generation before – I vaguely knew about the war. Holyhead was a town at war, like everywhere else. I can still remember the vile smell and claustrophobia of having my face covered in a gas mask. And picking up other people's fear as the air-raid sirens sounded. The town was bombed several times, the target being the naval shipping in the deep-water harbour. There was a lot of blue and khaki around. (I was especially drawn to the colour of those khaki uniforms, I didn't know why. I dreamed about it, and especially about motor cyclists in soldiers' uniforms. I would not understand the meaning of this most innocent of fetishes for another fifty years.) It slowly dawned on me that some families had a man as well as a woman in them. That seemed like a very good idea. But there wasn't one in our house. Also, it was a topic which was never to be talked about. I must have learned this very early on, presumably by talking about it. But I don't remember when that might have been. All I knew at the time was that there was one totally taboo subject in our household, never mentioned, never to be enquired about. By the time I got to school, and had to defend myself from the charge of being different, by not having a father, I had my answer ready. 'Killed in the war,' I would say. 'A famous RAF pilot, he was.' A prestige-building answer, among my peers. But that was playground gossip. At home, he had never existed. I was too young to notice that some of the photographs in the family album had an odd shape, as if they were cut down the middle (see plate 7.1).

My life was entirely Holyhead, as a young child, and for years I thought I had been born there. Not until I got a passport for my first trip abroad, when I was nineteen, did I discover that I had in fact been born in Northern Ireland. Why this was so was never very clear to me. Only much later did I learn that my soldier father had been there before being posted abroad. There was a barracks in Lisburn, and a hospital. I was born there. And my mother returned to Holyhead to live soon afterwards. So my earliest memories are all of Holyhead, and Wales.

I think of myself as, first and foremost, Welsh, even though I am genetically half Irish (the rather curious character of the other genetic half will be revealed later) and linguistically semilingual. My Welshness is one born of presence, within a land and a community. But you cannot ignore the fullness of a multicultural heritage. It is there, waiting patiently for you to draw upon it. When I go to Ireland, accordingly, it takes me only a few minutes to assimilate totally. If I am with a group of Irish, I know instinctively how they think and feel. And in Liverpool, where I would later acquire another heritage, I find myself unequivocably Scouse (not so far from Irish, actually, when you learn the history of Liverpool). I am, I suppose, what George Steiner once called 'extraterritorial'. He used this term in a 1969 essay to refer to those authors, such as Nabokov, Borges, and Beckett, who are linguistically 'unhoused' – to anyone 'not thoroughly at home in the language of his production, but displaced or hesitant at its frontier'. He talks of Samuel Beckett, 'fantastically proficient in both French and English, rootless because so variously at home'. And he concludes his essay:

> A great writer driven from language to language by social upheaval and war is an apt symbol for the age of the refugee. No exile is more radical, no feat of adaptation and new life more demanding. It seems proper that those who create art in a civilization of quasi-barbarism which has made so many homeless, which has torn up tongues and peoples by the root, should themselves be poets unhoused and wanderers across language.

That's good. 'Wanderers across language' is good. But Steiner's point applies to far more than authors, in the literary sense. It applies to anyone who travels around, and who doesn't stay long enough in a single place to become totally at one with its language – or even its dialect or accent. That's me, all right.

In my case, family connections and basic community life gave me an initial awareness and a basic ability in Welsh. By age five, my accent would have been fully North Walian, and I would have had a smattering of Welsh words, phrases, and everyday dialogue sequences at my disposal. I knew the rhythms of the place-names and the distinctive way Welsh people are called. (When every second person seems to be called 'Williams' – far more common than Jones, in our area – you slip very naturally into such designations as 'John Williams taxi' or 'Mary Williams Cae Mawr'; that is, 'the John Williams who drives a taxi', 'the Mary Williams who lives in Cae Mawr'.) I could pronounce everything as naturally as a native. Then, in primary school, this became overlaid with a more robust level of competence, which included the committing to memory of basic texts, such as the words of Welsh prayers, nursery rhymes, and the national anthem. The primary school I attended, St Mary's, did not teach through the medium of Welsh, but the walls were full of words in both languages. Everything was labelled. What you looked through was a window/ffenestr. You walked through a door/drws. This was so much the normal way of life that when I saw things that weren't labelled twice, I felt they were somehow incomplete. But we didn't *talk* about any of these things much. There's only so much you can say about a door, after all. The classroom world didn't seem to encompass the truly interesting things in life, such as the names for different kinds of marbles, or the rotting seagull found in the playground. When these matters had to be talked about, it was always in English. Very few children in the school had Welsh as a first language. As a result, comprehension soon hugely outpaced production, in both speech and writing. Still, down the road there was a Welsh school, and when you fought with their kids on the way home, it was a bilingual battle. You became fluent in insult, anyway.

The family movements which took me from Wales to Liverpool at the age of ten robbed me of a crucial period of consolidation in the language. Why we went there I'll explain in Chapter 4, but the effect on my development of the language was a disaster. The early teens is a crucial period for vocabulary development. It's a time when the child explores a vast number of linguistic worlds, and builds up a lexicon for talking about sex, politics, music, TV programmes (radio, in my day), sex, woodwork, stamps, sex, cars, boats, trains, planes, sex, and a great deal else. Some grammatical constructions, such as the passive (*The cat was chased by the dog*, as opposed to the 'active' *The dog chased the cat*) or the more sophisticated tense forms (*They would have gone*, *She might have been running*), don't receive much use until then. Even today I still have trouble with some forms of the Welsh passive, and there are several verb constructions that I've never tried to use. It's an unsurmountable difficulty when it comes to speaking formally, in situations where these usages are essential. I've only once given a TV interview in Welsh, and it was a linguistic disaster. Never again.

In those later years, annual holiday visits to Holyhead were enough to maintain my link with the language, but not enough to help develop it. Jumping ahead, my next close encounter with Welsh came when I was an undergraduate in London. Feeling the need for identity, I enrolled at the City Literary Institute and took some advanced classes. I religiously purchased the *Cymro* from the Welsh bookshop off Charing Cross Road, and a dictionary to work out what it was talking about. Still further ahead (see Chapter 7), and I found myself unexpectedly living for several months in a largely Welsh-speaking hospital environment, where I learned a great deal of medical vocabulary. And, even further ahead, when I got my first linguistics job, it was in Bangor, where I mastered the technical terminology of my subject, linguistics (*ieithyddiaith*), in both languages. So there we have it: fluent in nursery rhymes and linguistics, but not much else. What kind of language ability is that? The term 'semilingual' seems apt.

Today, my Welsh linguistic ability is curious indeed. I can (and have) read the Bible in Welsh in public. I attend bilingual public meetings, and rarely need to use the headphones to follow what is being said (though I usually keep them nearby in case things get lexically out of hand). I can understand most things on S4C (the Welsh television channel), though some of the fast-talking, slangy soap characters leave me struggling. I can even play with the language, to some degree, inventing new words to suit the occasion. But engage me in a Welsh conversation, and my lack of active vocabulary soon shows up. I keep forgetting the Welsh words for things, and end up using an English–Welsh mix. I have never had the chance to catch up on my lexical learning, and become really comfortable in the language. And as time goes by, and opportunities to do some really serious learning become fewer and fewer, I don't suppose I ever shall. It would only take a few months of solid exposure to get up to speed. But I've never had a few months. Also, in my earlier years, other languages got in the way, as I began to meet them more and more, and found myself devoting all available time and energy to 'getting by' in as many of them as possible. My poor old language acquisition device is now seriously worn out with all its language learning. It's not rust, but overuse. I would welcome a transplant. Or a top-up of the linguistic equivalent of distilled water. Or a language-boosting energy tablet.

Actually, I wouldn't be surprised if they invent some such tablets, one day. Here's an interesting story which suggests the possibility. It was in 1988, just after I'd been in France, in Nice, where I'd addressed a conference of *orthophonistes* (speech therapists). The organizers felt that the audience would have difficulty if I spoke in English, so they asked if I would give the lecture in French. I was dubious about my ability, but agreed, and painfully wrote out my talk in what would have seemed to any French stylist execrable (but, as it turned out, generally intelligible) French, then had it read through by someone from the French department at Reading University, who eliminated the worst of the errors. The lecture was quite an experience – a temporary but intense immersion, and really rather reassuring. People were there because they wanted to hear about my clinical work, and they didn't care if I got the grammar wrong as long as the points got across. Anyway, the occasion went well enough – or so they were polite enough to say. But at the end of it – even though the session lasted only a couple of hours – I had never felt so exhausted. I left the conference centre feeling quite shaky. But then I made a discovery: for the rest of the stay, domestic French proved to be a doddle. I felt I could ask for anything, and understand everything. Languages, shmanguages. Nothing to it.

Now, here's the point. We flew home, and during the drive back from Heathrow to Reading I turned on the car radio, and found it was tuned in to BBC Radio Cymru (Wales). The Welsh news was on. And as I listened, I realized that I wasn't having to concentrate in the same way as I usually did, during my (at that time, living in Berkshire) rare encounters with the language. I understood it all. It just flowed in, without trying. It was as if some of the effort devoted to French had unlocked a door behind which an accumulated mass of Welsh linguistic energy was waiting to get out. The concept isn't as bizarre as it might seem. Elderly patients who develop a loss of language (aphasia) following a stroke have been known to recall bits of a language unused for many years, even since childhood. We know so little about the way language is stored in the brain. And for those few minutes, I felt as though my lifelong sporadic exposures to Welsh had all combined into something powerful and coherent. I felt fluent. But it didn't last. The next day, I turned on the Welsh news again, and the feeling had gone. I was my old semilingual self again.

So I suppose the correct answer to my Chapter 1 questioner, asking me how many languages I speak fluently, is not 'one', but 'one-and-a-half'. That 'half', though, is enough to give me what everyone needs – a sense of identity. And I spend a lot of time these days trying to persuade members of the Welsh establishment that half-speakers are just as important, to the future development of a language, as full-speakers. Nobody should feel embarrassed because they haven't managed to achieve the full command of a language; and nobody should criticize them for being in that position. A confident language can cope with all kinds of variations in dialect, stylistic level, and competence. A blinkered purism, which denies life to all but a single traditional variety, is the death of any minority language. A language which is having to fight for its existence needs all the help it can get. Its mother-tongue speakers need to welcome all who show an interest in learning something of it, whether or not they have the opportunity to become fluent in it. I am one of the biggest friends the Welsh language has, despite my semilingualism. I talk about Welsh all over the world. It is, indeed, in the league of endangered languages, a great success story. Numerically, thanks to all the activist effort and careful planning over the past few decades, it is in the top 15 per cent of the world's languages now, and likely to stay that way.

So I cherish those early language-learning years, even though they never made me a balanced bilingual. But they did something else. You can never prove these things, but I'm sure the exposure to the welter of accents and languages in Holyhead developed in me a linguistic sensitivity which I have never lost. Give me a child until he is seven . . .? That might be the motto of any god of languages. As it was, even if this language awareness hadn't developed in my case by the time I was seven, it would have had no choice but to do so three years later. I didn't know it at the time, but my comfortably maturing linguistic intuitions would then receive a body blow whose impact, half a century later, I can still feel.

Chapter 3

New worlds

I bet I saw the inside of the front of the human mouth modelled in all its fascinating gummy detail, with every tooth in its place, at an earlier age than any other linguist ever. You want to take the bet? Can you beat age four? Let me explain.

You will recall that I was the youngest member of what later generations would call a single-parent family, and an only child. Grandma, who came to live with us as she became frailer, was the oldest. And on returning to Holyhead to live, my mother needed a job, to look after us both. She got one as a dentist's receptionist in Hamilton Jones's surgery at the end of the main street. Quite often she would take me there, and I would be left to look at the pictures in the waiting-room magazines while she went about her business. I remember the first time I decided to explore, and found my way up some steep stairs to the very top of the house. I was not prepared for what I saw. There, in the attic, was a Frankenstein laboratory. When I peeped round the door I could see him, a mad scientist, his face aglow in the flame of a hissing fire, and I smelled a horrid gassy smell, and he was burning human flesh! I could even see the different teeth on his table, spread out before him. I fled, had nightmares, and was never going back there again. But when it was coaxed out of me what had happened, I was taken upstairs to meet this other employee at the surgery. He was the man who made the false teeth. I can't remember his name now, which is sad, for we became great friends, and he would show me how he made a cast, and how the teeth all fitted into place, and how he could make moulds, and how his bunsen burner worked. As I got older, he made me feel my own teeth, and where they were, and told me what each one did. This was much better than Enid Blyton. I was definitely going to be a dentist when I grew up. As it happens, I became a linguist instead, but always with a special fascination for phonetics. Did it start then, in that upper room in Victoria Terrace?

Having a mother out at work every day isn't much fun. Grandma stayed mainly in her room, I didn't know why. I was on my own, most of the time. In the summers, I spent hours on the beaches, and explored the coastlines of the island and the back streets of the town, getting to know them in absurd detail. There would be occasional family trips (with various aunties and cousins) to the sandy bays at Trearddur or Porth Dafarch. Every now and then, a bus ride up to South Stack to see the lighthouse. Four hundred rapid steps down the cliff, a dozen or so frightened steps across the narrow suspension bridge to the lighthouse island, and another dozen or so squeezed steps within the lighthouse itself, up to the very top, where the lamp-cover slowly revolved around its enormous bulb. Afterwards, the four hundred painfully slow steps back up to the bus stop. Sometimes the trip would be by bus or train to Bangor, the metropolis. Sometimes, further afield. A weak left eye, and some long-sightedness, meant that I had to wear glasses when I was three, and so there was the occasional visit to an eye clinic in Caernarfon, usually with a look round the castle. There may even have been human habitation the other side of Caernarfon, but it seemed unlikely.

And once a week, there would be a visit to the world of the cinema. Ah, *cinéma*. When the French say it, the word seems to capture the magic more profoundly. Holyhead had three in those days. The Cybi (the saint would have turned in his grave) was for Saturday-morning serials and cartoons. The Empire and the Hippodrome were for the serious stuff. Always the same menu there: a cartoon or two, the cock-crowing Pathé news with its resonant masculine voiceover, a supporting film, a main film, and a trailer to bring you back next week. But what films, eh, Pip! Cowboys and Indians, escapes from German prisons, visitors from outer space, Robin Hood, Roy Rogers, Walt Disney . . . The chase across the desert at the end of *Stagecoach*. Hunting for Harry Lime in the Vienna sewers. The effect of some of these experiences was long-lasting, and in the case of *The Third Man* it provided me with my favourite obsession (as the Epilogue will reveal).

The glossy photographs advertising the films outside the cinemas were the most wonderful creations – though I never went so far as the young François Truffaut (if the dream sequences in his *Day for Night* are to be believed) and devised cunning ways of pinching them. But round the back of the Empire, there was a place where treasures could be found. In the cinema dustbin, you would find, if you were very lucky and the kids from Newry hadn't got there first, short strips of celluloid film (offcuts from the reels as they were prepared for projection). Hold them up to the light, and you had the magic of film in your hand. You could see the event captured there, frame by frame. We argued at length over whether you could see a face changing from one frame to the next. These clips were more valuable than gold, or marbles, in the children's barter economy of the town – much better, even, than the colourful tin fragments found in the equivalent bins outside the toy factory at the top of Kingsland Hill. They awakened an interest in the mechanics of film-making which has never left me. There could be no better life than to be a film cameraman, I thought, perched high on a boom above a set. (When I had the chance to sit on such a device, decades later, while making a film about the town, I found out it would not have been such a good career choice. Vertigo.) Given the way my later life went, I find it especially intriguing that I always paid special attention to the names of the sound men. Did you know that Bert Ross, Red Law, and George Adams were the sound recordists on *The Third Man*? I thought not. Even today, when the rest of the cinema audience has long left, you will see me still in my seat, following the details of the end-of-film credits to the very last one. I know all about best boys and gaffers. And I curse films, especially those made for television, that roll their credits so quickly that you can't follow them. The credits are part of the magic. To me, cinema has always been a magical art form.

But never the only one. Eventually, I discovered another magical world – the world of reading. I learned to read very quickly and, according to my mother, I was always reading. We couldn't afford much by way of books, but she brought back magazines from the surgery, and the local library was only two minutes away. I got to know every inch of its children's shelves, and steadily worked my way through them, using my allowance of two books per person per week. Apparently my favourite place to read at home was under a large stool in the corner of the sitting-room. I remember the stool very well. Turned upside down, it made an excellent tank, with the four legs acting as controlling levers. Right way up, and transformed into a tent by the illicit use of a bedroom sheet, it was a reader's haven. I treated it as a personal library alcove, and took it very badly if some grown-up ever wanted to sit on it. Perhaps it was this confined space that intensified the sense of the physical presence of books, which I now feel so strongly, and which gave me a passion for the antiquarian: their texture, their weight, their shape, their smell, their – satisfying page-turningness. No electronic product will ever replace that. And then there was the joy of ownership. A book was *my* book, even if it was due back at the end of the week. The words were mine. I was their master. Years later, when I came across Jean-Paul Sartre's *Words* (*Les Mots*), I was delighted and amazed. This was my story, too:

> I never scratched the soil or searched for nests; I never looked for plants or threw stones at birds. But books were my birds and my nests, my pets, my stable and my countryside; the library was the world trapped in a mirror . . . Nothing seemed more important to me than a book. I saw the library as a temple.

A temple indeed, but so much more. A library is a refuge, a second home, a leisure centre, a discovery channel, an advice bureau. It is a place where you can sit and draw the shelves around you like a warm cloak. Those who threaten any library service with cutbacks and closures are the most mindless of demons.

Then there were comics. *Dandy*, *Beano*, *Comic Cuts*, *Radio Fun*, and a host of others whose names I can't remember. I was comic-mad. Their stories were the soaps of the day, and they had the same function. You just had to know everything about the life and times of Desperate Dan, for example, because his exploits in the latest issue would be a leading topic of playground conversation the next day. Those who condemn comics as bad for children's literacy and oracy forget their extraordinarily motivating force. I was always getting told off for reading comics, but I didn't pay any attention. And then one day in April 1950, there was the comic to end all comics. *The Eagle* came out. It had a stunning full-colour front page, with a huge yellow eagle superimposed on a bright scarlet block in the upper left-hand corner, and intricate, meticulous drawings (Frank Hampson was the artist) of the saga of Dan Dare, 'pilot of the future', and his enemy, the Mekon. I kept every copy and read them several times over, often surreptitiously after bedtime. I must have had hundreds, at one time. I wish I still had them. Imagine what a copy of that first edition would be worth now! But my mother put them all in the bin, during a house-move when I was a teenager.

And when it was too dark to read, and the battery for the under-the-bedclothes torch was too weak, there was the radio. Yet another magical world. Like a book, a radio allows you to inhabit a universe of two: here, the person in the radio set, and yourself. Radio is such an intensely intimate relationship. It is one-to-one, person-to-person, and at its best you forget there is distance separating you from the speaker in the studio. As far as I was concerned, there was nobody else in the world listening in. There was only me. Whether it was the Children's Hour presenters, or the newsreaders, or the Goons, or Radio Luxembourg's advertising voices, they were all talking just to me. When Tommy Handley died, a few years later, it was like losing a favourite uncle. It was a John F. Kennedy experience: I remember the day, where I was, who told me. And when I started broadcasting myself, I always tried to remember what it was like for people at the other end. It's common practice for radio producers to tell their neophyte presenters to think of a studio as if it were a living room, as if you were talking to someone across a table. I didn't need to be told that. I'd been there.

The radio also introduced me to the fascinating unintelligibility of the world beyond Caernarfon. I must have spent hundreds of hours twiddling the dial on the set, in long winter evenings, tracking down fragments of programmes, and annoying everyone else in the house in the process. Droitwich, Athlone, and Hilversum were enchanting names. But it was the babel of foreign sound that was so riveting. I was mesmerized by the intonations and rhythms. Every now and again you could detect familiar words – often place-names, sometimes a general word. In the 1940s English was already having a noticeable impact on the other languages of the world. But it was the tangle of sounds which most impressed me. How could there be so many sounds, so many languages? And how could they all get into a small radio set? Later, as a teenager in Liverpool, Uncle Bill solved the latter point, showing me how a radio worked, and teaching me how to build a little one, using the simplest of components. Then, one day, my mother's sister moved to Hartlebury, in Worcestershire, and we went to visit her. From our bedroom, I could see two tall masts on the horizon. 'What are they?' I asked Auntie Audrey. 'That's Droitwich,' she replied. I thought I was in heaven, and stared at them for ages. (Today, driving past the masts on the M5, they seem somewhat forlorn, but they still retain their magic, as all radio masts must.)

Friday night was music night. That was the name of one of the programmes: 'Friday Night is Music Night', an hour-long event of largely light classical music broadcast at nine o'clock in the evening. The only problem was that Friday night was also cinema night, and by the time we got home there was hardly any of the programme left. I had never been particularly interested in music. Books were better. But once, when I was about nine, we got back and I switched on and I heard the end of the most wondrous, thrilling, breath-taking musical creation. After it was over, I waited open-eared to find out what it was. They didn't say! They must have announced it beforehand, or maybe they ran out of time afterwards. Or maybe it just wasn't their practice to announce a second time. Classic FM syndrome, we would call it now. Whatever the reason, I was furious.

My mother had been in the kitchen, so she hadn't heard it. I tried to sing some of it to her, but it didn't come out right. She had no idea what it might have been. There was only one thing for it: to listen, in the hope that it would turn up again.

I can't remember how long I listened. Every Friday I would tune in religiously to the same programme, not realizing that, having played it once, they weren't likely to be playing it again – not for some time, anyway. For a while, words weren't important any more. Music ruled. I must have listened to thousands of orchestral compositions, checking their names scrupulously against the listings in *Radio Times*, and as a result became a juvenile musicoholic. Some kids collect car numbers. I collected Mozart's Köchel numbers. I had them all, in a huge exercise book. Then, one day, not a Friday, I heard it again, the whole of it. This time the announcer did his job. 'That was the overture *1812*, by Tchaikovsky.' A few years later, when we bought our first record-player, and joined the World Record Club to get cheap records, *1812* was my first purchase. But, as so often, the technology got in the way. When the cannons roared, the needle jumped. I played the record repeatedly, and stuck chewing gum on the pick-up arm, to weigh it down, but the needle always jumped. Eventually, the grooves were so badly damaged that it seemed, musically at least, that Napoleon had won. The orchestra went straight from the 'Marseillaise' to the final dramatic chords. I have a CD version now. But I am still mildly surprised, listening to a live orchestra performing the work, to find that when the guns go off the players don't jump a few dozen bars in order to reach the end.

LINGUIST AS MUSICIAN

The link between music and language fascinates me. There's no simple or inevitable connection. Different areas of the brain are involved in processing music and processing language. You can have a good ear for music and be a weak verbal performer. And I know plenty of people who have great language skills and who can't sing a note – well, not in tune, anyway. Yet there are obvious points of connection. There is a sort of music in the voice, in the form of intonation. And it is possible to use the voice as a musical instrument – not only in the obvious way, through singing, but in the sense that a composer can explore its tonal properties, and use it to create effects unachievable through other means. The works written by Luciano Berio, with Kathy Berberian as the soloist, provide some stunning examples.

I was briefly in touch with this world. In the late 1970s, the linguistics and music departments at the University of Reading held a series of joint seminars on the relationships between language and music. The Canadian composer Istvan Anhalt was there. He was exploring the possibilities of speech-composition, in such works as *Cento* and *Foci*, using live performers and tape recordings, blending them in intriguing ways, and incorporating real languages, pseudo-words, tones of voice, and other effects. We had long conversations about the fuzzy edges between musical 'meaning' and linguistic meaning. I illustrated the various tonal patterns of different languages, and showed him how phoneticians wrote them down, and he made notes. He gave me some of his scores, and I tried to analyse their structure. I still have them: they are the craziest looking things compared with conventional musical scores, involving zig-zag lines and dots and curves and all manner of verbal instructions to the performers. But in their realization they create a new auditory world. You either hate this kind of thing or you love it. I love it. I once played a bit on a 'Private Passions' programme on BBC Radio 3. Michael Berkeley's face was politely inscrutable.

Cinema, books, music. Plenty to do while you waited for mummy to come home, even without television. And there were games, of course. Card games were a winner. There is something very satisfying about a crisp, glossy, fresh pack of cards. We played innumerable games of rummy. I was taught several types of patience, and quickly learned I didn't have any. Snakes-and-ladders, ludo, and other simple board games were good for long winter evenings. Jigsaw puzzles too, the ultimate preparation game for a life in linguistics. But the best of all – you will think I am making this up, but I swear I am not – was a game actually called 'Lexicon'. This was not something invented by a post-war pre-generative linguist. It was a simple pack of cards, with a huge red capital letter printed on each one, along with a number value. A kind of pre-Scrabble in cards. We played it endlessly. I must have worn out all my word-game cells in those days. Certainly I have none left now. I can't bear to play Scrabble, Boggle, and all the others, and I find myself watching in a mixture of admiration and horror as my wife and her mother engage in word-game marathons every time they visit each other. I don't mind collecting instances of word-games, and analysing them to see how they work. Indeed, writing my Penguin book, *Language Play*, which is full of examples of ludic language, was great fun. But I never play them. I think it's because they're too much like work. When I'm off duty, I want something as far away from words as possible.

Another art form was never far away in those days, one which perhaps had more of a shaping influence on me than anything else. Drama. I did, after all, end up as a university lecturer. And much of my life thereafter was taken up with various forms of public speaking. But what is a lecture, if it is not an attempt to engage with an audience? The content and style may be different from that of a play, but the actor and the teacher inhabit the same stable. They both have to put on a show. The headache that the actor has to ignore before walking on stage affects no less the teacher entering the classroom. They both have to deal with audience nuisances. They both have to watch out for the same risks – such as vocal nodes, or the other conditions which can affect the vocal cords when people strain their voice too much. The actor has to put on the same level of performance, night after night. The lecturer has to do the same, but often hour after hour. There were times when I would have to lecture to six or seven different classes in a day. That's six or seven shows to script and present. Ah but, you might say, the job of the actor is very different: it is to entertain, not to educate. Lecturers don't have to entertain. I beg to differ. For me, a class – or any audience – should leave a talk feeling both informed and entertained. They must have enjoyed the experience. How else can there be successful learning, if there is no enjoyment? And if the lecturer can foster this interaction, oh how much better is the result. I know the reality is often the opposite. I have attended many boring lectures myself. It is a crying shame when that happens, because it need not happen. But the sad fact is that most lecturers have never been taught how to lecture. It is assumed that the skill comes naturally; and, indeed, some people are gifted in this way, born communicators; but most are not. Yet there is vast experience in the world, dating back more than two thousand years, dealing with the subject of how successful communication takes place. It is called 'rhetoric'. A course in practical rhetoric ought to be an obligatory element in the induction of any lecturer. Failing that, experience in the world of drama will provide a good foundation.

I found myself near the boards very early on. Amateur acting companies were everywhere in the 1940s. Anglesey had its annual drama competition. In Holyhead alone, there were several lively groups. St Mary's parish had one, and my mother acted in it and went on to direct many of its productions. I remember seeing her in *Love from a Stranger*, in which she kissed a male lead, who happened to be Uncle Joe. From that moment on, I was convinced they were going to be married, and to this day regret that they didn't. The most spectacular production I recall was a Christmas pantomime, *Snow White*. The bravest and fittest of the parish were conscripted to play the seven dwarfs. They had to be fit, for each one had to crouch down within a basket-like framework, to appear the requisite size, and hop all over the stage. I saw every rehearsal. I could have understudied every part, including the female lead. I saw the rehearsal disasters, joined in the laughter, shared the pre-night nerves, was repeatedly told off for being in the way, and generally had a great time. I was on the boards, all right, albeit vicariously.

LINGUIST AS ACTOR

It must be helpful to have some acting in the blood, if you're going to end up a linguist. When you learn a foreign language you adopt a new persona. You don't just talk differently, you hold yourself differently, you look different, you talk about different things and in different ways. 'I think you always feel braver in another language,' said Anita Brookner, in a newspaper article a few years ago. This must be why there are so many quotations around by famous people explaining that they use different languages for different purposes, such as former UN secretary-general Boutros Boutros-Ghali's comment: 'When I have tense relations with my wife, we speak in Arabic. When we talk business, then we speak English. And when our relationship is better, then we talk French.' Or, even more famously, the remark attributed to Emperor Charles V, 'I speak Spanish to God, Italian to women, French to men, and German to my horse.' Later, I would indeed do a lot of acting, and the parallels continued to strike me. Entering into a new language is just like entering into a new character. You learn its foibles, its strengths, its weaknesses. And, when you try to speak it, you have to enter into the activity totally, otherwise you will not be convincing. In language learning, there is only the Method.

Being on stage. A different kind of stage now comes to mind, on which I appeared regularly from the age of about seven, and in yet another language not so far mentioned as part of the Holyhead mix. It happened like this. My mother was in the habit of visiting St Mary's presbytery, just along the road from the church. I don't know why. But I enjoyed the visits. Father Collins had a big red setter dog, excellent to play with. Father Clark was much involved with the drama group, and he was good fun, too. One day we arrived in the late afternoon, and there were a group of lads, all from St Mary's school, but older than me. They were learning to be altar boys. I must have looked interested.

'Would he like to join in?' I remember hearing Father Clark say to my mother.

'I'm sure he would, but is he old enough?' she replied. I drew myself up to my full height. This sounded promising.

'He can have a go, anyway. Can you read this?' And Father Clark thrust a Mass sheet under my nose. It was the first response by the altar server to the opening statement of the priest, at the very beginning of the Latin Mass. *Introibo ad altare Dei*, says the priest (made famous to all by its use at the opening of James Joyce's *Ulysses*): 'I will go in to the altar of God.' *Ad De-um qui lae-ti-fi-cat ju-ven-tu-tum me-um*, replied this auditioning server: 'To God who gives joy to my youth.' As the hyphens suggest, my first jerky phonic attempt at a Latin sentence was not likely to have been very accurate; but it was evidently plausible enough for me to be taken on. I learned the Latin in no time, and found myself on show, cassocked up to the throat, within a month. To any Martian observer, my interaction in the opening dialogue with the priest, over some half-a-dozen exchanges, would have seemed totally fluent. What our observer wouldn't know, of course, was that the fluency was tongue-deep only. I had only a limited understanding of what I was saying, and none at all of what the priest's words meant. Another sort of semilingualism.

That was the way of it, in those days. Latin was the everyday language of the Roman Catholic Church, and those who attended Mass and the other services had to cope with it as best they could. People followed the services in their Missals, and learned the words of the main responses by rote. The longer Latin prayers, such as the *Gloria* and the *Credo*, would be known by heart too. I thought the *Kyrie* was Latin, also, until somebody told me it was Greek. It was the best thing in the world when the Second Vatican Council initiated the movement in the 1960s which led to the vernacular becoming the language of the liturgy. I would be involved in that, too, in a small way, and would in due course write screeds supporting the need for liturgical intelligibility, and cautioning against the domestic use of a ritual language that nobody except a priestly elite understood. I learned the desirability of the vernacular the hard way. Latin is a much heavier language than English. This is not a psycholinguistic point. It simply reflects the fact that, in those days, it was the job of the altar server to carry the priest's Missal from one side of the altar to the other, when the time came to move from the Epistle (which was read on the right side of the altar, as you face it) to the Gospel (which was read on the left). The book rested on its own lectern. Together, they made a heavy weight for a young lad, already bogged down in a cassock several sizes too big for him (the other boys were older, as I've said). I became known as 'the altar boy who drops the book'. In the sacristy was an English translation of the Missal. It was half the size of the Latin one. I looked at it with envy. It would be fifteen years before Vatican II would take my unspoken wish on board.

The presbytery was near the parish hall, known as the Lounge, which was next to the church. And on top of the Lounge, on the first floor, was the primary school – just three classrooms. Of my early years in formal education, the least said the better. I don't think I can have liked my school much. I seem to have blocked out most of my five years there. Mostly all I remember is getting into trouble, and being made to stand outside the door as a punishment. Miss Durkan, the headteacher, scared the living daylights out of me, and had a wicked way with the wooden-backed board-duster towards boys who kept talking when they shouldn't. The palms of my hands ached so, after she'd dealt with them. I suffered for speech, for I was always talking. But I suppose the pain taught me that there is a time and a place for everything, including language.

School can't have been all bad, of course, and if I try really hard I can just bring to mind some good memories. Unsurprisingly, they turn out to be mainly linguistic ones. I can remember the thrill of learning to write, copying huge letters on the blackboard, working out how to scale them down to fit the lines in my exercise book (a task whose difficulty is often underestimated by those working with children with reading difficulties). I remember filling line after line with joined-up forms, and being praised for having an elegant hand. I thought the teacher meant my hand looked nice, until I realized she was talking about my writing. I remember the challenge of spelling lists. I never felt the confusion that spelling-reformers insist is part of every child's encounter with the English writing system. The written language to me was like an enormous, enticing jigsaw puzzle. It had no picture, but it did have straight edges, in the form of the various regular spelling patterns, and then it tried to catch you out, by leaving some pieces out of the box, and including pieces from other puzzles. It was a great puzzle, though, and I knew I would complete it. The question is, which is to be master? – that's all. I became an excellent speller, and seem to recall winning prizes. But more to the point, I ended up intrigued about why the system was the way it was. Why were there so many odd forms? How on earth did *fuchsia* and *boatswain* come to be written so? The teachers couldn't tell me why, when I asked such questions. So I asked my friends sitting in nearby desks. They didn't know either. 'Crystal! You're talking again. Outside!'

And I wrote my first poem. I can remember only the last line of it, 'At the Battle of Trafalgar'. It had a dozen or so verses, each I think of four lines, and it was all about – well, the Battle of Trafalgar, I suppose. I know the final syllable of *Trafalgar* was stressed, and that it ended each verse. It must have been awful. I can hear myself reading it in front of the class, and having praise heaped on me by, no it couldn't have been, Miss Durkan. It was some sort of competition, and I think I must have won it. It was my first taste of fame. In Wales, to win a poetry competition, at any age, in English or Welsh, is a Great Thing. My name got into the local paper. I became known. People nodded at me. I was a Poet. I would Go Far.

There was one other world I encountered, during those years in Holyhead, though I did not then enter it. It came about through a discovery so enormous and mind-shattering that I would not talk to anybody about it for years, and even then only to a select few. When I got home, after school in the afternoons, I would open the post. My mother never seemed to mind. One day – I must have been about nine – there was a large, official-looking envelope, and I opened it as usual. I never forgot what I saw, and can report it now exactly, for a copy was still among my mother's papers when she died in 1999. It was a document, printed on a kind of crisp creamy paper which I had never felt before. At the top was a kind of print which I had never seen before – big, black lettering with curls and jagged edges. I could decode the words. They said: 'In the High Court of Justice'. Underneath, in ordinary print, there was 'Probate, Divorce, and Admiralty Division', and then, in a capitalized parenthesis, (DIVORCE). I recognized one of the names that followed: Marcia Agnes Crystal. ('Marcia' was odd – I had always known her as 'Mary Agnes'.) There were other large words, 'Referring to the Decree made in this Cause whereby it was decreed that the Marriage had and solemnized . . . between the Petitioner and the Respondent . . . be dissolved by reason that . . . said Respondent had been guilty of adultery . . . by final Decree pronounced and declared the said Marriage to be dissolved.' I did not know what most of it meant, but I knew what a divorce was (I had seen it in films), and I knew that adultery was something one should not commit, for I had the Commandments off by heart. One thing was evident. There was a man mentioned. His name was Samuel Cyril Crystal. He had to be a husband. And that meant he had to be a father. And if there was a divorce going on, he had to be alive.

My mythological world was overturned in an instant. All my carefully constructed RAF-daredevil fantasies came tumbling down. I sat staring at the paper for ages, until I heard my mother returning, and I stuffed it back into its envelope. I didn't see her read it, so over tea I waited to see what she might say. She might be cross, to know I'd opened such a thing. But she didn't show any emotion. She didn't say a word about it. So I didn't.

Next day, the same. It was as if it had never happened. And it stayed that way for the rest of her life. She had never spoken to me about my father before that day, and she never would after it. The taboo remained, growing in power, as taboos do. But I had changed. For the first time, I knew I had a father. I was like the other kids. He wasn't dead, after all. I might even meet him, one day. I was thrilled, but scared stiff. My mother's reserve was unnerving. She was keeping all this to herself. It evidently wasn't any of my business. I would look at the photo album. There was a lovely picture of her holding me, I must have been less than a year old. One side straight and neat; the other side cut away. I now knew who was on the missing side. I suppose I sensed, through the cut, the profound hurt she must have suffered, and I felt I could never reach out to it. So I respected it, instead. If she didn't want to talk about it, that was fine by me. I wouldn't interfere. I wouldn't upset her, even by asking. That's the way it was going to have to be. It was somebody else's world, not mine. I wasn't part of it. It would be more than twenty years before I dared to even knock on its door. And linguistics had its part to play in that too.

Chapter 4
Liverpool school

It wasn't a bad life, really, those early years in Holyhead. We weren't well off, but within the limits of the family budget I managed to get some early glimpses of the artistic worlds of film, music, literature, and theatre. Outside, and there was another world, one you could have for nothing – beaches, blackberrying, exploring, rock climbing . . . Who would ever wish to leave it? How could anything ever disturb it? The questions aren't rhetorical. I didn't. And something could. Another black-lettered word beginning with D.

One day, when I was nine, I was at home, and heard a crash from the upstairs room, and grandma calling my name. I ran to see what had happened. She had fallen out of bed, but she couldn't get up. She told me to fetch my mother. I ran the length of the High Street in record time, and she came rushing home from the dentist's. The doctor arrived. There had been a break – a hip, I think. She was taken in to Stanley Hospital, down by the port. From then on, she just deteriorated. A short time after, I was the altar server at her funeral. It was January 1951.

Things then happened in a rush, and those final months in Holyhead are a complete blank. The family context becomes important at this point. My mother had two siblings, both of whom turned up briefly in Chapter 3. There was a younger sister, Audrey, who'd married a few years before and gone to live in Manchester with her husband, John Meade, an ex-naval man who was training to be a teacher. Remember that name: it figures large, later on. And there was an older brother, Bill, ex-RAF sergeant, then living in Liverpool with his wife, Anne, and their two children, Sheila and Stephen. I never found out exactly how the whole thing happened, but it was agreed after the funeral that we should move to Liverpool to stay with them. And within six months it was all done. By August I found myself living at the top of a terraced house in Thorndale Road, Waterloo, one of the northern suburbs of Liverpool. A month later, I started my final year of junior school at the local parish of St Edmund. It was time to learn another art – of survival.

The new junior school was no better than the old one. But there was a difference. This time I was the new boy, entering a world where everyone else knew everyone else. Worse, I was an alien, someone from the hills with a funny accent. They knew where. I was called Taffy from the very first day. They all knew the rhyme: 'Taffy was a Welshman, Taffy was a thief, Taffy came to my house, And stole a leg of beef . . .' Ironically, the nickname is derived from *Dafydd* (= David). As Meic Stephens circumspectly puts it, in his entry on *Taffy* in his *Oxford Companion to the Literature of Wales*, the name 'is used by the English both good-humouredly and pejoratively'. I would have to wait twelve months for signs of any good humour. In that first year in Liverpool, I learned the physical meaning of 'pejorative'. And also something about the pragmatics of questions. 'Can dey fight in Wales?' said one of the kids in the playground. Naively, I answered yes. 'Let's see yer, den,' came the reply, and I suddenly found myself in the middle of a circle of shouting kids facing the hardest-looking ten-year-old I had ever seen in my life. I can't imagine I put up any impressive sort of defence. I had never been a fighter. But I instinctively did something right. Because suddenly the circle around me had gone, and I was being picked up off the floor by one of the teachers. As I wiped some of the blood off my shirt, the teacher asked me who'd done it. I said nobody had. I'd just fallen over and banged my nose, that was all. And then, after he had gone, everything was suddenly fine. 'Dat Taffy's awright,' said one. And the kid who had bashed me came over to check my nose was mending and ruffled my hair. I hadn't told. It was all some kind of subcultural test. I sported my bruise proudly. And if my mother didn't believe my story, as she washed the shirt that evening, she never let on.

There were some very good things about Thorndale Road. It led on to a thoroughfare in which there were lots of shops, including a small secondhand emporium into which came regular supplies of a truly wondrous creation, 'American comics'. 'Horror comics', they were often called, for they were indeed full of ghouls, demons, monsters, murderers, aliens, and other eminently desirable beings. *Eagle* had been founded to provide a moral alternative to this ghoulish onslaught, but it had never supplanted them. These comics were numerous, cheap, and immediately resellable.

They were also useful as aids to survival, because the toughest family in the area happened to live in Denmark Street, unfortunately and unavoidably on my way to school, and their main aim in life, or so it appeared to me, was to ambush me and beat me up. The problem only lasted a year, because then I went to a different school, in a different direction. But during that first year, survival was the daily priority. I learned several strategies. Bribery was a good one. Letting them have a few pages from one of the horror comics in exchange for safe passage. If you passed across all but the last few pages of a story, you could get by for two days or more. They wouldn't kill you, I reasoned, before getting to the end of a story, and there was always a better story to follow. Looking back, I realize I'd invented 'A Thousand and One Nights' before ever having heard of it.

But even better, I found, was to put my new, thick Scouse accent to work, in the form of abuse. Linguists call it 'verbal duelling' – the sophisticated swapping of insults between members of opposing groups or gangs. It can often be highly alliterative, metrical, rhyming, inventively figurative. It may even be found in literature; a famous example is the ritual insulting (or 'flyting') compiled by the sixteenth-century Scots poet William Dunbar. 'Rank beggar, ostir, dregar, foule fleggar in the flet.' You don't have to know what all the words mean. The consonant repetitions, rhythm, and rhyme pack the punch. My abuse was not so well developed as Dunbar's, but it was enough. I was articulate and could produce a quick riposte about the parents, physiques, or pathetic sexual prowess of any of the Denmark Street gang which was sharper than theirs. Linguistically, I proved to be a born Scouser. It had the desired effect. It's funny how well-wielded words, even if you don't know what they mean, can have the same effect as a well-wielded weapon. The gang always kept a respectable verbal distance from me, after I learned, Caliban-like, how to curse.

We stayed in Thorndale Road a couple of years before moving to a separate flat, a few streets away. By then I'd changed schools. I took my 'eleven plus' exam, and must have passed it, because I was summoned for interview at St Mary's College, Crosby, a grammar school run by the Irish Christian Brothers. The headmaster at the time, Brother Gibbons, gave me a book from his shelves – I had never seen so many books, outside a library – and asked me to read an extract aloud. That was easy. Then he picked out some words from the passage and asked me what they meant. *Conviviality* and *jollity* were two of them. That was hard. Did he sense a future lexicographer, that he should have given me definitions to do? But I must have given a plausible answer, for he let me in. Moreover, I was placed in '1 alpha', the top stream, and found myself sitting next to Peter

LINGUIST AS READER . . .

Just across the road from the second-hand shop was Wilson's Bookshop. This was actually a small lending library. His shelves were packed full of war novels, detective stories, thrillers, historical romances, and every other imaginable popular prose genre. My mother took out a lending card. She was determined to wean me off American comics – and, I have to say, she succeeded. I discovered *The Saint*, Leslie Charteris's brilliant creation, whose adventures (by the early 1950s) numbered more than two dozen stories, and read the lot. Richmal Crompton's *William*, likewise. Paul Brickhill's war stories were just beginning to appear – *The Great Escape, The Dam Busters.*

Another thing about Wilson's: he sold stamps. Foreign stamps. Within a week of entering his shop, I had become a philatelic anorak. My collection numbered only about a dozen items, but they were treasures. I got a stamp album for Christmas. All available funds thereafter were devoted to stamps. Six months later I had an albumful, mainly British Empire (remember that?), which was the fashionable thing to collect, but with a sprinkling of other countries. And stamps had to be read. I kept an index of the country names in English (Nyasaland, Southern Rhodesia, Straits Settlements . . .), and another of the names in foreign languages (Sverige, Polska, España . . .). The names in indecipherable alphabets were more difficult to index, but I copied them out anyway. (Good training for linguistics and palaeography, I would think later.) That was the magic of stamps. Their foreign names, exotic pictures, and unfamiliar values (piastres, yen, escudos . . .) carried you abroad, and made you a part of their world. I wanted to visit all of them. And for a fair number, eventually, I would get my wish.

Callaghan, my best friend from St Edmund's, whose Hornby train-set had the most sidings in town.

It's fashionable, these days, to knock the Christian Brothers, and all such schools, especially after the bad publicity they've had, with reports of sadistic punishment and of boys being abused. There was enough truth in the allegations to make the superior of the order, Brother Garvey, issue a public apology a few years ago. I must say I was puzzled. There had never been any sign, at our school, of abuse. It would have been known, at least on the school grapevine. And as for sadism. Well, yes, it has to be admitted, there was the occasional brute. But I recollect only two in all the years among a changing congregation of a dozen or so brothers and twice as many lay staff, all of whom were firm but caring, and with a good sense of

. . . AND ENTREPRENEUR

Reading can get you into serious trouble, though. In a newsagent's, further along the road, they sold a few books. A new edition of the *William* books came out, with bright red covers. I never wanted any books so much. Just one would do. But my pocket money fell far short of the two shillings needed. Then I had a brilliant wheeze, worthy of William himself. Nearby there was a pawn shop. It seemed, from the window, as if they would buy and sell anything. Old cameras, for instance. Now, I had seen an old camera in our house. My mother had never used it, as far as I knew. It was an eyesore, anyway, cluttering up the place. It was in her way. I'd be doing her a favour if I got rid of it for her. So I took it into the shop and got four shillings for it. That was enough for two books! I chose them with great joy, brought them home to be the jewels in my meagre collection, and showed them proudly to my mother when she came home from work.

But I had, it seems, made a slight miscalculation. It wasn't an old camera, but a new one. I hadn't seen it used because it hadn't been used. It wasn't worth four shillings, but something more like forty-four. Uncle Bill went round and sorted it all out. The camera came back. My books were taken back. And I never went back. I've not been into a pawn shop since.

humour. The atmosphere was one of discipline, indeed. Caps were worn (at least until well away from the school premises). Brother Francis, the new headmaster, would stand at the main gate, at the end of the school day, and check each of the nine hundred or so boys as he left. He knew every name, and first names, too. 'Cap, David.' You straightened it. Prefects patrolled the bus stops. There were detentions and lines for bad behaviour. And there was the strap.

When two or three ex-pupils gather together, the conversation, sooner or later, always turns to the strap. 'You went to the Christian Brothers?' 'Sure, I can show you the marks.' Such are the jokes, as far from the truth as in any other school where caning reigned; and yet, containing enough of the truth to produce solidarity in memory. For what did the bard say? 'He today that sheds his blood with me shall be my brother' There is a brotherhood that comes from shared pain, as everyone knows; and there was certainly enough of it at my school to ensure lifelong fraternity. Yet it was a fine school, judged by what schools are supposed to do. The proof must be in its roll of eventually eminent alumni. Sociologist and broadcaster Laurie Taylor. Liverpool poet Roger McGough, four years ahead of me. Archbishop Vincent Nichols, four years behind. BBC director-general John Birt, three years behind. That reminds me. During the period when Birt was in post, and broadcasters were reacting to the reforms at the BBC which became known as 'Birtism', I was doing a fair bit of broadcasting. Somehow it became known that we went to the same school, and somebody worked it out that I would have been a prefect when he would have been a naughty fourth former. 'You probably kept him in after school,' said one of my producers to me one day. 'Very possibly,' I replied. 'Not for long enough,' added the producer, wistfully.

I bumped into Birt, Taylor, and several others at the school foundation anniversary Mass in Liverpool Cathedral in the mid-1990s, and we reminisced a bit. It was a splendid event, in fact, with Vincent Nichols celebrating, and fine musical performances from the students. I'd been at the opening of the cathedral crypt in the 1950s, and seen the cathedral in action on television, but had never attended a live service there. It was a packed, powerful occasion. Later, there was a formal dinner at the Blundellsands Hotel in Crosby, a place so grand to a teenager's eyes that I would never have dared to enter it. I'd been asked to give the after-dinner speech on behalf of the old students. I was proud to do it, and as I toasted the school, I looked round the room. Hardly any brothers present. None teaching at the school now; it was entirely lay staffed. A head *girl* as well as a head boy. A couple of still familiar faces, teachers from my day. And, good grief, yes, Brother Sullivan, in the flesh – my old history teacher, and an excellent one.

Does one ever forget one's teachers? Evidently not. McGough has even written poems about some of them. For me, they are the subjects they taught. They had no life, no identity, outside those subjects. The language classes and teachers I remember very well, for their subjects gripped me. Maths, history, geography, and general science, not so much. The English classes, curiously, I remember less well. The O-level curriculum had both English language and English literature in those days, so the course had two strands. I remember some of the set books for Lit – *Hamlet*, *Wuthering Heights* – and greatly enjoyed that kind of detailed investigation. But surprisingly, the language work – full of the strictures of prescriptivism, the parsing of boring texts, the counting of metrical beats, and the spotting of similes – I found uninspiring. I say again: linguists are made, not born. Unless one's language is presented enticingly at school, in a way which shows its dynamic variety, its creative potential, and its relevance to the real world, it will deaden the linguistic interest that I am sure lies within everyone. It virtually killed mine. I ended up finding mother-tongue grammar a big bore, like everyone else in the class. I would have a similar negative moment at university, but then I would be saved from linguistic dissolution by a prophet. At St Mary's there was no prophet, and gradually my English interests veered more towards literature than language. Only the foreign languages kept my language impulse going. Fortunately, there were several of these.

In the first year, we had French, and my first exposure to phonetic symbols: [y] for the rounded front vowel of words like *tu*, [~] put on top of a vowel for a nasal sound, and a sprinkling of others. I didn't have much trouble making these sounds, but I was very impressed that there was a special way to write them down. I was also very struck by the fact that these were 'new' sounds. They didn't turn up in any English I'd heard before. Or in Welsh. French, and the France reflected in Whitmarsh's text-books, was my first conscious linguistic love. Years later, I would listen to Orson Welles doing a voiceover for a film documentary on France. 'Every-one has two homes,' went the commentary, 'his own, and France.' It was certainly true for me. I began living in France from page 1 of book 1. And I actually did get to live there for a while only eight years later.

The next language, introduced in the second year, was Latin. I found myself completely in awe of Latin, and swallowed whole the traditional way it was taught. *Amo, amas, amat* . . . and all the rest. I was there. I thought it was great. Here were jigsaw puzzles on a supreme scale. Patterns, more patterns, and patterns within patterns. Oh, the holy elegance of it all. And enough exceptions to fill a bucket, just to keep you on your toes. And *three* genders! (Try harder, French!) And the stories. What stories, eh, Pip! The fragments of the Roman world began to piece together. These were the people who had built the fort in Holyhead. They were the ones who appointed Herod. From their letters and essays, you could tell they were real people. (Or at least, from the crib we weren't supposed to be using.) It was all good, and in some ways I regret not taking it past Ordinary Level. I never did enough at school to get a real sense of Latin style. The intricacies of its poetic metre remained a closed book, for a long time. And the Church pronunciation we were taught I eventually discovered didn't exactly correspond to the classical model used in academic circles. But I learned a Great Truth, that first year. Those altar-serving words did mean something after all.

Brother Petit was the teacher. Was it unfortunate we had him for Latin? Maybe I wouldn't have learned it so well if I hadn't been so scared of him. He came closest to being my generation's 'occasional brute'. I sweated blood over the vocab which had to be assimilated each night. The language was fascinating, but I didn't see why you should get hurt in the process of learning it, so I kept my head down, and absorbed words. I sat at a desk to the side, and was able to keep out of harm's way, for the most part. Even so, I got hammered once for my old weakness, talking in class. And, as in earlier days, it wasn't fair. Petit had set us all a translation task, and left the room for some reason, with an injunction of death if there should be the slightest noise while he was gone. There was total silence. Then I hit a snag with one of the words. The relevant glossary page was missing at the back of my book. It was a crucial word, without which the sentence wouldn't construe. I asked my neighbour. Unbeknownst to me, yer man was listening outside the door. In he blasted. 'Who was talking?' Now, the irony was, that I didn't think I had been. What I'd been doing wasn't 'talking', in the sense he meant (i.e. time-wasting, for-fun talking), it had been an intellectual enquiry. I assumed he must have heard somebody else. So I didn't put my hand up. But nor did anybody else. If 'ballistic' had been around in the 1950s as a term for human behaviour, he would have gone it. He threatened us with every evil imaginable. We would be kept in until kingdom come. He would give us all one chance, and that was for the culprit to turn up at the brothers' house by the end of the lunch break. He stormed out of the room. And I realized that everyone was looking at me.

I had to own up, of course. I went across to the house, feeling sure he would understand. 'Is Brother Petit there?' He came to the door. I explained what had happened, and that I hadn't been 'talking' really. Well, blow me down, he understood perfectly. He accepted my account. He sympathized with my problem. We talked about the meaning of the word I didn't know – *duco*, 'I lead'. I walked away unsteadily, thinking he wasn't such a bad chap after all. My class-mates were equally amazed. This was so out of character. We waited in wonder for the afternoon Latin class. In he came. He told us all there would be no detention, as the person talking had confessed. 'Confessed'? I didn't like the sound of that. 'Crystal, come up here.' And then I got the biggest beating I ever received in my whole time in school – six on each hand. A distinction plus of a beating. It went down in the annals of the second year. People talked about it for days. And then, at the end of that school day, when I could hardly pick up my satchel, my hands still throbbed so much, he waited for me in the corridor, and asked me if I was all right. I asked him why he'd punished me. Hadn't he believed me? And then I learned a bigger lesson. 'Oh yes, I believed you,' he said. 'But that was as an example to the others. You can't have people not owning up.' He hoped I understood. It was a ritual act, no more. Later, I read *Candide*, and noted the bit about killing an admiral in England from time to time, 'pour encourager les autres'. Later also, I would find out that *duco*, when used with reference to metals, also meant 'shape, beat out'.

Language teachers thrive on ritual; and so it was with my next language teacher, who taught us Greek. At the end of the second year, we had our first choice of examination subjects. Why did I choose Greek? I didn't. Our linguistic future was already decided for us. If you were in '3 alpha', you 'chose' Greek; if you were in '3 beta', German. And thus I entered the world of the tall, gaunt, skeletal Mr Lawlor. His balding head spoke intellect. In the first lesson we were introduced to the Greek alphabet. I can't remember how he did it, but by the end of the lesson I knew it by heart, and how to write all the (lower-case) letters. I went straight home and compared the symbols in my school jotter with those on the stamps stuck into the Greece page of my album. It checked out. This language looked even more promising than Latin. It was supposed to be Classical Greek, and a dead language, but the same letters were on my stamps. Greek was evidently still around, even though it was 'Classical', whatever this meant. I would have to think about that. And in the meantime, every lesson began with the same ritual. In strode Lawlor. His fingers would snap, and we would chant 'Dei graphein kata tous nomous' – 'It is necessary to write according to the laws.' We would then solemnly recite the Greek 'laws of concord'.

Latin and Greek together turned me into an amateur philologist. I found it curious that there should be so many similar-looking words. French words looked like them at times, too. Even German seemed to have some similarities. German? But that was not my class, surely? True, but you see my friend Mike Houghton was in 3 beta, and as we cycled home together, he would show off what he had learned in German class that day. My exposure to German was thus second-hand and sporadic, dependent on the traffic flow, the weather, and Mike's memory, but I picked up *bitte* and *danke*, *ich bin* and *du bist*, and a fair bit more. I made a mental note. This sounded like a good language, too. I recognized some of the words. Those soldiers in the war films and novels evidently weren't making it all up.

I prodded all these languages, I imagine feeling a similar (albeit much younger) amateur enthusiasm to that of Sir William Jones, the founder of comparative philology, when in 1786 he drew his momentous conclusion about the common origins of Latin, Greek, and Sanskrit, and thus launched Indo-European philology. French, I had already been told, came from Latin. Could Latin and Greek have sprung from some common source, which, perhaps, no longer exists? I worked out this theory in woodwork lessons (a subject in which I was genetically deficient), and spent several happy classes inventing a new old language, a sort of Graeco-Latin, full of cases and tenses and moods and genders, and writing it out in my jotter. I then realized that a new language was of little use unless I had somebody to talk it to, so persuaded a friend, who was smaller than me, but no better at woodwork, to learn bits of it. We copied out chunks of this tongue, and exchanged coded messages in it until the woodwork teacher found out. He was Polish, and the news on the street was that he had been in a concentration camp during the war. You did not mess with him. I went back to making book-ends. We left our manuals in our desks. Then, as examinations drew nearer, we found fewer and fewer opportunities to refer to them. In such ways do once great languages fall into disuse.

That virtually completes a memorial to my St Mary's language syllabus. But I mustn't forget elocution, which we had in the first year. Imagine it! A class of Scouse gits being taught to speak in unison in a southern accent. 'King's Cross! What *shall* we do?' we all had to say together, with a high note on 'What' and a dramatic falling tone on 'shall'. We worked our way through Palgrave's *Golden Treasury*. And yet, if it was useless, how is it that I can still remember most of the poems we read in that class? Or those read to us? When that teacher read 'The Burial of Sir John Moore at Corunna', you could have heard a pin drop. I knew, from Denmark Street, that the voice had expressive power; but this was different. She stretched my voice in ways I hadn't felt before. She could make a voice sound – beautiful. I suppose I must have been read to as a little child, but I don't remember any of it. That elocution teacher was the first person to show me the compelling force of a good literary reading. I wanted to be able to read aloud like her. And I think I also got from her the notion that the voice was a tool, whose use you could explore and totally control. Once again: 'The question is, which is to be master – that's all.'

These were some of the memories which came flooding back as I sat and drank port at the anniversary do. In fact, that occasion wasn't the first time I had been back in touch with St Mary's. The first time had been a couple of years before, when I'd been asked to give a talk to the Old Boys' annual dinner. One of those coincidences. I was back living in Holyhead by then (as I'll explain later). One of the St Mary's College teachers, Paul Kindelan, had family in the town (in fact, his brother had taught me for a while when I'd been at the other St Mary's, the primary school), so he would visit from time to time. He was a member of the Old Boys Association, and one day he turned up at my house and asked me whether I'd come over and talk to them. I hadn't been near the school in thirty years, but I had good memories of some early contacts with the Old Boys. I was curious to find out how the school was doing, and there was a chance I'd bump into some old friends. I was, he assured me, guaranteed a good evening.

Then there was one of those surreal experiences which I imagine often happens when you 'go back'. I was given instructions about how to get to the Old Boys. Their premises were in Moor Lane, half a mile from the school, and his instructions seemed clear enough. I left Holyhead by car, anticipating a slow journey, and of course there was no traffic at all, so I found myself leaving the Mersey Tunnel with over an hour in hand. I decided to visit the school itself, to check that it was still there, and drive round through Waterloo (but avoiding Denmark Street, just in case). All went well until I arrived at the junction with Moor Lane where, in my memory, there was a simple right turn which would take me in the direction of the school. There would be no problem. I had walked the route a thousand times. And I knew where I should prepare to make my turn for the school, too – just past the Regent Cinema, on the right. But arriving at Moor Lane, in the dark, was to enter an alien world of new roads and new traffic lights and new buildings and new road signs. It seemed impossible to turn in the direction I wanted. There was no Regent Cinema in sight (it had closed, I learned later, years before). I took the exit with fewest buses and lorries – a survival tactic which works very well in Wales – and tried to keep my eye on the stars in order to move in a generally southwards direction. But it was cloudy, and the roads are not straight, round there. They curve, interminably, and you quickly lose all sense of direction.

I was too proud to stop and ask the way. Why should I? This is where I had lived for years. I knew where I was. How could I look assorted Old Boys (and probably Girls, now) in the face if I had to ask the way to my old school? Still, it would have been helpful if I could have recognized just one of the roads along which I was driving. There was no sign of the school. There was no sign of anything. I looked at my watch. My suburban excursion was steadily eating into my spare hour – and I still had to find my way back to the Old Boys address. I began to panic. Any familiar landmark would do. Anything. My imagination started to run riot. Maybe the school didn't exist. Maybe nothing exists. At last, a noticeboard. Perhaps it would give me a clue. A church name, perhaps, which I might recognize. I stopped the car, wound the window down, and peered out. The letters formed themselves in the gloom. The noticeboard told me I had reached St Mary's playing fields. There was a God.

But a God of ironies, for I had not often visited the playing fields, in those far-off days. Wednesday afternoon was sports day, and I hated sports, and would do anything to get out of them. The brother in charge of rugby (he was the other exception I mentioned) harangued us about being aggressive to win. Kill! Kill! I didn't want to kill anybody. Please could I read a book instead? 'You're a weed, Crystal.' 'Yes, sir.' 'A pathetic weed.' 'Yes, sir.' Fortunately, the weed needed to wear his glasses, and also suffered from a touch of asthma. With judicious exaggeration, and a persuadable note-writing mother, it proved possible to get out of virtually anything. I ended up as a linesman for rugby for a while, until my penchant for flagging fouls for perfectly normal rugby savagery demoted me to the bench as a substitute lineament carrier. Then they gave up, and let me off games. I read, instead. But the sight of the playing fields noticeboard still brought me out in a cold sweat, even after thirty years. I needed the drink, when I finally made it to the Old Boys, and because I was staying the night (their reputation had preceded them, so there was certainly no driving home until the levels had gone down), it was a Drink. I don't remember if I gave the talk, but I got a thankyou letter some days later which said it had been very entertaining, so I must have.

LINGUIST AS FIELDWORKER

It's surprising how often language rears its head in unexpected places. Take the field trip organized by our geography teacher, 'Titch' (he towered above other teachers) Phillips when we were in the lower sixth. The whole class wanted to go, mainly I think because Titch took his family with him, and his daughter was known to be gorgeous. Eventually we went off for the weekend, with the aim of studying U-shaped valleys, terminal moraines, other glaciated phenomena, and the daughter. The obvious place was Snowdon, and because I was still the professional Welshman in the school, I became the specialist adviser for this trip. We stayed in a large rented cottage in the village of Llanrug, near Caernarfon. All day Saturday we climbed and clambered, including all the way up to the top of Snowdon, and made copious notes. That evening we were allowed out, with a strict curfew and an even stricter warning not to go into any of the pubs.

We left the Ship and Castle in good time to get back for the curfew, sucking mints to hide the unsteady walk. Then, on the way back to the cottage, some bright spark decided he wanted to hear some Welsh. 'Taffy will know where to find some.' This was a challenge. I dredged up some relevant sentences about asking the way to Llanrug, and waited for someone to come along to ask. But the road home was deserted. A large house loomed up ahead of us. We could try there. The gang waited at the gate while I advanced to the front door, and knocked. 'Yeah?' said the man who opened the door. I asked my question, and waited, hoping the answer wouldn't exceed my limited vocabulary, which was even less now than it had been some years before.

'Hey, Robbie,' shouted the man. 'Dere's someone 'ere talkin' Welsh. Come an' lissen.'

It was a Scouse accent you could sharpen razor blades with. Another man, in a uniform, came out of a back room, and stood expectantly. I asked my question again.

'Hey, it's good dat,' he said. Then he saw my friends. 'Do dey talk Welsh an' all?'

'No,' I said, 'they're from Liverpool.'

'So are we,' said the first man.

It turned out they were from a scout troop doing some badge-work, there for the weekend just as we were. We exchanged brief biodata, and went on home, still looking out for a stray Welsh speaker, but never finding one. Still, the fact that I had tried was enough for my mates. 'Hey, sir,' they said when they got back, 'Taffy Crystal was talkin' real Welsh.' Titch's daughter looked impressed. Multilingualism, I began to realize, evidently had pulling power.

Several of the other extra-curricular activities in school had, I can now see, a relevance to my later career choice which I didn't appreciate at the time. My theatrical family background, of seven dwarfs' calibre, must have prompted me to respond to a request for volunteers for school plays in the mid-school years. I was evidently a striking Fred, the press photographer in *The Winslow Boy*, bringing great depth of understanding to that significant and much neglected character, even though he is only on stage for a minute and a half. And the way I held that camera obviously showed great potential, for I was upgraded to extrovert and madman parts in *1066 and All That* and *Arsenic and Old Lace*. The experiences were useful. I learned you could get away with virtually anything on stage, as long as you kept in character and were positive enough. A mistake is only a mistake if you treat it as one. During the dress rehearsal of 1066, in which I was playing an Indian colonel in the days of the Raj, I glimpsed Brother Sullivan in the wings, got distracted, and came out with his name instead of the one I should have said. It got a great laugh. Then I had an idea. The following night, at the point where the colonel was ranting away, I put Sully's name in on purpose. My mates thought this was great fun, and the next night spurred me on to greater efforts. 'Bet you can't get Sullivan and Phillips in,' they would say. 'I bet I can.' 'Oh no you can't.' 'OH YES I CAN.'

Nobody ever noticed, apart from the chosen few. But it showed me a world of creative possibilities, which in due course transmuted into a lecturing game I still quite often play, just for fun. It's a way of keeping a lecture fresh, especially when you have to give it several times in a row, as often on tours. I set myself a challenge before the talk starts – say, to bring in a reference to Superman or to Woolworths, or whatever attracts attention on the way to the venue. Then I try to make it come up in the talk as naturally as possible, so that nobody notices, and turn it into a sort of subplot. It's probably easier with linguistics than with most other subjects, because linguists tend to use lots of examples of usage in their lectures; and it's just as easy to illustrate the passive voice with a sentence like 'Superman was chased by the Penguin' as with 'The cat was chased by the dog', and a whole lot more interesting. The game became a real battle of wits for me in Australia in 1997, when doing a bookshop promotional tour on behalf of Cambridge University Press. Son Ben had come along, and he thought I should adapt the game so that the talk would include a famous quotation, which he would supply. If I managed to get it in, I won. If not, he did. It seemed a fair challenge, and once, just once, he nearly won. It was at Gleebooks, in Sydney. Five minutes before I'm due to go on, Ben sidles up and says, 'My God! It's full of stars!' – the climactic last words of astronaut David Bowman as he approaches the planet Jupiter in 2001. A tricky one, given that the subject of my talk was 'The future of the English language'. Then I realize where I am: in a bookshop. I nip quickly over to the astronomy section, find a copy of *The Cambridge Encyclopedia of Space*, and place it on a shelf next to where I'm going to be standing. After I'm introduced, I stand up to begin the talk, accidentally knock against the book, look at it, open it briefly, and react to the pictures, getting my quote in before the audience has even settled down in their seats. A hit! A palpable hit! DC 1, BC 0. Devising ways of staying ahead of your children is not restricted to linguists, of course, but it's just as crucial for them as for anyone else.

Is it part of a linguist's early training to sing in the school choir? Alto, in my case. I doubt it. But it was all part of a rich musical experience at St Mary's which consolidated and hugely developed the interests which had started with the 1812 some years before. Everyone was taught to play an instrument, from the very first week. If you had a particular interest, you could ask for it, otherwise you were assigned to the violins (unless you were tall, in which case it was the double bass). I asked my mother what I should opt for. 'Why not try the clarinet again?' she suggested. Again? Yes, I had had a clarinet in my mouth once before. A visiting clarinettist, Frederick Thornton, had once performed at a school concert in Holyhead, I think as part of an eisteddfod occasion. At the end of his performance, he talked to us all about the instrument, and asked if anyone wanted to blow it. This was my post-1812 period, so my hand was up first. It looked so easy. The long shrill squeak I produced immediately showed that it wasn't quite as simple as it seemed. Thornton showed me how to hold the instrument differently, and to blow more gently. A wondrous quivering note came out, wavering gently before it died, out of breath. I had wanted to play the clarinet ever since, and here was my chance. Mozart concerto, stand by. Fortunately, nobody else in my class seemed to know what a clarinet was, so I got my choice. The consequences of that decision were immense, and seven years later my graduation from clarinet to saxophone would nearly keep me out of linguistics and lecturing for ever.

Chapter 5
Extra-curricular acts

I often wonder where particular linguistic abilities and strengths come from. Linguists have to be interested in studying every aspect of language, but how do they acquire all the different skills they need to do this job well? I guess nature and nurture combine here, as always, but only nurture provides a level of explanation that can be put to use. I've already reflected on the value of a bilingual environment, and on the way certain kinds of early encounter seemed to relate to the subject. But an awful lot of the time, when you're doing linguistics, it is simply hard slog. How do you train for that?

Some examples. You obtain a tape recording of a speaker, and then have to transcribe it, sound by sound, listening to it repeatedly to make sure you've got it right. It can take ages, and you've got to have an industrious temperament, otherwise you'll never get through it. Where does that industriousness come from? Or: you collect a pile of written material in which you want to find examples of a particular kind of vocabulary, so you work your way through it, line by line, to make sure you don't miss any. It's meticulous, systematic, painstaking work. How do you learn to be painstaking? Or: you want to find out how an area of grammar works, so you put together a questionnaire and ask a group of people to react to a particular usage. It could be anything – an interesting word order, a split infinitive, an unusual word ending. It might be noun plurals. 'Is *a criteria* acceptable?' Some say the usage is acceptable; some say it isn't; some say they'd never use it, but they know a man who does; some just don't know what they do. You end up with a huge pile of questionnaires that has to be worked through. Maybe men use it more than women? Or maybe young people use it more than old? Or maybe it depends on where you come from? It all has to be checked out. There are lots of things to be borne in mind simultaneously. You mustn't lose track. You mustn't panic. How do you prepare yourself for that – other than by taking as your mantra the 'Don't Panic' slogan of *The Hitch-hiker's Guide to the Galaxy*?

I've always been a great data collector. I've never been drawn to thinking great theoretical thoughts, devising innovative super-schemes to explain The Way All Linguistic Things Are. Some linguists have a real penchant for it. Not me. I'm happiest when I have a drawerful of material to sort out – or fileful, as it more often is these days. The finding of a pattern is the thing. Seeing the regularity within a mass of apparently random data. Identifying things which don't fit the pattern and seeing whether you can make them fit, or whether they are genuine exceptions. Sometimes the task is purely of linguistic interest, an end in itself. When you finish the job, you've shown how a bit of a language works that nobody has shown before. That's a fine feeling. At other times, the task can have immense practical value. For instance, you carefully analyse a sample of recorded speech, and discover that every time certain sounds, or words, or grammatical constructions are used in a certain way there's a breakdown in the speaker's ability to use the language. The sample might come from a child of five. His parents are worried sick over his inability to speak properly. After you do your linguistic analysis you've found a reason. That's a fine feeling too.

But how do you become a data collector? How do you learn to tolerate – welcome, even – the slog? How did I? Was it the stamp collecting? The Köchel number trawl? The strap-induced Latin lexical acquisition? Is it something you learn at all within the school curriculum, in fact? Or is this where all those extra-curricular activities come in – the ones that are supposed to build up your strength of mind, curiosity, stamina, fortitude, planning, self-discipline, and all the other attributes listed under 'individual volition' in Roget's *Thesaurus*. I don't know what the recipe is. I certainly had no shortage of these activities, and any of them could have contributed an ingredient to the eventual mixture, or brought it to the boil.

Perhaps it was the cycling. That might account for the stamina training. We used to go to Holyhead a couple of times each year, to keep up with the family. We stayed at Uncle Joe's, and apart from anything else, that kept my Welsh batteries topped up. But I'd learned to ride a bike, and then got rather keen on it. A friend of my mother's did some racing, and he showed me how to take bikes to bits and put them back together again. One summer, I decided to cycle to Holyhead. My mother was persuaded, and off I went. It's a hundred miles, more or less, and it took me all day, and up some painfully steep hills, especially at Colwyn Bay and Bangor. But I did it, and then several times more over the following years, and also once to Hartlebury in Worcestershire – you remember, the place near Droitwich? – which we used to visit every Easter, staying with the Meades. Uncle John had finished teacher-training, and was working in a school there. Those visits were always a treat. They coincided with the end of Lent, so there was always a sweet-buying expedition to Worcester. And most of all, they had a television set, something I'd never seen before. I would spend ages just watching nothing happen during the programme interludes.

Perhaps it was the mountain climbing. Maybe that inculcates a belief that even the greatest of heights can be scaled. I remember the first time I climbed a big one (Holyhead Mountain not quite falling into that category). A friend of the family, Norman Jacobsen, used to visit the Snowdon range regularly, and one fine weekend he invited me along. As we drove up the A5, the hills started to grow, and by the time we passed Capel Curig they were looking disturbingly awesome. There was one with a particularly ferocious jagged peak. 'What's that one called?' I asked.

'Tryfan.' The Welsh pronunciation, '<u>truh</u>-van', makes it sound as abrupt as it looked.

'Looks quite high,' I added nervously.

'Not as high as Snowdon.' That sounded promising. 'But much more difficult.'

Why wasn't I surprised when he stopped the car at the foot of Tryfan? It looked even more ferocious bottom-up.

'See that bit sticking out?' I followed his finger. 'That's the Cannon. You'll be sitting on that in half an hour.'

I took his word for it. In fact, thanks to Norman underestimating my lack of hands–feet co-ordination, it took an hour. The Cannon turned out to be a narrow rectangle of tilted rock, a few feet long, sticking out from the side of the mountain like – well, a cannon. It was evidently a mountaineering rite of passage to sit astride it. And why is it when someone says 'Don't look down' you always look down? The cars on the A5 were like grubs. I edged out, holding on like grim death – and then suddenly realized there wasn't a problem. This climbing business might actually be quite fun. When we got to the top, I was introduced to the two large rock pillars, Adam and Eve, and invited to jump between them. I declined, preferring to be a live weed than a dead hero, and spent my time eating sandwiches and taking in the amazing views. We were lucky; it was a splendid day, and you could see the whole way across to Anglesey. After it was all over, I was left with two things. An unprecedented sense of achievement. And an Important Discovery – that coming down a mountain is a great deal harder on the legs than going up.

If not the cycling and climbing, then perhaps it was the school cadets that added to the mixture? I joined the RAF section, and learned how to march, how a combustion engine worked, how to take a rifle to pieces (much easier than putting it together again) and name its parts, how to make a glider crash, and how to be sick in the front cockpit of a trainer aeroplane. The experience, you perceive, wasn't an entirely positive one. I learned I did not like to be upside down in an aeroplane any more than in the school gym (where an ex-army gymmy would try to force somersaults out of us all in absurd locations, and would grind his teeth in fury when I produced the magical maternal note – 'you're an unbelievable weed, Crystal'). There were a few good things, though. Linguistically, I discovered drill-sergeant language and air-force slang. Non-linguistically, I discovered that, despite my glasses, I was a reasonable shot with a .22, which has stood me in good stead in the occasional fairground (at least, when the rifle and stall-holder are not bent). And there were some good out-of-the-ordinary activities.

Like the initiative test. The task was to get as far away from the school and back again as we could, within a weekend, and spending no more than, I think, five pounds. We went in pairs, and in uniform. It was a time when hitch-hiking was commonplace. My mate and I decided to head south, and the hitching went very well. We eventually found ourselves late at night on the Plymouth road, and arrived in the city centre, near the docks, about two in the morning. The lorry driver had dropped us by a sailors' doss-house, costing a few pence a night. In the morning, we went down to the port. We had to find some way of proving we had reached Plymouth. The *Ark Royal* was in, so we asked the man at the gate (of the dock, you follow, not the ship) if we could pay it a visit, explaining who we were and what we were up to. A junior officer came out, and invited us on board. We passed the galley, where everyone was eating. Our faces must have told a story. We were given enormous breakfasts, a tour of the ship, a certificate to say we'd been there, and a merry wave of farewell. God bless HM Navy! We hitched back, convinced we'd won. You can't get further than Plymouth, after all, we reasoned. We had a slight delay, because we accepted a lift into Sheffield, which we thought was somewhere south of Liverpool, and then found we had to walk all the way round the city to get a westward lift out again. But we got back to school by the end of Sunday, and went in on Monday confident of collecting the prize. No chance. We'd forgotten that Britain goes north as well as south. Somebody else had gone somewhere ridiculous in Scotland, and easily beaten us.

Perhaps it was the Baden-Powell treatment which laid down the data-collecting abilities? All that work for the different badges. I'm in two minds. It couldn't have been the wolf cubs. I joined the St Edmund's troop soon after arriving in Liverpool, but a few months later Akela married Baloo and the troop was never quite the same again. No, it wouldn't have been the cubs. Maybe the scouts, then? I joined the scouts twice, in fact. Once at eleven for a couple of years, at which point I got fed up and left. Missing the company, I rejoined a couple of years later, learned to tie knots and do all sorts of other clever things, and went on summer camps. I have some nostalgia now for the places we visited – Church Stretton in Shropshire, Coniston in the Lake District. My response to the English lakes is today worthily Wordsworthian. On the whole, though, I didn't enjoy camp very much. For one thing, I was regularly sick in the truck on the journeys there and back. Apparently, motion side-to-side in a big vehicle had a similar effect on me to being upside down. Then, when I got to the camps, I found I was homesick. And, to add insult to injury, one of the senior scouts (a relative of Brother Petit, I suspect) kept putting me on fatigues – for talking in the tent after lights out. I did my best (as all young scouts had to promise to do), and managed the odd grade or two, but I don't think my overall contribution to the scouting movement was up to BP's highest standards.

Father Barry was the scoutmaster. He was one of the priests at St Edmund's. A wiry, dark-haired man, with flashing eyes, full of energy, and definitely a role model. I remember his sermons. No, I don't. I remember just one linguistic point he made in one of his sermons. He was talking about swearing, and he pointed out how stupid it was. 'Don't you realize what you are saying when you say *Cor blimey?*' he thundered. 'You are calling on God to blind you!' Eh? Really? I hadn't realized that swearing was anything to do with real language. I resolved never to swear again. And yet, the reasoning didn't seem quite right, because I knew I'd sworn at lots of people, and they at me – the Denmark Street gang, for a start – without knowing what on earth the words meant, and the result was nonetheless effective. Swearing seemed to be a totally different use of language from anything else. It didn't have the same logic as other uses. It was a long time before I understood what I then vaguely felt, that different language functions do indeed have different rationales, and that etymology never provides the answer to a linguistic problem. The history of a word is no guide to the way the word is used now. Still, at the time, I made jolly sure I didn't swear when the Rev was around. Nor did the others. We may not have won prizes for ropework, but we were the best-spoken troop in all Liverpool.

There was a hall attached to the presbytery, used for small-scale parish concerts, meetings, and the like. I came to know it very well. For one thing, it had a piano. As a member of the scouts and other parish groups, my face was known well enough, so none of the priests were ever surprised to see me there, if they happened to pass through. I went every day, and taught myself scales and riffs. Then one day I thought to look in the piano stool. It was full of music. I rifled through it. A collection of classical themes. *Moonlight Sonata* . . . Mozart . . . *1812* . . .

1812!

I couldn't believe it, but yes, there were all the chords from the rousing finale, dozens of black notes, but all organized into sevens or eights. I stretched my fingers out, worked out where each one should go, and pressed hard. An *1812* chord came out, loud and clear. Then another. And another. It took about half an hour to work through the first ten chords, by which time I'd forgotten where my fingers went for the opening one. But I persevered, and within a few weeks I was erratically fluent. I was definitely going to be a pianist. I asked my mother for piano lessons, but they proved to be too expensive. I tried the music teacher in school, but he said stick to the clarinet. And eventually, the impulse died. I can still do some of the riffs, though.

The Legion of Mary had their meetings in that room. This was a church organization which met once a week to foster a special devotion to the Virgin Mary. There would be prayers, discussion, and a programme of social activity out and about. Doing the shopping for old people, a bit of gardening, that sort of thing. I stayed in it for years, and made some good friends. A side-product was the opportunity it provided to meet girls. St Mary's was useless, from that point of view. There was only the school librarian as an agreed object of veneration, and she was totally unattainable outside the world of fantasy. Church choir was good, too, for a teenage alto – and even better, when the alto's voice broke at sixteen, and he became a spasmodic bass. But the Legion was best of all, especially when, after a year or so, I was given officer status (I was appointed treasurer, and collected the weekly subs). This meant I was entitled to go to the monthly meetings of the Curia, the combined body of all the Legion groups on our side of Liverpool. The talent there was phenomenal. But it was a watching brief only. In all my time as a senior Legionary, I never asked any of them out. And they never showed any interest in me. By no stretch of the imagination, with my glasses, big ears, and freckles, could I have been said to have been good-looking. I had no physique, and no special skill to pull them in. Being Welsh didn't seem to work, either. It was all very dispiriting. It was probably God's will, though. Maybe he had it in mind for me to become a priest.

Priests I got to know very well, especially the Montfort Fathers, a missionary order founded by the seventeenth-century French saint, Louis Marie de Montfort, with a special Marian devotion. This was one of the Legion's activities – to visit Montfort House in Blundellsands and weed the garden. It was a big garden, so a small army of us was there most weeks. The priests were – I expect, still are – the very best of company, warm-hearted, lively, full of great stories. People were always coming through from overseas with tales to tell. I felt an affinity with them, and was drawn to their spirituality. I went there as often as I could. And opportunities increased when the monthly issue of their magazine, *Queen and Mother*, was being prepared for distribution. Several thousand copies arrived from the printer's. The envelopes and labels had to be printed, then individual copies put into the envelopes and larger numbers into parcels, for sending out all over the world. Address changes had to be noted, and new address plates stencilled. Meticulous stuff. Volunteers came to help from as far away as Bootle. It took two days to do the lot, in a real party atmosphere. We Legionaries would deliver copies by hand (by bike, really) to local addresses in Waterloo and Crosby, to save postage.

All of this may seem beside the point, but the Lord works in strange ways. For it gave me my first opportunity to write. Well, I say first. The epic of Trafalgar must not be forgotten. And I had had a second experience, which had actually put me off writing. I was about fourteen, and my mother and I had recently returned from a visit to Holyhead by train, which had gone very well. The *Sunday Express* the following week ran a piece on how awful British train travel was, and it just didn't fit in with our recent experience at all. So I decided to write a long letter to them about it. On the Wednesday, there was a knock on the door. A telegram. It was from the *Sunday Express*. It said, 'May we print your letter?' I was overjoyed. There was a pre-paid reply. 'Yes,' I cabled, journalistically, and could hardly wait for the next Sunday. We found the letters page. There was my name sure enough, and above – a set of dots, a fragment of one sentence, and another set of dots. It was one of a sequence of extracted remarks from several letter-writers. Of the rest of my carefully crafted letter, no sign.

How could they do that?! I complained at length to anyone who would listen, and was told about the ways of newspaper editors and the power they had. 'But I spent ages on my letter,' I moaned. People sympathized, but the consensus was that there was nothing I could do about it. I should be satisfied. I'd made my point, and got my name in the paper. True. I'd not seen my name in print before. But it left me with a deep suspicion of editors, which I've never entirely lost.

LINGUIST AS EDITOR

Editors can be very helpful, but they can also do you harm. I learned that lesson at fourteen, and have never forgotten it. It remains true. Never trust an editor. When I became one myself, editing academic journals and series, I didn't trust me either. But I tried to remember the basic principle: the author rules. Never change a text without discussing the point first. It is the most basic of courtesies. Most newspaper sub-editors still don't observe this principle, which is why I write as little as possible for the daily press, and have never done much reviewing in popular newspapers and magazines. It has to be a really special reason before I will take something like that on. And when I do, I know there is only a small chance that it will be published without raising my blood pressure.

I'm by no means the first, of course, to get upset when somebody with a distorted or ill-formed sense of language decides to impose their own idiosyncrasies of taste on your writing. (The green squiggles which appear underneath my screen typescript now – or at least they would if I hadn't switched them off – imposed by the pedants at Word, are the contemporary manifestation of this disease.) I'm reminded of Raymond Chandler, who wrote a letter in 1947 to the editor of *Atlantic Monthly*, in which he sounded off at length: 'Would you convey my compliments to the purist who reads your proofs and tell him or her that I write in a sort of broken-down patois which is something like the way a Swiss waiter talks, and that when I split an infinitive, God damn it, I split it so it will stay split.' All linguists feel that way too.

Fortunately, the editor of *Queen and Mother* was different. The sun shone out of his dog-collar. In fact, there were a couple of editors, during my time there, and I can't now recall which one it was, for I don't have the copies, but one day I was moaning to him about the quality of one of the short stories in one of the issues, and he stopped me in my tracks by saying, 'So why don't you write one yourself?' Did he mean it? He meant it. I was in the lower sixth form by then, and had developed the beginnings of a style. I did my first story – on what I can't recall, something science fiction-ish, I think – about a thousand words, and sent it in. It was well received. I nearly framed the issue of the magazine it appeared in. Perhaps I should have done, for it's lost now. He asked me to do another. That was accepted too. I was all set for a literary career. I was doing English literature as one of my A-level subjects (along with history and geography), and this success confirmed me in my vague thought that I might in due course apply for an English degree at university. Virtually everybody in the sixth form went on to university from St Mary's. I had done reasonably well at O-level, though not brilliantly, getting seven respectable passes. It was time to buckle down, and get some serious work done. 'You could do well, Crystal, if you work.' A unanimous view. But there was a difficulty. Its name was Bill Haley.

The year was 1957. Bill Haley and the Comets had erupted on to British screens two years before, when *Blackboard Jungle* brought 'Rock Around the Clock' to everybody's attention. I had been in the Corona cinema when they had to call the firemen to hose the audience down. Too much rocking in the aisles. This was something very special. And everybody in Liverpool wanted to be in on the act. A few of us had already been meeting in each other's houses, trying out our various musical skills. I would take my clarinet round to Tony Garrigan's, and play in with his accordion, but that was Irish lilt, not rock. The occasional Gilbert and Sullivan soirees with interested local families hardly counted, either. Lonnie Donegan and his skiffle group had taken everyone by storm, and we all knew the words of 'Rock Island Line' by heart. But it was rock that was slowly getting into the blood.

Several of us went to a weekly youth club at English Martyrs in Litherland. Dancing was in. If you can call what the men did 'dancing'. As far as I can remember, the aim was to stand as still as possible, and let the girl do all the moving. Well, it was only fair: to move about too much could ruin your hair-style. Also, I didn't dare move too much myself. I had dispensed with my glasses, to look suave, and therefore couldn't see where I was going. It was a real relief when I discovered in due course that it was possible for a girl to like you without you having to take your glasses off.

The group changed all that. What do you mean, 'Which group?' *The* group, of course. Following in the footsteps of the Master, Haley, and noting that none of the other primitive rock groups in Liverpool had anyone who could play a saxophone, I decided it was time to graduate from first clarinet. The music teacher had shown me that the fingering was virtually the same, using an old alto saxophone they had in the school. Then I heard that someone had an alto for sale, £30. I saved, borrowed, squeezed money out of whoever I could, and got it. I don't know whose idea it was to form the group, but somehow four of us found each other. Apart from me, there was Dave Lovelady, who had a fine set of drums, Bernie Mohan, who played a cool piano, and John Kennedy, who played guitar and sang. And someone else, too – but the name escapes me. We called ourselves The Zodiacs – not to be confused with two other groups of that name (led by 'Ian' and 'Jimi' respectively) who later came on to the pop scene. We were the *original* Zodiacs. We rehearsed at all available hours, wherever we could find a piano. Bernie was the most musical, and he did most of the arranging. Dave did some stunning drum solos. John could take off pretty well every well-known rock-and-roller. But my sax, I like to think, was what made us distinctive. Nobody else at that time had one.

We played our first professional gig in Maghull, not far from Crosby, in the church hall, and got £5 for it. It was a princely sum. Then we played in our own school hall. And suddenly, we found ourselves in demand. There was a regular spot at St Luke's Hall, in between the school and the (RIP) Regent Cinema. That Hall is RIP now, too. But in those days it was a swinging place. Paul McCartney talks about it, so it must have been. Eventually, our reputation grew, and we went further afield. I also did some busking on my own. There were jam sessions at the Jacaranda Club and the first Cavern, all dark and sweaty and claustrophobic, and once with my trumpet-playing school music teacher in the orchestra pit at a Liverpool theatre (not such a successful occasion, as I couldn't keep up with him). It was all very enjoyable, really. At the Zodiac gigs, I'd never had anyone screaming for my body before, and now there were dozens of them, all at once. At least, I think it was mine, but on reflection it was probably John Kennedy's, who could wiggle his hips like Elvis.

I did get a girlfriend out of it, actually. A Seafield girl called Molly. Seafield was the girls' equivalent to St Mary's, on the other side of the road, and every day dozens from both schools would mingle at the same bus stop to get home. The school prefects were there from both schools to stop any hanky-panky. But when you became a prefect yourself, you were entitled to hanky-panky. By the time I was in the upper sixth, and a prefect, the group was getting well known. At a joint-school gig, I heard the news (via a series of friends – you know how it happens) that there was someone out there who fancied me. This had never happened before. I wasn't like Pete Callaghan, who'd been dating a Seafield girl for years, or Mick Murphy, who seemed to have a different girl every time you saw him. This was worth exploring. I explored. And before the evening was out I found myself assigned to the category of lads who had 'gotta judy'.

In my upper sixth year, the list of gigs was building up nicely. There was just one thing getting in the way, a little matter of the A-level exams. Dave Lovelady, who was a bit younger than Bernie and me, didn't have such a problem. But we were under severe pressure to get our heads down. There were state and county scholarship exams to be taken as well. Nobody was going to get to a university without a grant, and that was dependent on results. It was time to start revising. Everyone has their favourite place. Mine was the Picton Library in the centre of Liverpool. A wonderful echoing building, with a domed roof, and books all around you, in a huge tiered circle. The whole place smelled of book. You couldn't fail to learn there. You just had to breathe the learning in. Mind you, there were distractions. The clacking high heels of the librarians brought a universal raising of male student heads. And then there were the 'other' books – in my case, the ones unconnected with Eng lit, history, and geography. My near-downfall was to discover the philology section. This was an Aladdin's cave of linguistic delights. I remember finding A. S. Diamond's new (in 1959) book, *The History and Origin of Language*, and reading it from cover to cover. A sociologist and lawyer, he provided an account of the subject which I found enthralling, with examples from all kinds of languages and a historical perspective which carried me back towards the beginning of people. I read it again, many years later, and found its speculations disappointingly amateurish, by the standards I had by then learned to respect. But at the time, it was an eye-opener to the possibilities of a serious study of language. My first real encounter with philology.

I applied to various universities to read English, did some scholarship exams, and was called to interview at Liverpool and London. I'd chosen them because the courses seemed to offer both a language and a literature component. I remember the Liverpool interview very well, and the interviewers. Simeon Potter was the professor there, and he gave me a grilling on poetry and style. I thought he was great, and resolved to read his books as soon as I could. (Our paths would almost-cross again. After his death, some twenty years later, I took on his role as co-editor of the Language Library.) The London visit, for some reason, I don't remember so clearly, probably because there were so many interviews. I'd applied to two of the constituent colleges, and the scholarship system required a further 'federal' university interview as well. It all took place in a huge room at the Senate House, and you raced from one interviewing panel to another. It was my first visit to London, though, and I was greatly impressed. If I was going to go to university, this was a much more exciting location than Liverpool, it seemed to me. I rather liked the thought of 'going away' to college. I was used to seeing older generations of local lads turning up in Waterloo during their vacations with their swish scarves and their romantic tales of the orient. Staying at home was not really an option.

Between the interviews, The Zodiacs played on. I was eventually offered places at Liverpool and University College London, and accepted the latter.

The group became more successful. A-levels, grant applications, and all the other school-leaving events came and went. The group was beginning to play really quite well now, and had built up a wide repertoire. Liverpool groups were getting known. It wasn't quite Beatles era yet – that didn't take off until 1960 – but there was an enormous amount going on, and it all seemed very lucrative. We talked about it at the beginning of the summer vacation. Should we carry on with the group, and forget all that tosh about going to university? There was an 'opportunity knocks' sort of competition we could enter. Reps from recording companies were known to be trawling about. There was a rumour of an invitation to play in Germany. I decided to leave it in the lap of the gods. If I did well at A-level, I'd go collegewards. If I didn't, I'd go Cavernwards.

When people can't make up their mind what to do, they often run away to sea. I did that, too, at the beginning of the long hot summer of 1959, before the results came out. The activities of amateur pop groups are always badly disrupted by school holidays, so there was nothing to do in Liverpool for a few weeks. And I was broke. I had the option of extending my Saturday job. A couple of years before, my friend Anthony and I had landed Saturday afternoon jobs at Littlewoods in the city centre (only afternoon – we had school on Saturday mornings). Even though it was my mum who had made the link (she was working for the firm at that time), it was Anthony who got the plum job – controlling the lift up to the stock room. I was placed in the bacon-preparation room at the back of the store. I know his was a plum job because part of my work was to take the trolley up to the stock room to bring down boxes of butter, sides of bacon, and the like, and that meant using Anthony's lift. The plumness showed up in the regularly appearing lipstick on his shopcoat. Nothing like that ever happened in the bacon department, I have to say. Ours was a serious vocation. I wasn't allowed near the slicer, but Joe, the supervisor, taught me how to sharpen knives and to bone a side of bacon. I became quite expert. That must qualify you for something in linguistics, but I'm not quite sure what.

I was just about to sign on for the whole summer, when I heard they were looking for extra staff on the mail boats between Holyhead and Dun Laoghaire (pronounced 'leeree'). I applied and got a job, joined the National Union of Seamen (another unusual linguistics qualification), and for the next six weeks worked behind one of the bars on the *Hibernia*. A shift was one journey there and back – about four hours each way – plus a stopover at the Irish end. That was the best bit. There was a marvellous record shop in the town, with really cheap jazz records. And you never knew what might happen in Dun Laoghaire. Once we were all brought in as film extras. Robert Mitchum was escaping, in some Irish historical saga, and he ran all the way along the railway lines to avoid the police and into our boat. Oh yes, I've filmed with Mitchum.

It was good being back in Holyhead for six weeks – the longest time I'd been there since leaving. I got digs with the Hutchinsons – Alf was the chief cook on the boat – and he showed me the ropes. I met up with Mike Dolan, an old friend from primary school (we'd had our tonsils out on the same day, when we were three – you can't have much more of a shared history than that!). He was on the boats, too – as indeed were all kinds of former acquaintances. Wenglish, a fascinating mix of Welsh and English, ruled on board, interspersed with chunks of Gaelic. I learned to sell things in three languages. And the views of Holy Island as we left port were stunning. It was a *very* hot summer – so hot that more than once we could see the gorse on Holyhead Mountain burning, from way out at sea. It looked like a volcano.

In view of my bad aeronautical and scouting experiences, I was relieved that the weather was so good. It was a memorable summer. The sea was as flat as any nautical neophyte could have wished. Fortunately, it stayed that way until the very last week of my contract. Unfortunately, the weather changed on my very last shift. It was a double shift, too – there and back twice – and I had to do the lot because I didn't want to lose the extra money. It started out well enough, but on the way back the wind got up and the heavens opened, and verily I learned the meaning of being seasick. I lasted only a few minutes, and spent virtually all of the remaining three journeys on my back on the floor of my bar. Seasoned customers would knock on the counter, ask if there was anyone there, note my posture, and find their way to the other bar. At one point I looked up, and there was Alf, leaning over me, and saying that it wasn't any good lying there like that, and the stomach needed something to work on. I appreciated the theory, but not the practice. He had brought me a fried egg.

My A-level results came through while I was on the boats. I got three As, and so it would be bye-bye Cavern. I often wonder, did I make the right decision? Certainly, a couple of years later, living the archetype of a penniless student in a shabby flat in North London, I wondered moodily about it, especially when I heard what had happened to Dave Lovelady. The Zodiacs of course broke up, when we went our respective ways. Bernie Mohan went to Oxford, and eventually into linguistics. (Who says there's no relationship between pop music and linguistics? Fifty per cent of our group entered the subject.) But Dave stayed in the business. He went on to drum for another group we'd shared the stage with – 'Kingsize' Taylor and the Dominoes – and then later joined the Fourmost, and was part of their flurry of hits in the 1960s. Somebody told me what his group had earned for a single gig somewhere on the continent. It was more than my entire three-year grant.

It was the end of the summer. I left Holyhead once again, and went back to Liverpool. Then, still not entirely sure whether I'd made the right decision or not, I packed my bags, picked up my saxophone, and left Merseyside for London.

Chapter 6

Learning, and not learning, about language

I didn't go to London alone. Pete Callaghan, whose companionship dated from St Edmund's, had also got into the same course, at University College – or UC, as we learned to call it – and so we took the same train down to Euston, and found our way to the same digs which the university lodgings officer had assured us were 'quite close to college'. UC is in Gower Street, in central London. The digs were in Finchley, which seemed to be seriously close to Scotland. This was obviously some special London sense of the word 'close'. We endured the hour-long journeys into college for a term, then found ourselves a place nearer in, along with some other students, in Tufnell Park. My three years in London were spent there and in nearby Finsbury Park. Always bedsits. Residential university accommodation was virtually non-existent in London in those days, and is still pretty thin. Having since seen the intimacy of an academic life where you live on campus or in college, I'm sorry I never had the chance to experience it for myself. On the other hand, living out in the London suburbs did provide a chance to get to know the city well. And we took it. Each weekend we would choose a tube station, go to it, then try to find our way back to the city centre on foot. As a result, I still feel very much at home in London, and know parts of it as well as I know anywhere.

I fell in love with university life as soon as I arrived, and fifty years later the love affair is still as strong as ever. I walk into the cloisters of University College now, and feel immediately and emotionally at home. Indeed, when I walk into any university anywhere I feel at home. I suppose it is the proximity to so much knowledge which is so affecting. The palpable respect for knowledge, perhaps. But it's also the wonderful diversity of people you encounter there, and the readiness to treat others as equals. Differences of class background become unimportant. Ethnic difference is seen as something positive, as a means of encountering other worlds, and not as a focus for knee-jerking, mindless, racist antagonism. In my English class in the Foster Court building I found myself alongside a chap from the South Wales valleys, another from Yorkshire with an impeccable knowledge of real ales, the son of a Berkshire country doctor with an extraordinary range of artistic talents, a mature student from the Caribbean ('Shake' Keane, who had already made a jazz career as a professional flugelhorn player), and a host more. It was a class of about forty altogether. The accents were from everywhere.

Outside the department, there was the UC Student Union, and across the street the 'federal' University of London Union (ULU – or 'yooloo', for short), both with their multiple activities. These were crucial centres for developing any sense of student community, given that most students lived well away from the college. A modern jazz group played in the UC Union each week. I'd discovered jazz during my sixth form years, having fallen in with a group of older lads, some of whom were already at (Liverpool) university. We would meet at David Peat's house and listen to his Brubeck and MJQ (Modern Jazz Quartet) records, of which he seemed to have an infinite number. When Brubeck played at the Liverpool Empire we were there. Egged on by the gang, I'd used every ounce of linguistic creativity penning a letter to the theatre in advance asking to meet him, and telling him which seats we were in. We then forgot we'd sent it. As a result, we nearly missed our moment when an usherette called out our seat numbers during the interval. We thought we were going to be told off for something or other, so we pretended we hadn't heard. But she was persistent, and dragged us out of our seats. We were taken backstage and into a dressing-room, and there lolling about was the entire Dave Brubeck Quartet, as laid back as anyone would wish, ready to sign our programmes, and asking us who we were. None of us could remember even our names, of course, and it was all a bit of a blur. For my part, I copied Paul Desmond's saxophone style from that night, and became a jazz freak for several years. London was the place to be, from that point of view. Basie, Ellington, all the big bands came through during my time there, and I saw them all. Ronnie Scott's Club – in Oxford Street, in those days – was not far away from college. My new English Department chum, Shake, was known there, of course, and he introduced me to several of the players of the day – Tubby Hayes, the tenor saxophonist, I remember with special admiration. And Shake's own playing was ethereal.

There's something about a flugelhorn, as Miles Davis aficionados don't need telling . . .

So, it was only natural to gravitate towards the UC jazz club. I was always in the audience. They already had an alto saxophonist, unfortunately, so there was no scope for an itinerant ex-Zodiac. Some of us got together, nonetheless, and made up a 'second eleven', playing on happily in an upper room in the Union. I found a double bass stored in the music room, and took it up, even to the extent of standing in once for the main jazz group's bass player when he was ill – but much to the regret of my fingers, which were virtually shredded by a whole evening's plucking. Not my metier, I concluded. In my second year, I went down to Selmers, and part-exchanged my alto for a baritone, hoping this might get me more front-line opportunities. That experiment didn't last long, either. Apart from anything else, it took far more puff than I had anticipated. A baritone is a big piece of machinery. Then, later that year I got woefully short of money, and had to sell it back to Selmers in order to live. A quite Dickensian moment, really. Bring on the violins.

The artistic richness of London was both a plus and a minus – a plus, because there was so much, in every conceivable genre; and a minus, because it was all so expensive. In Liverpool, I'd often been to the Philharmonic Hall with my mother, and I remember the Promenade Concert seasons there with special affection, but as she'd always been paying I had no real idea of the true cost of the sound of music. Still, I managed to get to the occasional London concert, including one memorable evening when Stravinsky's *Firebird Suite* was being played, and I found myself in the gods with a perfect view of a tiny old man in the front row of the circle, who stood up and took a bow at the end of it. The composer himself. Not everything was prohibitively expensive. The London Prom Concerts, for instance. But I never got to Covent Garden, for example – and, given the present-day prices, am still not sure whether I can afford to go.

The routine student outing was to the cinema, where foreign films in black and white were all the rage. The cult film of the day was *L'année dernière à Marienbad (Last Year at Marienbad)*. We went to see it in a cinema on Regent Street just after its premier, and it blew us all away. We went back to our digs and spent the whole night working out how it was that the ominous character in the film was always able to beat everyone else at 'the match game'. This was a simple game in which four rows of matches (or cards, or counters) were laid out in the sequence 7, 5, 3, 1. The two players take it in turns to remove any number of matches from any one row at a time. The object is to make the other person take the last match. In the film it is played at Very Significant Moments, and as I say, the 'bad guy' (or is he a bad guy?) always wins. How did he do it? By the end of the night, we had worked out all the possible combinations and strategies. We understood how he did it. And this knowledge stayed with me. Years later, when parish priests were looking for events at local fêtes, I was able to offer 'Beat the Master', taking on the role of the bad guy and daring anyone to beat me. It seems so simple, but unless you've done your homework you'll always lose. Of course, some of the people I beat didn't take their defeat lying down. One student, a computer buff, got out his calculator and got so good so quickly that the only way I could beat him was to add extra matches randomly to the rows before we began. He said it was cheating! As if using a calculator wasn't? And I remember one man, at a church fête in Holyhead, who took himself off to the Seaman's Club, got all his mates together, and several pints later came back determined to win. He was a belligerent-looking brute. He won.

But what about work, I hear you murmuring. Is not that why you went to university, to read an English degree? Why are you not enthusing about all the wonderful linguistic experiences of that first year? Well, sad as it is to report it, that first year fell far short of the promise I'd expected from my earlier sporadic and amateur encounters with philology. There were some great names in the department – Hugh Smith, for example, who was indefatigably working his way through the place-names of Yorkshire, and who taught us the development of the language. There were classes on Old English, Old Norse, and Middle English, as well as several on literary topics, and some on creative writing. But with just a few exceptions the linguistic subjects did not come alive. The languages remained resolutely dead.

I remember the puzzlement and increasing frustration as I got closer to classical philology. The books would present an old language solely in its written form. One of the books had a paradigm of an Old English noun, *cyning*, the word for 'king'. It gave us no indication of how it should be pronounced. The notes said that the *y* symbol represented a certain type of 'fronting' of the vowel, but in the absence of any phonetics training at that point it was not clear what 'fronting' was, and the book did not tell us. I went and asked my lecturer, Geoffrey Needham, 'How do you pronounce this word?' His answer was accurate but evasive. It was a mini-essay on the difficulties of ever knowing exactly how Old English was pronounced, on the nature of sound-change and how everything was a hypothesis based on spellings, many of which were of uncertain status due to scribal inconsistency . . . I persisted. But please, can you not give me even a rough idea? Reluctantly, he pronounced it, then said it in two or three different ways, but my ear wasn't good enough to pick the distinctions up. Still,

I had got the general idea: *cyning* had the stress on the first syllable, and the *y* sounded a bit like the vowel in the French *tu*. That's all I wanted. An approximation. But I was depressed at the reaction I'd had, and didn't ask again.

Throughout my first year, I treated Old English and the other old languages we were exposed to as a kind of written abstraction, a set of symbols representing a world which probably had no real existence at all. So there was a thing called *Beowulf* written in it, but that was just shorthand for a vast number of abstract sound-changes. The introduction said it had been spoken or sung, but nobody in our department seemed to know or care how it might have sounded in real life. Philology seemed like a phonetically alien world. It could make a chap broody. I could quite see how, as Eugène Ionesco had put it a few years before (in *The Lesson*), 'philology leads to crime'.

Looking back, I can see that it was John Dodgson who kept my faith in philology alive. A bluff, jovial northerner, whose every movement spoke 'down to earth'. He was into place-names in a big way, and a few years later would produce a fine account of locations in Cheshire. 'Who would like to come on a place-name field trip this weekend?' he announced one day. This sounded interesting. I put my hand up. 'We meet at the Lamb and Flag at one o'clock on Saturday,' and he told us where it was. Somewhere in the direction of Abingdon, the other side of Oxford. It turned out that he was doing some work on the place-names of Oxfordshire, and he had arranged to interview some people in the pub. There were three or four of us, and by the time we got there, he was well into it. As far as I could tell, the research methodology was to pour pints of ale down the throats of anybody over seventy, and get them to talk about the names for the four-acre field, the local wood, and everything else that could be located on a detailed map of the vicinity. It was amazing the stories that these old men came out with. Extraordinary memories they had, and a real enjoyment in talking about their local histories. It was a lunch full of reports of gossip, past scandal, lawsuits, slander, illicit marriages, murders, hangings, and much more. I had never imagined that places could have so much dramatic history encapsulated in their few sounds and spellings. Here was a philology of the real world, with a vengeance. Lunch lasted till about ten o'clock that night. What happened to afternoon closing time I have no idea. John Dodgson seemed to have fixed it all up. His enthusiasm for the subject was obvious. His single-mindedness and meticulous probing stayed in my mind. This was how things should be done, I thought, blurrily, as we found our way to the late-night bus back to London. We could do with more trips like that.

But that was the only one, for the whole year. And the other lecturers didn't operate in that way. Philology remained buried in its books, with one finger always in the glossary at the back. I remember John Dodgson's lesson, though; and many years later would use it myself, when I did some dialectology work. Others did, too. Alan Thomas, when he was working on the Welsh Dialectology Survey in the 1960s, used to tell me how important it was to make sure that any research grant in that field allowed for the beer-money which would be an essential means of lubricating the inhibitions of local informants. The point would have to be phrased circumspectly in grant applications, of course. I can't imagine a Social Science Research Council responding favourably to 'Item: 250 pints of dark ale – £100'; but they might not worry too much about 'Item: elicitation materials – £100' under 'Methodology'. The point is a serious one. When you are investigating language, you are investigating people. Language has no existence apart from the people who speak it. To get to know a language, you have to get to know the people. There is no other way. And what better way is there of getting to know someone than over a glass or two in a snug?

Some classes went on all year, some lasted just a term. One course looked especially interesting, in the third term. It was called 'introduction to linguistics'. I had heard the name, and come across it occasionally in my Picton Library delving, but had no real idea what it was about. It turned out to be the science of language – so Jeremy Warburg told us in our first lecture. This sounded like the most wonderful idea, with unlimited possibilities. A science, of language! A subject exclusively devoted to the study of these most amazing of human creations. I don't think I ever looked forward to a lecture series so much. But the lecturing strategy was to expound the thinking found in some of the most influential books on the subject. They included Ogden and Richards' *The Meaning of Meaning*, Ferdinand de Saussure's *Course in General Linguistics*, and Leonard Bloomfield's *Language*. Today, I regard all these books with deserved awe. The Bloomfield, in particular, is one of the top half-a-dozen books on language of the twentieth century. But I would never, in my wildest nightmares, think of introducing first-year students to my subject by using any of these books as their very first initiation into it. I had been so impressed by the title of the Ogden and Richards book that, having seen it on the reading list, I had chosen it as my State Scholarship prize from St Mary's, but after a few pages I wished I'd chosen Wordsworth instead. I found its abstract reasoning unappealing and its disambiguation difficult – they do, after all, distinguish sixteen different major meanings for the term *meaning*. As for Saussure, I think I sensed his pioneering spirit, but I found the exposition intractable (it is in fact a compilation based on his students' notes, made after his death), and felt completely out of my depth in his abstractions. And I found the breadth of Bloomfield unnerving. There was so much in that book – more than five hundred pages covering the subject from every conceivable point of view. Definitions of morpheme and phoneme, inflection and derivation, metonymy and metaphor, and all to be assimilated in a week. I bought my copy, and read obediently, but felt the subject slipping out of my grasp. I could not see the wood for the trees, and there were so many trees. We were given an essay at the end of the course, by way of assessment. I can't remember the title of the essay, but I remember my mark. It was a D. A fail.

I have no doubt that it was a fair mark. I had found the subject confusing, ponderous, and unmotivating, and it must have showed. There were some good bits, of course – the exotic language examples in Bloomfield were eye-openers. Imagine: languages with pronouns for 'you two, 'you three', a fourth person ('him here' vs. 'him over there'), and more besides. The American Indian languages were amazing in the differences they displayed from the familiar world of Indo-European. But the phonetics was the killer, or rather, the lack of it. Repeatedly I found myself involved in passages where I couldn't understand what I was reading because I couldn't hear what the text was saying. There were too many symbols. It was all going too fast. I wasn't intellectually ready to handle the abstract reasoning. And it just wasn't – well, it just wasn't fun. If there's one thing I believe in now, more than anything else, it is that linguistics is fun. When Andrew Radford got the chair of linguistics at Bangor in the 1980s he believed this too, and actually went so far as to have a T-shirt made on which the slogan 'Linguistics Is Fun' came across loud and clear. It raised a few academic eyebrows, but he was absolutely right. The sad thing, of course, is that it needed to be done. Nobody would doubt the point if there hadn't been several generations of linguists and philologists who believed that fun has nothing to do with it. The tradition, especially in Germany (where so much philology began), is that the study of language is a serious business. By contrast, undertakers have a ball. That at least is the impression one gets after reading nineteenth-century philologists. It is certainly no laughing matter. There has to be balance in all things, of course: language study requires serious commitment and discipline, as I said in Chapter 5. But it is so central to everything we do that its study should be capable of reflecting everything we do – and that includes the enjoyment which comes from investigating how things work, how people behave. Language is full of surprises, and courses and texts should go out of their way to capture them.

LINGUIST AS COUTURIER

There have been some fine T-shirts in the history of linguistics. One I especially remember. It was during a visit to Georgetown University in Washington in the 1970s. It's a Jesuit university, and several of the linguists there were priests, such as Frank Dinneen and Walter Cook. One of the linguistic theories which was achieving a widespread application in those days was called tagmemics. It was an approach devised by Kenneth Pike which came to be used throughout the world as part of the activities of the Summer Institute of Linguistics – an organization whose chief aim is the translation of the Bible into as many languages as possible. It made use of several technical concepts, including the 'tagmeme' – a notion which allows the analyst to link the forms of a language with their functions. It is a kind of basic unit, from which all grammatical things stem. I walked into the department one day, and there was Walter proudly sporting a new T-shirt. It said, 'God is the ultimate tagmeme.'

Some of the tenets of the way I practise linguistics were fuelled, I can now see, by that negative first-year experience. I learned there how NOT to do linguistics. I learned the importance of the overall view, the necessity of introducing the subject slowly, the crucial need to balance theory and practice, the benefits of working from understandable examples towards theory and not the other way round, and the desirability of injecting as much enjoyment into the encounter as is possible. Many linguists recognize these principles now, and there are several fine published introductions based on them. But at the time I had only a vague intuition about these things. There were no 'easy' introductions to linguistics, in those days. The subject wasn't even an undergraduate degree subject then. And my sporadic reading around the subject wasn't enough. I did find some books whose genius lay as much in the writing as in the content – Edward Sapir's *Language* remains a light in an otherwise dark term. And the study of individual languages remained as fascinating as ever. I wandered into some weird parts of the UC library, where all kinds of languages were on display. I bought second-hand books on Gaelic, Polish, Russian, Spanish, and anything else I could get cheaply. As I mentioned, I topped up my Welsh batteries by joining the Welsh group at the City Lit. And I applied for a grant to go to France. But after failing my first formal meeting with linguistics, I concluded it wasn't for me. I had met my lady, and she had found me wanting.

It was time to do something else. The literary side of the course had been much more appealing. Everybody found the language side deadly. The lit courses, by contrast, were full of interest, and prompted many late-night discussions. They had reading lists of obscene length, and there was no alternative but to get on with them. That first year – indeed, during all three years – I began to read my way through English literature. I blessed my decision to choose Legouis and Cazamian's *History of English Literature* as a school form prize a couple of years before. Plays, novels, poems, essays, letters, diaries, short stories, British, American, English, Scots, Irish, Welsh . . . 'Twas all one. And, of course, there was the accompanying 'critical apparatus'. I initially made the mistake, as many do, of reading the literary criticism before reading the authors, thinking it would be easier. What a blunder. The right way, I soon learned, was to put the criticism in the middle of a creative sandwich. Read the text first, then the crit, then the text again. That way you get a triple discovery, and a triple pleasure. There is the basic delight of the first encounter – finding out what happens. There is the reflective delight of the second encounter, having things pointed out to you that you missed. And there is the creative delight of the third encounter, as you re-engage with the text, in the light of that process of reflection.

There is a fourth encounter, too, when your re-reading makes you query the judgement of the critics – a process fuelled by the lecturing method itself, which routinely passed judgement, often clinical and unforgiving, on the authors. I learned early: nothing, no one, was sacrosanct. The result was a growing confidence in my own judgement. I could feel myself being shaped, and it was great. I became intensely self-critical. I have only one record of my undergraduate writing to support this memory. I have long since lost or destroyed all my essays. But a few years ago, I was looking again at some Old English textbooks to find examples for *The Cambridge Encyclopedia of the English Language*, and I found, tucked into the back of one of them, a neatly folded tutorial essay. It was on 'The character of Old English poetic diction'. Six foolscap pages of unbelievably neat writing. Then, at the bottom of the last page, a note from me to me: 'Rewrite the whole bloody thing with the emphasis on the Christian impetus to most of this poetry.' This is followed by a comment from the tutor: 'A severer comment than I would make.' I think it was Geoffrey Needham, bless him.

Shakespeare was a central element of the course – as he should be (though this sentiment is honoured too much in the breach, these days) – and he was given an in-depth treatment. There were no fewer than three specialists in the department – Arthur Brown, Winifred Nowottny, and

Hilda Hulme. Brown taught us the necessity of understanding as much as possible of the social and historical situation of the time – and, not least, the world of the Elizabethan theatre, publishing, and printing. We revelled in Henslowe's Diary. One of Nowottny's books, *The Language Poets Use*, was later a major influence on my developing views about style. That book begins, 'In considering the language of poetry it is prudent to begin with what is "there" in the poem – "there" in the sense that it can be described and referred to as unarguably given by the words.' It seems to be stating the obvious, but when you read just how much criticism relies on an unsubstantiated personal response, and how much of its terminology masquerades as objective statement, you can see the point. I learned the importance of evidence in stylistic judgement from her, and as the book was being written during those UC years, the point came across with freshness and urgency. It's so important that lecturers should introduce some of their ongoing research findings, problems, and feelings into their expositions, and take their students into their intellectual confidence. And it's such a shame that this happens so infrequently.

From Hilda Hulme came another important message – the importance of placing Shakespeare fully within the language of his time, 'putting him into his linguistic context'. Her book, *Explorations in Shakespeare's Language*, was also being written then (it came out in 1962), and here too I remember the way in which she would talk in tutorials about fragments of her research. Putting language into context is as critical with reference to Shakespeare as to anyone – if not more so, given the amount of minute attention paid to the language of his texts. 'Language into context' is a rather intimidating way of putting it. What it really means is to try to see the way Shakespeare chose his words in the light of the way everyone else was choosing words at the time. It takes only a moment to appreciate that there were many others – probably some four million, in the reign of Queen Elizabeth I – who spoke 'the tongue that Shakespeare spake' (as Wordsworth put it); but once the point is grasped it becomes obvious that the only way to appreciate his genius is to find out as much as possible about the language of his time. Only in that way can we be accurate in our judgement about his linguistic uniqueness and impact. The point would not have to be made if it wasn't so often overlooked.

LINGUIST AS QUANTITY SURVEYOR

People both underestimate and overestimate Shakespeare's effect on the English language. At the moment, we seem to be going through a period of severe overestimating. I wrote this paragraph a day after watching an edition of ITV's *South Bank Show* on the continuing popularity of Shakespeare, in which I heard one of the literary contributors holding the view that 'Shakespeare invented a quarter of our language', while another germanely observed that 'Shakespeare *is* our language'. Neither point stands up to even a superficial examination. Shakespeare's total vocabulary (measured by the number of different words he used in his works) is in fact rather small, judged by present-day standards. It approaches 20,000. The latest edition of the *Oxford English Dictionary* (*OED*) contains some half a million. A modern medium-sized college dictionary contains some 100,000, about half of which are in the active vocabulary of most graduates (that is, words they are likely to use), and a further quarter additionally in their passive vocabulary (that is, words they know but do not use).

Great writers don't need to have their contribution exaggerated. All we need do is tell it as it is. Shakespeare's long-term linguistic contribution is not so much in the words he gave the language as in his demonstration of how it was possible to be creative with language. Many words attributed to Shakespeare (in the sense that his use is the first one attested in the *OED*) could have been routinely used by others of his time – 'everyday' coinages such as *hopeless* and *successful*. Then there are all the words which appear first in Shakespeare and which do *not* remain in the language, such as *indirection* and *impartment*. Many of his especially brilliant creations, such as *incarnadine* and *cerements*, are not part of modern English; they have not been an influence on the language; they remain Shakespearean. All this has to be considered in any evaluation. Without a doubt, we are left with a core of lexical poetic creativity which is unparalleled in the history of English. But a great deal of this is to do with fresh uses of older words (the 'functional shift' of *uncle me no uncle*), new senses for older words (*scandal*, in the sense of 'damage to reputation', as distinct from its earlier, religious senses), inventive images (*the morn in russet mantle clad*), and insightful observations, some of which have become proverbial (*love is blind*). Only a relatively small part is to do with the construction of brand-new words from scratch.

I had consciously discovered Shakespeare, as so many young people do, a few years before as part of the 'set text' ethos of examinations. But my first real meeting with the plays was at Stratford during my A-level year, when my mother and I stayed there for a week. One of the A-level texts was *Othello*, and it was being produced that year. Paul Robeson starred, and his performance stays with me, as does Sam Wanamaker's (Iago). It was a great week. We visited all the usual places, and by the end of that week, Shakespeare lived. I read as many of the plays as I could, bought a complete works, and was thus more than ready by the time various university lecture courses began. Because the author had come first, the intellectualizing of the commentators and critics fell into place. I had none of the difficulty that I encountered with my first exposure to linguistics. Indeed, I think a lot of my eventual ability to handle the abstraction of linguistic reasoning has to be put down to the literary critical discipline which I took on board in those first university years, especially in those Shakespeare classes. I can't otherwise explain why Shakespeare has stayed so much with me, intellectually. I don't have a 'favourite author' – I have too many competing for that title – but he is certainly the author I have found myself most often coming back to, over the years, and the one I always turn to first when I am searching for illustrations of linguistic points. This is a dangerous manoeuvre, though, if you are in a hurry. You pick up a play to search for a quick example at the beginning of Act I, and put it down three hours later at the end of Act V.

A linguistic interest in an author can be risky. You can get so interested in the process that you forget the content and disregard the drama. Fortunately, UC had an excellent theatre group, and there were regular chances to see some of the plays performed. I remember a splendid Hamlet from Tony Garnett. There were departmental opportunities, too, for anyone with an acting interest to have a go at reading various roles, and I seized them whenever I could. At the end of the first year there was the usual departmental party. Somehow I ended up writing and directing the first-year contribution – *William Shakespeare, This Is Your Life* – with the role of the interviewer thrown in for good measure. It was a hit, and I was warmly congratulated by all three professors, Sutherland, Smith, and Brown – though the meaningfulness of the latter's effusive language was somewhat diminished when I found myself stepping over his gently snoring frame in the Foster Court corridor a few minutes afterwards. More later on the intimate and interesting relationship between alcohol and literature.

The end-of-year party settled it, as far as I was concerned. It was a literary career for me. Language, to the blackest devil. Linguistics, to the profoundest pit. I looked at the specialist options available in the second year and knew what my decisions would be – all literary ones. Languages were all well and good, but they were practical tools, no more, worth polishing, but of no intellectual interest at all. And as it happened, during the first year an opportunity had come up to do some polishing. One of the big London livery companies had made bursaries available to enable students to travel abroad; you had to come up with an interesting project and to write up a report at the end. The bursaries were advertised, and one of the lecturers drew my attention to them. I found an organization which arranged programmes for travelling students. It was called Concordia, and among their offerings was a three-week stay in Les Contamines-Montjoie, in Haute-Provence, France, working on various environmental projects. Concordia looked after the food and accommodation if someone else paid the travel. I put together a proposal and it was accepted. A few weeks later, I packed my old scout rucksack, picked up my saxophone, and took the train for Dover.

It was on the train from Calais that I first sensed the real magnitude of a language – and especially the enormity of the gap between my schoolboy French and what everyone else seemed to be speaking. It wasn't that ticket inspectors, coffee-sellers, and all the rest weren't able to follow my painfully constructed sentences; they simply adopted a brave expression and waited for me to get to the end. It was their responses which did for me. At the station change in Paris, I nearly missed my connection through a total comprehension breakdown. It got worse at Chamonix, where there was another station change. And when I was exposed to the rural speech of Les Contamines, I gave myself up for lost. I was one of the first to arrive, and was met by our team supervisor, who took me by téléférique to the chalet which we were using as a dormitory. The others turned up during the next day or so – a mixture of nationalities, but mainly French and Algerian. My linguistic salvation came when I was assigned to share with one of the Algerians. He had Arabic as a first language, and French as a second, so he spoke the latter more slowly than the Parisians had done, and in a staccato style which I found both pleasant and highly intelligible. I picked up all his colloquialisms in no time, including (I discovered much later) some interference from Arabic. From him I learned how to end French sentences with a preposition. I still remember the first time I dared to end one with *avec* – it was like gaining my linguistic spurs.

There was so much of linguistic interest in that cabin. From my Algerian friends I gained my first experience of a mixed language and saw how well it worked. They were inveterate code-switchers, using their Arabic whenever they wanted to set themselves apart from the French nationals in the group. I soaked up as much Arabic as I could, and learned to sing 'Moustafa' – the bilingual pop-song hit of the year – as lustily as the best of them. (I bought the record when I got back to England, and it remains a piece of nostalgia in my collection.) One of them – a wiry, mischievous lad called Moq – was very anxious to learn English, so I traded him English in exchange for Arabic, when the work got boring. We kept it up for a while afterwards, too. In an early example of distance learning, I would send him lessons by letter in English and he would reply in Arabic. But the effort involved in an impromptu correspondence course was very great (oh, for email then) and didn't survive the onset of the new university year.

Because of my musical companion in her case, I was called 'David Saxo' by the group, and the instrument did sterling service in the evening sing-songs. During the day we would troop down to one or other part of the hillside where we cleared paths, dug out new walkways, built bridges over streams, and generally prepared this corner of France for the tourist season. It was harder work than I thought it would be, but linguistically it was a pleasure-dome. At the end of the three weeks, I was aching, but reasonably fluent. We split up, some of us arranging to meet on the Pont Neuf in Paris a few days later – one of those meetings that somehow never happened. I hitched down through Avignon to Marseilles, then tried to hitch to Paris. After a fruitless day standing at a roadside waiting for a lift which never came, I cut my losses and took the train. I had enough for a ticket to Lyons. I stayed on the train after Lyons, and found that my French had improved enough to argue my poverty to the ticket-inspector on the Paris leg. Linguistic fluency is never a guarantee of railway generosity, however, and I was about to be thrown off the train at the next stop when some American tourists came to my aid, and paid the excess for me. God bless America. But I missed my tryst with them in Paris and then lost their contact details. I have always wanted to pay them back. So it goes.

The judicious use of the saxophone on the Pont Neuf earned enough to keep me alive in Paris for a couple of days, until it was time to take the train to Calais. Then it was back to Liverpool for a few days before the new term. I remember walking past St Mary's, still cherishing my newly honed French skills, and thinking: what a let-down the five years of school French had been. I should have been able to do better than that, after *five years*. A long time later, when I'd had a chance to study the language of teaching materials in detail, I could see why it hadn't worked. The grammar-translation methods which had performed so well for Latin had been a disaster for French. I could read the language fine, and spell it well enough. But I doubt whether I spoke it in real conversational settings for more than a few minutes in total during all those school years.

Then it was October, and a new term began at UC. A new set of courses on a variety of topics. Some new lecturers, it seemed, from the schedule. But the balance more or less as before. Literature options were beckoning sexily, in their best dresses. I turned up for the obligatory course on the history of the language with gloomy anticipation. Linguistics was a receding dream.

Then the doors of the Foster Court lecture room burst open, and Randolph Quirk walked in.

Chapter 7
Becoming academic

Well, I say 'walked'. Did you ever see the cult series *The Prisoner* from the 1960s? At the beginning of each episode we see Patrick McGoohan striding purposefully along a corridor to confront his spymasters with his resignation. He reaches the double doors to the inner sanctum, and thrusts both panels open at once, standing there framed in the doorway like an avenging angel. Quirk (see plate 1.1) arrived like that. He incarnated himself into the room, enthused at us about the history of the language, harangued us to take the matter seriously, and in one hour changed my life. I don't remember much about the topic that day, or his approach. I can recall only one thing clearly. In the middle of the lecture he spoke some sentence and told us to write it down in phonetic transcription. We looked at each other. What on earth was phonetic transcription? He saw our blankness. None of us knew even where to begin. He blasted us. 'How can anybody study the English language without knowing anything about phonetics?' I write the sentence with a question-mark, though the intonation was that of a parade-ground sergeant. I took the point, but how to do something about it? The solution came a sentence later. 'If you want to get somewhere with my subject, get over to Gimson and O'Connor in Phonetics and sign on!' Who? Where?

This, it emerged upon enquiry, was A. C. Gimson and J. D. O'Connor ('Gim' and 'Doc', as they were universally known to their colleagues), two of the lecturers in the UC Phonetics Department. I didn't know it at the time, but this was *the* Phonetics Department – the place where Daniel Jones, *the* Daniel Jones, had achieved his reputation as the leading British phonetician of the twentieth century. Five years later I would review DJ's eightieth birthday volume for *le maître phonétique* ('The Phonetics Master'), and would get a charming little thankyou card from him, in spidery handwriting. He died not long afterwards. But back in 1960, I had no sense of the latent power of those emphasized definite articles. Quirk's power, on the other hand, was by no means latent. As soon as his lecture was over I made my way to the Phonetics Department, located in an unprepossessing building down one side of the UC site on Gordon Street. The shortest way from Foster Court was up a fire escape through the back door. I found myself in an old building, full of steep narrow staircases and dark dusty corridors. A secretary told me where to find Gimson, and after a bit of a search I discovered him behind a desk in a tiny room on the first floor, surrounded by mounds of paper, and facing a small blackboard covered in esoteric symbols. I explained who I was. Professor Quirk had sent us. 'Us?' It dawned on me that I was the only one there. 'Maybe others would be following on?' Maybe. I explained what Quirk had said. A tired look crossed Gimson's face. He had evidently heard this before.

It turned out that it was so unusual for someone from the English Department to take the phonetics option that they weren't entirely sure what to do with me. I was indeed the only one who had responded to the Quirkian invite. I found myself attached to a couple of other students who were doing an MA in phonetics, John Wells and Eleanor Higginbotham. I got to know John well in later years, often finding myself at the same conferences or committee meetings. He went into academic life, too, and indeed became professor of phonetics himself at UC in 1988. But their timetable was very different from mine, so I often turned up for my weekly classes – one with Gim, one with Doc – and was the only one there. I didn't realize at the time just how privileged a situation that was. One-to-one tuition is critical in phonetics training, but few students have the fortune to benefit from it – especially these days. The ear-training side (where the teacher articulates all kinds of weird and wonderful sounds) can be done in groups; but the performance side (where the hapless student has to pronounce the sounds back) is unavoidably face-to-face – or perhaps mouth-to-ear would be more precise. It turned out I had something of an aptitude for the subject. I could mimic most sounds quite quickly. I was told I had a good ear for pitch contrasts, and indeed I found the intonational side of speech particularly interesting. That interest would prove to be lifelong.

The phonetics classes were wonderful, largely due to the brilliant teaching. Gim and Doc were very different, physically (see plates 1.2 and 1.3). Gim was a sturdy man in his mid-forties, with a slight cast in his left

LINGUIST AS PHONETICIAN

Phonetics, I quickly learned, was far more than copying sounds accurately. It also meant being able to analyse them into the factors involved in their articulation. That took longer. A precise knowledge of the different vocal organs is fundamental – which means more than just knowing where they are and what they do; it means knowing how they feel and how they sound. One of the most important skills in learning to be a phonetician is the ability to work both ways, from articulatory position to sound and from sound to articulatory position. You have to be able to produce a sound, at will, by putting your vocal organs in the right place. Then, you have to be able to work out from hearing a sound which articulatory organs are involved. This isn't so hard when you're dealing with consonants, because in most cases you can feel the parts of the mouth touching or coming close together – or even see them, when the sounds are at the front. But when you're dealing with vowels, it's the devil of a job, for all you have to go on is a sense of where your tongue is in the middle of the mouth, and sensing small tongue movements isn't so easy. It took me ages to get the vowels right. Fortunately, there was a lifeline. Daniel Jones had devised a 'cardinal vowel' system for working out where vowels go, based on the theoretical limits of tongue movement that the human being is capable of. It was probably the most useful single piece of linguistic apparatus I would ever learn.

eye which gave him a perpetual twinkle. Doc was slightly older, tall, with hair rapidly receding, thick-rimmed spectacles, a moustache, and a broad smile. They were both genial, warm, patient (an essential attribute for any phonetician), and with a great sense of humour (an entry qualification to the subject, it would seem, when in later years I met the rest of the Phonetics Department). Another of Doc's distinguishing features was his eyebrows. A lecturer's eyebrows can be an invaluable tool to neophyte phoneticians in their early encounter with ear-training. In Doc's case, whenever the pitch of one of his test sentences went up, his eyebrows did too. When my ears let me down, I watched those eyebrows – and blessed them.

As someone from the English Department I was taught only the basics about the sounds of the world's languages, but – for the same reason – I was given an in-depth introduction to English accents. It's a magical moment when you follow the instructions, put your tongue and lips in the right position, and blow – and out comes a perfect bit of Birmingham, or Australia, or wherever. Developing a conscious sense of how all the sounds (especially the vowels) in a particular accent fit together is highly satisfying too. It's a point, I would later find, that is often missed in the training of actors. Actors can be very good at imitating accents, and learning dialogues off by heart under the tuition of a dialect coach. But the real test of whether you have mastered an accent is whether you can identify words in isolation – and, moreover, words that aren't in the script. How would someone from Birmingham say 'suit'? How would someone from Edinburgh say 'put'? How would someone from Newcastle say the sentence 'Can we go now'? That's what a professional knowledge of English accents involves. Today, of course, a thorough course would have to include accents related to English-speaking populations all over the world – South Africa, Canada, Singapore . . .

Meanwhile, back at the Foster Court ranch, my forays into the phonetic darkness had attracted not a little comment from my literary friends, many of whom found themselves struggling with the technicalities of the language side of the course. By contrast, as I took to it more and more, it became increasingly easy. Classmates sensed this, and approached me for help. It was all fair trading. As I spent progressively more time on the language courses, so there was less time for the literary ones. I remember swopping information on Middle English grammar for good sources on the nineteenth-century novel, and there must have been hundreds of such bargains made during my second and third years. The Quirk course just got better and better. And the splendid thing was that its content spilled over into the other language courses. Old English pronunciation was becoming a doddle. Sound changes were beginning to mean something. Even the Bloomfield mountain looked climbable. In my second year I followed an optional course on comparative philology given by Oswald Szemerenyi, a scholar whose accent was almost as unpronounceable as his name, and it was bliss. Soon after, I picked up Saussure again, and found myself sailing through it, even daring to write critical remarks in the margins. I did very respectably in the second-year examinations, and my tutorial essay marks were apparently building up nicely. I was awarded the annual Early English Text Society prize. Linguistics looked as if it might be Fun after all.

There wasn't one single moment when I decided on an academic life of language study. The feeling just sort of grew, during the third year. I became more involved in activities which gave me an insight into how the 'system' worked. I helped run the English Society for a while, though the only event I recall was my failure to outploy Stephen Potter in correspondence inviting him to talk to us about one-upmanship. I found myself acting as a student spokesman in departmental discussions about course structure, and getting into trouble with James Sutherland, the literature professor and head of department, for insisting (on behalf of my class) that lecture courses about authors were more (or was it less?) rewarding than lecture courses based on themes. I got into debating a bit, and found my Liverpudlian oratorical skills a boon. I was told so often that I was a 'born lecturer' that I began to believe it. People would start making remarks about it. Fellow-students would joke about it, and call me 'Prof'. Gim and Doc seemed to take my academic future for granted. There was a departmental opinion that I might do well enough in finals to stay on and do research. Quirk had just begun planning his Survey of English Usage (see Chapter 8), and had some money to appoint a couple of junior research assistants. He nobbled me in the corridor one day. Was I interested? Was I?! It would need a first, of course. Of course. The lights began to burn very very late. I had written some scripts for the university film group, which had been well received, and in my final term they offered me the chance of directing one of them. Another of those moments. I said I couldn't. Too much work. Could I come back to it after finals, in the summer, 'if all went well'? It sounded like a great way to spend a bit of the summer. We left it that way.

If all went well . . .

It was two weeks before finals. People were telling me I needed a break. They were right. There was a table in the English Department library where you could read my elbowprints. I was feeling a bit down, too. Tired. A visit to Holyhead seemed the answer. John and Audrey Meade had returned there to live. John had quit teaching a couple of years before and had gone back to the town to set up a chandlery on Newry Beach. They'd found a house in Gors Avenue, near their old family home, and it had a spare room. I got in touch. They'd be delighted to have me stay for a few days. So I packed a few books, and got the train from Euston.

I think it was the second night there. I brushed my teeth as usual and noticed some blood in the wash-basin. Must be more gentle, I thought. Lousy gums. More there the next morning. Ah well. It'll go away. And it was a lovely day. John had to paint a boat down at the beach, so I went along to help, and we started to cycle down the road. We'd just turned the corner into South Stack Road when I felt a bubbling sensation in my chest. I had to stop, and found myself coughing up blood at the side of the road. This didn't seem to be teeth. I went back to the house, and they called a doctor. Dr Bryn Evans lived just across the road. He came over straight away, and had no trouble with his diagnosis. A couple of hours later, I found myself in an ambulance being taken over to Llangwyfan hospital, near Denbigh. It was a sanatorium for TB.

Where *did* it come from? Nobody could ever tell me. Did I pick it up in France? Certainly, I felt that I had been steadily losing stamina since then. I seemed to get tired more easily, but I put all that down to the workload. I had no special licence for tiredness. After all, everyone else on the course had been feeling tired too! I thought I had always looked after my health while a student, and had never needed to visit a doctor. The TB must have been building up for ages, nonetheless, and then, bang, it just blew up. The haemorrhage was quite a serious one, said the consultant, after all the X-rays – at the top of my left lung, it turned out. Fortunately there was a drug cocktail that was proving effective against TB in those days – daily injections of streptomycin (along with daily jokes about buttocks and dartboards), with two varieties of accompanying horse-pills. They slammed the drugs into me over the first few days, and the bleeding stopped. I was let out of the intensive room, and found myself on a ward with about fifteen others. This was to be home for what I thought would be just a few days, but which turned out to be six months.

I can imagine the scene at t'mill, when the news broke. My mother had come across from Liverpool, a couple of hours away, like the proverbial lightning. She phoned the English Department. The most urgent question was what to do about the examinations – two weeks away. Doing them in the official hall in London was out of the question. Should I simply not do them, and ask for the award of an aegrotat – an unclassified degree awarded when illness prevents someone from taking finals? Or would I be well enough to do them in the sanatorium? The consultant left it up to me. The drugs had begun to work quickly, and I actually wasn't feeling too bad. I opted to take them. The university arranged to have a set of papers sent up, and the hospital fixed up a system of invigilation. Each day I was driven in a little two-seater electric trolley from the ward to a room in the staff quarters, where one of the senior nurses would look after all the necessary arrangements. At the time, I suppose I just thought of it all as part of the National Health Service; only later did I appreciate just how much administrative complexity must have been involved. Everyone wished me well. The day before the exams started I received a telegram from the department. It consisted of just one sentence – a quotation from *Henry IV Part 1*. 'How has he the leisure to be sick / In such a jostling time?' It did me the world of good.

I don't remember anything about the written exams, but the phonetics oral is impaled in my memory. They must have had an awful time finding an examiner. But in the end it turned out that Eileen Whitely, one of the phoneticians from the School of Oriental and African Studies, was going to be on holiday in North Wales, so she was cajoled into making the visit.

A time was set and in she came. I don't think it was my best phonetic performance, by a long chalk. And she didn't seem to enjoy it much either. Can't understand it, really. Maybe it was the fact that it had to take place with me in my bed surrounded by screens, and a permanent backdrop of coughing and commentary from the passers-by. Doubtless none of them – nurses or patients – had ever heard noises of the kind that examiner and examinee were exchanging. Everyone seemed to want to stop and listen to what was going on. Or maybe what put her off was the unpleasant-looking phlegm ('sputum' in the trade, don't you know) that emerged every time I tried to produce a post-velar fricative? It all had to be kept, I explained to my examiner, for analysis. I half hoped that I might get away with a half-size exam; but phoneticians are made of stern stuff, and she persevered. I got a good half-hour's grilling.

Anyway, the whole exam business took about three weeks, and then another couple of weeks while I waited for the results. James Sutherland was kind enough to write a personal note to my mother, letting her know. I'd managed to get a first, apparently without any special pleading on their part to the examining board. And Quirk had agreed to keep his offer of a research assistantship on the Survey open until I was out of hospital. An officer and a gentleman. I was delighted. All I had to do was get better.

It took longer than I thought, as you know. Six months. A long time for someone to be out of action, at that age. I had my twenty-first birthday party a few days later. Bit of a non-event, really. Then I heard from some UC friends about the end-of-term parties I'd missed, and was in a foul mood for days. Still, needs must, and routine took over. I did all the things one is supposed to do in hospital. Fell in love with one of the staff nurses – and out again when I saw the size of her boyfriend. Fell out seriously with the people in the neighbouring beds, and became their best friend a day later. Fell in line with the bizarre sense of humour of the male charge nurse, Glyn Jones, who thought it would be a good jape if (you will recall the acting skills) I dressed up as a foreign visiting consultant and took a ward round one day. Of course, virtually everyone recognized me straight away, even with a surgeon's hat and mask covering my face, but they all played along. The best bit was when one chap didn't. Tommy, a wiry diminutive Welsh ex-slate-miner from Llanelidan. He took the visit very seriously, even when I recommended to the nurse (who stood behind me, in the official way, carefully writing the instructions down) a treatment regime which involved, inter alia, Tommy standing on one leg and reciting the Welsh National Anthem before his daily injection. He took it all in, and when I asked him whether he had any questions, the rest of the ward, who were avidly listening, just fell about. 'Did it matter which leg?' he asked. When the truth came out, he vowed he would get his own back, but TB has a way of not letting you keep your promises. He was one of two men who died while I was there.

Despite the black cloud hanging over the heads of the older men, it was a merry ward. Almost all were Welsh born and bred, and most spoke Welsh as a first language. It proved to be a good time to get some more Welsh inside me. I began learning the medical terminology from a dictionary, until I realized that nobody understood it or used it. According to the dictionary, what we received every day in our buttocks was a *chwistrilliad* or a *mewnsaethiad*, but every man jack of them said 'injecshun'. To be fair, they were impressed by the dictionary words, and there was some debate one day about which was the more 'correct' word to use. There was a vote, and *chwistrilliad* won – it 'sounded more Welsh', they said. One chap decided to use it from then on – but his resolve lasted only a day, after saying to one of the staff that 'it's time for my chwistrilliad now, nurse', and she brought him a bedpan. He didn't use the word again. Of course, with my semilingual background, I was quickly at home in this kind of environment. Mind you, some of the patients had a highly irreverent attitude towards the language of heaven. One of them was a farmer called John Hughes. He was strongly Welsh nationalist. His bed-neighbour, Robin, wasn't, so there was a running political row between them – though all very good-humoured. Robin's main ground for condemnation was that, if Hughes was a true 'Welsh Nash', he would pronounce his surname correctly. Welsh is a highly phonetic language – one letter, one sound. So, Robin reasoned, the name *Hughes* should be pronounced 'hig – hess' (the letter *u* in Welsh is pronounced similarly to the *i* in English *big*). The point was still being debated when I left.

As I got better, I used the time to write. I wrote more scripts, a couple of stories, a radio documentary, and a novel. All for internal use only, you understand. I just *had* to write. What happened to the writing afterwards wasn't so important. It was during those six months, when I didn't have much alternative, that I think I found my métier. I suppose I could have done other things. There were games to be played, radios to be listened to, and plenty of things to read. I may have done all of these, but I only remember the writing. Looking through my dust-laden bottom shelf now, I see only the radio documentary has survived – a piece on Giraldus Cambriensis, the twelfth-century Welsh chronicler. The novel was consigned to perdition after I read it again in my late twenties and couldn't believe how awful it was. I suppose it's a rite of passage. Everyone has a novel in them, they say. And some people feel a lot better once it's out of them and placed on the garden bonfire. Only one person ever read it, one of my fellow-student visitors. I wish I hadn't burned it. I would have found it stylistically intriguing now.

I watched the summer of 1962 pass by. By September I was well enough to get out a bit. One of the charge nurses, David Buckley, gave me the treat of my life by taking me out on the pillion of his motor-bike, and we toured some of the Denbighshire lanes – along with a visit to Owen Glyndwr's house in Glyndyfrdwy, and the prehistoric fort behind. There were sporadic visitors from Liverpool and Holyhead – and sometimes further afield, when student buddies took the trouble to call in. The worst part was feeling back to normal again, but not in the eyes of the doctors. The last few weeks were deadly. Apart from anything else, I was so looking forward to getting down to London to start work. The Survey of English Usage had begun its year's activities. One of my student colleagues, Judith Godfrey, had also been offered an assistantship, and she had already started. Time passed. I heard it. Time passed.

Then, suddenly, I was out of there, briefly visited Molly and her family in Liverpool, and took the train down to London. My mother had been working hard, too, passed some civil service exams, and got herself a job in the East End in one of the 'labour exchanges', as they were called in those days. She'd found herself a flat in Leytonstone, and as there was a spare bedroom I went there too. Time to become acquainted with the Central Line now, for the daily journey into the Survey, housed on the first floor of Foster Court in the English Department (see plate 1.5). The morning rush-hours were no different from those on the Northern Line. I checked out my old haunts at the college. The place looked the same, but everything was subtly different. It hadn't changed much, but I had. I was a member of staff now, albeit the most junior of all – a research assistant at £67 a month (I thought it a princely sum, let me say). Doors in the buildings which I had never dared enter were now open to me. The people who had taught me were now colleagues, and expected me to use their first names or nicknames. An inevitable distance stepped in between me and the students in the year behind me, some of whom I'd got to know very well. I wasn't a student any more, I found. No more student union. No more student societies. I tracked down the film group, but the people had changed, and anyway, by the time I got back to UC, in November, they were into new projects. No film career now.

But it was just as well, for there wouldn't have been time. My illness had cost Randolph Quirk a month in lost research assistance. I was determined to make that up to him, over the duration of the assistantship – if I remember rightly, I think there was money for three years. I owed him. So I expected to start early and finish late, and that's how it was. The nature of the work, and some of the unexpected things that happened during that research year, deserves its own narrative (see Chapter 8). But it was, indeed, a hard-working year. RQ had courses to teach, and wasn't able to get into the Survey to work with me until late in the day, so it was often nine or ten o'clock at night before I got away. Monday, Tuesday, Wednesday, Friday . . . I got used to it. Slog away at my tasks during the daylight. Then checking and discussion into the long dark evenings. 'Take it easy,' the docs said on my monthly check-ups, as they renewed my supply of preventative horse-pills. 'Yes, doctor,' I would reply meekly, for indeed I was taking it easy – at least, by contrast with the examination-dominated world of six months before. I found the research world exhilarating, liberating, relaxing. Long hours were not the point. It was what you did with them that mattered. If this was working for a living, then it was a very palatable sense of the word 'work'. The possibility of a lifetime doing this sort of thing was extremely appealing.

You will have noticed, no Thursday. Thursdays were different. For on Thursdays there was the English Department Seminar.

Everyone on the staff went to the Seminar. I don't know how long it had been going as an institution before I first attended it. Probably for ever. I remember the first time I went. I was working away with RQ as usual, in my first week at the Survey, when he looked at his watch, unexpectedly turned off the tape recorder, and said, 'Right, time for the Seminar.' Odd time for a seminar, I thought, six o'clock in the evening. But I was in the earliest stages of learning what academic life was all about, so I made no comment. I tagged along, expecting to turn right and go upstairs into the department. But we didn't. We turned left, and out of the building, and into Torrington Street. I was puzzled, but trusting. Within two minutes we were at the Seminar. A series of tables pushed together, with chairs all round, and a highly convivial atmosphere. Hugh Smith beaming away at the head, Arthur Brown at his left. Most of the departmental staff, as far as I could tell, along with some faces I didn't recognize. I was formally welcomed, and – as the most junior member of staff present – given the honorary position of 'pot-boy'. Pot-boy? Oh, sorry, did I forget to tell you? We were in the back room of the Marlborough Arms.

I learned that the Seminar had begun as a domestic strategy on the part of some of the staff. Aware of the sensitivities which can surround a late-night arrival home, and anxious to give an honest answer to the loaded question, and its variants, 'Where have you been until this hour?', my new colleagues had evidently introduced the Seminar as a routine part of their working lives. 'At the Department Seminar, my dear' – I always imagined it said in the tones of Mr Pugh in *Under Milk Wood* – was a cast-iron excuse.

If any spouse, suspicious of the answer, were to check with the department, there would be ample confirmation. Thursday evenings were, indeed, Seminar evenings. And if the facilitation of academic interchange required regular phonetic maintenance, in the form of the routine application of hops, juniper, barley, and grape in their fermented liquid state to the hard and soft palates, uvular, and pharynx, then so be it. That, at any rate, was what 'pot-boy' meant. It was the privilege of the newest member of the department to trawl between bar and table, carrying the pints as required. A privilege indeed.

At that table I learned what academic life was really about. Only occasionally did the conversation turn to anything I would call 'the subject'. It was a rapid quick-fire introduction to the world of academic politics, finances, scandals, condemnations, complaints, sadnesses, and fun. I was taught what to moan about and why. I discovered the other side of the coin: I found that the staff had opinions about the students which were sometimes even more vitriolic than the opinions we students had held about the staff. These were people who had to teach and administrate, certainly, but their main aim in life was the pursuit of knowledge, and, frankly, the students would often get in the way. There were immense labours of – love, is the clichéd way of putting it; compulsion, obsession, would be more accurate – going on in that department. Huge surveys taking place of place-names and English usage. Editions of old texts being meticulously edited. I could see why they were all at that Seminar, away from the dusty manuscripts and the transcriptions and the deadlines. It was an escape, a lifeline, a means of staying sane. Here I encountered the real cut-and-thrust of the academic world. The interchanges were incisive, ferocious, unconstrained. No sign of the genteel criticism of the lectures: 'One may perhaps be permitted to doubt aspects of the reliability of Cholmondley's conclusions.' Here it was unequivocal: 'Cholmondley is a prat. He doesn't know the first thing about Chaucer.' (This said of someone whose books I had read on Chaucer.) There was a critical world here that I had never dreamed of in my philosophy. And there too I discovered the opposite – the welcome, supportive, sympathetic reality of academic camaraderie. It only took a couple of hours. By the end of my first Seminar, it was as if I had always been there. I found my way to Holborn tube station and woke up at Wanstead, fortunately only just past the stop where I should have got off.

Chapter 8
Surveying

In the meantime – between Seminars, as it were – I got on with my work at the Survey. RQ had set up this ambitious project the year before. Its aim was breathtakingly simple in conception, and mind-disturbingly complex in execution: to provide a description of the grammatical features of all varieties of spoken and written English. Surprisingly, this had never been done. The grammars of English that had been written in the past all suffered from different handicaps and limitations. Most were highly prescriptive, aiming to tell people how they *ought* to write and speak according to the author's opinion about what was correct and incorrect. The complex and varying realities of everyday spoken and written usage would not be found in those pages. Most were based on the written language, with little or no attention paid to the very different ways in which grammar was used in speech. But even within those approaches, there was an enormous selectivity – whole areas of grammatical construction (such as the way in which sentences combine into discourses) simplified or disregarded. There was distortion, too, with English sentences being forced to fit the straitjacket of Latin grammar. Several of the better books were pedagogical grammars, orientated towards teaching English as a foreign language; this made them speech-aware, but at the same time highly simplified. And the linguistically inspired descriptive accounts, such as Charles Carpenter Fries's *The Structure of English*, were programmatic in character. Nobody had previously attempted to adopt a linguistically principled grammatical perspective, and apply it systematically and comprehensively to a large and representative collection (or *corpus*) of English data. This is what the Quirk Survey was intending to do.

By the standards of the time, the corpus was certainly large. The plan was to compile a million words of spoken and written text, split into such domains as instructional prose, newspaper writing, prose fiction, broadcast news, spontaneous commentary, and telephone conversation. Each domain was represented by a set of samples, taken from recognized sources within the field. So, for instance, there would be samples taken from different legal texts, or recordings made of different kinds of sports commentary. Because of my phonetics training, I was given the job of adding a prosodic transcription to the various spoken texts, and developing the transcription so that it could cope with all the different intonations and rhythms and tones of voice that the speakers used. The basics of the intonation system had been worked out by RQ and his first research assistants the year before, but it was crude in many ways, and left a great deal out. 'It ain't what you say but the way that you say it.' My remit was to sort out 'the way that you say it'. And to make sure we covered 'all possible ways of saying it'.

The procedure involved listening to conversations and monologues on tape, transferring a short segment (usually about five seconds in length) to a device called a tape repeater, then listening to it over and over until I was absolutely certain that I had heard every little nuance of expression in the voice (see plate 1.5). I would mark the vocal effects on to a typed transcript of the words, using a special notation, and this would in due course be typed up by another member of the team. My transcription had to be checked, of course. One of the things about listening to such vocal effects as intonation is that they aren't always easy to hear. The changes of pitch, loudness, and speed which convey differences of meaning (often referred to cumulatively as the 'prosodic features' of speech) can be very subtle. It's not like listening to the words on a tape, where everyone hears *cat* as *cat* and *dog* as *dog*. With a prosodic analysis you're trying to decide whether *dog* is rising or falling in pitch, and, if rising, whether it is relatively high up or relatively low down compared with *cat*, and, if high up, whether it is forte or fortissimo, shortened or lengthened, and all sorts of other things besides. Second opinions are the order of the day – and on the Survey it was routine procedure. RQ himself was the second listener, much of the time – and I learned an important lesson in that. Even if you're the boss, you still do some of the dirty work. The day the lead researcher lets all the basic analysis and transcription be done by research assistants, that day the research starts to go downhill. If you want to be really in control, you have to be hands-on. Apart from anything else, it keeps you in touch – real touch – with your research team. And from the junior researchers' point of view, it lets you get to know in intimate detail how an experienced research mind works.

What was it like, working with Quirk? Quirking, we research assistants used to call it, though not when he was around. It gave new meaning to the word 'intensity', certainly. The man had enormous energy and enthusiasm, as I had encountered when an undergraduate, and he was able to focus that like a laser on the task in hand. When he bent his head down over a piece of transcription or grammatical analysis, it was as if everything else ceased to exist. He was in another world – and when he was concentrating in that way visitors would tend, for reasons of self-preservation, not to interrupt him. When sharing that world, as in the task of transcription-checking, I found this concentration contagious. He might come in at half past five in the afternoon, and we would start working through a text, and the next time I looked at my watch it might be eight or nine. I didn't notice time passing. The target was to reach the end of a passage, or a text, and that became the oasis in the distance. Nor, especially on Thursdays, was the oasis solely a metaphor. And yet, there was never a sense of urgency or rush. RQ must have had his deadlines and schedules, the same as everyone else, but while working on texts it was the nature of the problem which dictated the pace of the work. If he listened to an extract, and disagreed with the way I had transcribed it, he would write his version down, and then we would listen to it again . . . and again . . . until we were both satisfied with it. At the beginning I found it difficult to disagree with his interpretations – after all, he was the boss, and had twenty years more experience of data analysis than I did. But my phonetics training was solid, and I grew in confidence as I realized that I did actually know more about the prosodic field than anyone else on the project, and probably had the best ear. Before too long, he was deferring to me as much as I was to him. Disagreements still occurred, and these were marked in the margin; but they were disagreements between peers. That was the thing about Quirk: he had the gift of making his juniors feel equal.

One reason I was becoming so knowledgeable about prosody was that I'd chosen it as my subject for a doctoral thesis. It was standard practice to sign up for a PhD when becoming a research assistant, and this I'd done as soon as I arrived. I had had no difficulty in choosing a topic. My allocated task at the Survey indicated an area ripe for investigation. There was as much data around as any research student could wish for. Only the grammatical aspects of the use of prosody were being used by the Survey – those aspects, in other words, which enabled speakers to express such differences as questions and statements, or positives and negatives. Are you asking me or telling me? In speech, it can be the intonation of the voice that conveys the difference, and the Survey was anxious to find out just how many areas of spoken grammar relied on melody in this way. But other questions – how many kinds of pitch movement are there in English? which are used most frequently and why? what emotional meanings do they express, and what other vocal effects are there which also express these meanings? – were not part of the Survey's remit. These were questions to do with the nature of the English sound system, or phonology, as such. This was the area I adopted as my own.

At the beginning of the doctoral road, in the first months of 1963, the research task seemed to be unassailable – a bit like Tryfan from the A5. My first duty was to the Survey, and that left little time at the end of the day for private study. The main benefit was that I could do two jobs at once, as it were – preparing transcriptions for the Survey while choosing extracts for a more intensive analysis for my thesis. I hoped to have the data for my study collected and fully transcribed by the end of my first year – and so it proved to be. But I managed hardly any of the other tasks – the kind of background reading that needed to be done, and the detailed quantitative

LINGUIST AS DOCTOR

A doctoral thesis is an amazing thing. It takes at least three years of steady work, and in the UK that is usually the minimum period of registration. However, unless you're a full-time student it will take you longer, because you have to earn a living. It took me four years (it was 1966 when I finally presented it) – and that was short, compared with some. It's by no means unusual for people to take five years or more to finish their doctorate. Sadly, some never finish, as life gets in the way. But if you are able to maintain a steady involvement, there is nothing quite like doctoral research as a new postgraduate. It's your first opportunity to become really focused on a subject. And it gradually dawns on you that, for a fragment of intellectual time, you know more about a particular subject than anyone else in the world, because of the depth of investigation you have been able to achieve – and that includes your examiners, who encounter only those aspects of your research topic that you have chosen to let them see. Having supervised and examined many doctoral theses, over the years, I know how much I do not know, whenever I have the privilege of evaluating a project. The encounter with the knowledge it contains is always a humbling experience.

analysis and interpretation. All this would take up a lot of midnight oil in the ensuing three years. In the meantime, I burnt the UC mid-evening oil. The Survey room on the first floor of Foster Court became a home from home. Dimly, from time to time, I heard of a new Liverpool pop group that seemed to be doing quite well. But that was some other world. For me, 'the 60s' didn't begin until mid-decade.

Some very strange things happened, during that year. Once, I'm on my own in the Survey room, late in an afternoon, when the phone rings.

'Is that the Survey of English Usage?'

'Yes,' I say, in my most helpful tone.

'Ah, can you help? This is J—— & Co. of the Strand, shoe retailers.'

'Yes,' I say, rather more cautiously.

'We're told you deal in English grammar?'

'Yes.'

'Good. You see we're launching a new range of shoes next month, and we're just beginning to put together our marketing material. But we've hit a snag.'

'Oh yes?'

'We can't think of the best kind of words to use to describe these shoes. Can you help?'

'Adjectives, you mean?'

'Exactly, adjectives. Do you have any?'

'Excuse me?'

'Do you have any adjectives that you could send us?'

'Adjectives?'

'Yes' – the tone was beginning to sound irritated at my obtuseness – 'Could we order some adjectives?'

I began to stammer. 'How – er, how – many would you like?'

'Well, how many do you think we might need?'

'A couple – a couple of dozen, perhaps?' I was beginning to feel a bit dizzy, and was not sure what I was saying.

'How do you sell them? By the dozen?' asked the voice.

'Probably,' I said very huskily.

'Well, we'll have two dozen then – no, make that three, to be on the safe side.'

Then something clicked. Of course. This was a jape. It was a mate of Judith's, probably, who had been persuaded to ring me up. Brilliant. I decided to play along. I became more business-like.

'One moment, sir, while I find our order-book . . . That's three dozen assorted English adjectives. For Messrs J—— & Co. The Strand, did you say?' I was given a number. Then I took the initiative.

'Of course, you do realize that adjectives by themselves may not do the whole task?' This time it was my caller's turn to say, 'Excuse me?'

'Oh yes, sir, you'll need nouns and verbs as well, perhaps even some adverbs.' (I remembered Humpty Dumpty, paying his parts of speech their wages on a Saturday night.) 'We do a very good line in nouns, actually, sir,' I say.

'How much are they?'

'Well, adjectives are threepence each. Nouns I'm afraid are sixpence. Verbs are ninepence. But we do have a special deal going this month, and if you order all three, we throw in the adverbs for nothing. That's quite a saving, as adverbs are normally a shilling. They're longer, you see,' I added helpfully. 'Because of their endings.'

'That's very useful,' said my voice. 'I'll take two dozen of each.'

'Thank you, sir,' I say effusively. 'A pleasure doing business with you.'

'That'll be . . . £1 19*s*. exactly, then.' (He was good, I'd give him that.)

'Shall we say £2, for postage and packing?'

'Excellent. We'll send you a confirmation of the order tomorrow.'

I put the phone down and laughed until I cried. It was Seminar night, and I told the others what had happened. Everybody agreed it was an excellent jape. Then, two days later, in the morning post, arrived a letter, from Messrs J—— & Co., the Strand. Our secretary, Joan, opened it: it was an order for three dozen adjectives, two dozen nouns, two dozen verbs, and two dozen adverbs, with a request that early fulfilment of the order would be appreciated. We looked them up in the phone book. There was a Messrs J—— & Co. And they sold shoes.

We had a hasty meeting. Should we ring them up and explain? It was a genuine interest, and a genuine order, whatever the context of it. They evidently did really want some good words to sell their shoes. Someone pointed out that advertising copywriters sell their linguistic services in this way all the time. We decided that we should meet the needs of Messrs J—— & Co. As I was the sales assistant in the case, I was deputed to trawl through Roget's *Thesaurus* and pull out the relevant items. Anything which stood a reasonable chance of collocating with *shoes*. It didn't take too long, and I solemnly presented the others with the fruits of my research. Each word was carefully scrutinized for its shoe-relatedness potential. Joan typed them up neatly on Survey notepaper, constructed an invoice, and put it in the evening post. Two days later, a cheque arrived for £2, made payable to the Survey of English Usage, and a nice thankyou note saying how helpful I had been. We had evidently given a good impression. And, I liked to think, having tracked down the shop in the Strand some time later, that its window texts were actually effective in an above-average sort of way. They call it contextual advertising these days – a domain which would engage my attention again forty years later.

Something out of the ordinary happened most weeks, on the Survey. That's often the way with language projects. Because language belongs to everybody, everybody has an interest in it. And when people learn that there are surveys and enquiries taking place into language, they like to find out about them, interrogate them, maybe even contribute to them. Sometimes the surveys welcome this interest, and foster it – as in the case of the dictionary projects run by such firms as Oxford University Press or Longman, where it is possible for 'word-watchers' to contribute their observations. Our Survey didn't actively look for a popular response; on the other hand, it always dealt with public enquiries sympathetically. Apart from a general sense of responsibility towards the people who actually foot a certain amount of the bill (as tax-payers), there is always the thought that the next phone call might be from an interested future sponsor. Surveys are expensive projects, and the long-term financial planning is always at the back of the mind. Good publicity is always a plus, and we knew to be especially solicitous when the enquiries from outside came from the media.

The press and the BBC were regularly in touch. Often it was just a factual enquiry. A paper or programme might have been sent a letter about split infinitives or prepositions at the ends of sentences, and a reporter would be assigned to find out the 'facts' of contemporary usage. Often, in those early days, there was little to be said, other than to acknowledge an ongoing trend in the language, and to combat virulent prescriptive attitudes. The real statistics about points of contentious usage would take a long time to compile, and indeed it was more than thirty years before grammars were able to incorporate quantitative data into their descriptions on a truly major scale. Sometimes there would be a visit. A reporter would make an appointment to look round the Survey. RQ would give an interview, and the research assistants were left to show the visitor the 'hands-on' side of the work. It wasn't as easy as it seemed. You had to be careful. I learned this the hard way – by getting it wrong.

It was the day of the *Guardian* visit, and my turn to take over after the RQ interview. The reporter wanted to see samples of the different kinds of written language we were processing. I obliged. And some spoken examples? I dug into the file, and brought out some material we had recorded from the BBC's *Any Questions* discussion programme. Our practice was to delete the names of the participants, replacing them by arbitrary symbols. For us, it wasn't important *who* said something as the way in which something was said and the occasion on which it was said. But the reporter was particularly interested in the 'who'. I looked them up in our index. One of the texts was a splendid interview between the political commentator Bernard Levin and the MP Gerald Nabarro. The reporter made notes, and went away happy. I forgot all about it.

A few days later, we were all called into RQ's office. In one hand he was holding a letter from Mr Nabarro, expressing his fury at the way the Survey of English Usage was criticizing his English. The point made no sense at all, until we saw the *Guardian* article which RQ had in his other hand. It was headed 'English Up With Which We Will Not Put'. The reporter had taken the message about the Survey trying to replace old-fashioned prescriptive views about language with a modern descriptive account. His editor had remembered Winston Churchill's oft-quoted explosion after discovering that someone had corrected one of his sentences which had ended in a preposition: 'this is the kind of English up with which I will not put!' This being the *Guardian*, a jokey headline was obligatory. The only problem was that, within the article, several people were named as providing source material, including the aforesaid MP – and he, presumably missing the joke, didn't take kindly to being listed under such a headline. Result: explosion. It could have been very awkward – but RQ was a master at defusing awkward situations. He wrote to the MP, explaining the context, and pointing out that, along with the Queen and other notable members of the British establishment, certain people had been included to represent the language of the age, and that he hoped very much Mr Nabarro would approve of this initiative, and so on and so forth. It was enough to smooth the ruffled feathers, and we were allowed to continue using the sample. Which was just as well, as I'd taken hours to transcribe the thing, and I would have taken it very personally if we'd had to throw it away.

From then on, we were scrupulous in our concern over anonymity. If you use a piece of someone's speech or writing, then – certain well-known cases aside, such as a famous sports commentator or the Queen – it should not be possible to work out from the words used who said it. This means doing more than just removing the name at the top of the page. If a speaker says, 'So I said to my brother Fred', you have to change that name too. If the point is made, 'I lived near Reading for ten years', likewise. All proper names need to be replaced by their phonetic equivalents – 'Fred' becomes another monosyllabic name, such as 'Ted' or 'Jim'; 'Reading' becomes a location with two syllables in it, such as 'Swindon' or 'Bolton'. It makes no difference to the grammatical analysis of a sentence, whether the noun one lives at is called Reading or Swindon. But it can make a lot of difference to the bona fides of the project.

The anonymity principle is especially important when making what we called 'surreptitious' recordings. The Survey was anxious to describe what happened when people used language naturally, spontaneously, informally. It was a kind of English which had never been written down before – very different indeed from the careful grammar used on formal occasions, or the kind of grammar encountered in writing. But the fact of the matter is that people don't talk naturally when faced with a microphone. If you've had to do it, you know just how self-conscious you get, and how non-fluent or very formal your speech can suddenly become. The kind of speech heard in *Any Questions* was good stuff, but it was articulate and reasoned and certainly not the kind of everyday desultory chat which actually forms the bulk of our speaking lifetime. Any survey which ignored that side of language would show only the tip of the speech iceberg. The problem was: how do you get at the rest of it? How do you record natural everyday speech without interfering with it?

Hide the microphone, is the obvious answer. And indeed, in the early years of the Survey, this is exactly what was done. It was a dangerous time to be visiting the Survey office. You would never know whether your conversation was being recorded or not. Of course, the news got out around the English Department, and it was soon assumed that *anything* you said in RQ's office would be part of a Survey text, sooner or later. In fact, only a small amount of material ever came from this source, and its anonymity was carefully secured. But the belief nonetheless grew that the tape recorders were always on. Of course, this was a Challenge which some members of the department could not resist. I remember RQ expressing bewilderment once about a colleague who had called in to see him for no other apparent reason than to slander as many members of the university as possible. Another arrived and swore more than usual. It all came out at the weekly Seminar. The sport of Quirk-baiting.

We junior research assistants didn't approve of such goings on, of course. We had subtler ways of getting an enjoyable RQ-reaction. Mine was to introduce rare grammatical constructions – ones which are hardly ever used in English – into my conversations with him whenever possible, just to see the effect. My favourite was the perfect continuous passive. Let me explain. *John has kicked the ball* – this is a form of the verb usually known as the 'perfect' (traditional grammarians called it this, because in their view the action is 'perfectly over'). *The ball has been kicked* – now the 'active' construction has been changed into a passive, allowing the speaker to say that a ball has been kicked, but without having to say who did it. It is a 'perfect passive' construction. Now add an element of continuity, emphasizing the duration of the action – *The ball has been being kicked*. This is the 'perfect continuous passive' construction – and it is not used very often, for the obvious reason that the concept involved is not something we need to talk about very much. But in RQ's office, things were different. 'By the way,' I might casually remark, 'I see that the Foreign Office has been being repeatedly criticized for its stance . . .' A Quirkian eyebrow would twitch. Construction noted. Important not to overdo it. Leave it a minute or two. Then: 'It's not often that new tribes have been being discovered over such a long period of time.' Another twitch, the moustache this time. Splendid. Stay looking innocent. Whatever you do, don't catch his eye.

My usage didn't have any world-shattering consequences. The construction is still labelled as 'rare', in all the modern grammars. (Though it has to be said that a 1999 descriptive grammar, the *Longman Grammar of Spoken and Written English*, has replaced the 'extremely rare' gloss in a previous grammar by 'generally rare' – a modification for which I take personal responsibility.) And I'm not sure that RQ didn't see through the whole thing all the time. But it was an enjoyable game – the kind consenting linguists love to play, though usually in private.

There was a down side to those surreptitiously recorded conversations, though. I was the one who had to transcribe them, and they were terrible things to do. For a start, the participants spoke much more rapidly than people do on such occasions as *Any Questions* – well over 300 syllables a minute at times, instead of the sedate 200 or so used on the radio. Words ran into each other, and some proved very difficult to disentangle. There were hesitation noises I'd never heard before, and intonation patterns to die for. Worst of all, there was extraneous noise, lots of it, obscuring crucial bits of the speech. It's all very well hiding a microphone inside a desk drawer, but – over and above any other consideration – it doesn't produce a recording of very good acoustic quality. The sound is muffled, the voices are distant, and every time somebody moves something on the desk or scrapes a chair you can't hear a thing. When more than one person is in the room, you often can't distinguish who's saying what. That's why, a decade later, I worked with Derek Davy on what we called the 'Advanced Conversational English' project.

By the early 1970s, the grammatical character of everyday conversation was becoming clear. All kinds of fascinating results were emerging, which had never been written up in grammars before – like how people use such 'filler phrases' as *you know, you see*, and *mind you*. These are an important feature of casual speech, and there are rules governing the way they're used. For instance, you can put *you know* at the beginning of a statement with ease (*You know, I think you're right*); but it's unusual to put it in front of a question (*You know, is it six o'clock?*) or a command (*You know, shut the door!*). It's a fairly obvious point, once your attention is drawn to it – but grammar books didn't draw your attention to it, and foreign learners of English often over-generalized their use of *you know*, using it with all sorts of sentences in unnatural ways. Longman, the publishing house that had been one of the sponsors of the Survey, was anxious to get out some teaching materials which were more authentic in their representation of everyday conversational English. Derek and I decided to take the job on.

The year was 1974. I had long since left the Survey by that time, but Derek – another English Department graduate, a year behind me, though (as a mature student) some years my senior – was then its assistant director. I was living at Reading, and he in London, so we could meet regularly. We had already collaborated once before, writing an introduction to stylistics which we had called *Investigating English Style*, so we knew we worked well together. We also knew how poor, acoustically, the conversational data had been that we had used for that book. The question we had to answer was therefore this: how do we record conversations surreptitiously but ensure they are of excellent acoustic quality – good enough to put on an illustrative tape which might be sold along with a book? We would need the microphones virtually in front of the mouths of the participants – but seeing the mikes there would surely destroy any semblance of a natural situation?

We devised a cunning plan. I invited small groups of friends round to my house for an evening, telling them that I wanted to record their voices for a project I was doing on English accents. They would arrive and be shown into the front room, where they would see microphones in front of each armchair and a tape recorder in the middle of the room. After they'd sat down, I would turn the tape recorder on, and ask them in turn to count from one to twenty. This they did, with great care and attention. The accents were, indeed, excellent. I would then turn the tape recorder off, thank them for their trouble, and get the drinks out. Everyone would relax, and people would fall to a-talking about sport, politics, and a host of other daily issues. At one point I would be called away into the other room, to answer a long-distance phone call from abroad. When I returned, I would apologize that this call had taken me away for so long – half an hour, usually.

Of course, as you have probably already worked out, the microphones were not connected to the tape recorder in the middle of the room at all, but to a different tape recorder purring away in the kitchen. But, having seen the machine in the sitting-room turned off, everyone promptly forgot about the microphones, which were left right by their chairs, just to one side and on a level with their mouths. There was no need to be suspicious of them. After all, they had observed the turning-off with their own eyes. As a result, I got the best quality recordings of natural, everyday, spontaneous speech that I have ever had, before or since. To avoid myself influencing the way the conversation went, the period when I was out of the room proved to be especially important. And the ethical issue? At the end of the evening, I admitted to the subterfuge, and explained what I had really been up to. I offered to erase the tape if anyone felt unhappy about it. Nobody ever took up the offer. On the other hand, I was not to be allowed to get away with it. I was warned that it was always going to be my round – for ever. And indeed, twenty years after, when I bumped into one of the participants in a pub in Reading, his first words to me were: 'You've not forgotten it's your round?'

The exercise was immensely worthwhile. We obtained some superb data, and the tape of extracts accompanying the book was as good as we had hoped. *ACE*, as it came to be called, sold very well for several years, went through several printings, and even parented a useful practical workbook for students, written by Keith Morrow. Then Longman, for reasons I have never fully understood (for even in the 1990s people were writing to ask me where they might get hold of it), let it go out of print. The recordings ended up as a part of the Survey archive. But the findings, relating to pronunciation, grammar, vocabulary, and patterns of conversational interaction, kept me in lectures for years, and still do. There is an almost inexhaustible mine of linguistic nuggetry in real conversation, and something about the naturalness of unselfconscious speech which is compelling. No matter how hard you try to make up plausible sentences for teaching materials, they are always a remove away from the earthy dynamism of unconstrained domestic spontaneous conversation. What is so sad is that most foreigners learn English without ever having the opportunity to hear this conversational reality, as part of their training. They learn a pastiche, or stereotype, of it – adequate enough for most purposes, but still some distance away from how native speakers actually talk on informal occasions. I had found the same gap between stereotype and reality in my own French learning in the 1950s (see Chapter 6). *ACE* was a chance to draw attention to the nature of true authenticity, and I found the exercise salutary.

While at the Survey, I encountered a major exception to what I have just said – a foreigner whose command of English, in all the years I later knew him, came as near to impeccable as it is possible to get. This was Jan Svartvik, a tall amiable Swede who had worked with Quirk on the Survey during its first year. Today I have got used to Swedes and Danes, in particular, producing English of stunning quality – by which I mean being in control of not just the formal varieties of the spoken language, but the informal ones too. Along with the Norwegians and the Dutch, they provide evidence of the levels of native-like fluency it is possible to achieve in foreign-language learning, and give the lie to those who think that foreign learners will always be at a disadvantage when they interact with native speakers. They also disprove another myth – that learning English means giving up your cultural identity and adopting an Anglo-Saxon mentality. Jan was as fluent as anyone could be, but he always stayed resolutely and incontestably Swedish. I did once ask him whether there was any sphere of life where he felt he would be incapable of using English. He thought solemnly for a moment, and then said slowly, in an inscrutable Scandinavian manner, 'Making love.' A new domain of practical English teaching opened up before my eyes!

Jan was part of the cosmopolitan atmosphere of the English Department in those days. Several students from abroad were working there, doing an MA or a PhD in English grammar, and they were the best of company. From them, on many an evening, I learned about Europe and other educational systems and cultural differences and similarities. And once a week, everyone met up at RQ's postgraduate seminar. Friendships formed in postgraduate seminars last for ever, I discovered – years later, of course, when I would from time to time meet up with people from that group, and find the years just falling away. On a visit to Zagreb in May 1999 I met up again with Vladimir Ivir and Damir Kalojera, both distinctly greyer than me (I maintain) but otherwise not much different. A few years before, I had found myself corresponding with Ranko Bugarski, from Belgrade, another ex-seminarian, who was leading a team translating one of my books into Serbo-Croatian. In the early 1990s, Croatia and Serbia had been at war. In May 1999, NATO was bombing Serbia. My Croatian friends were as concerned for Ranko's safety as I was. Such links cross frontiers and political boundaries.

They were great seminars, attended by all kinds of interesting people, and it was there that I got a proper grounding in linguistics. That's where I first heard Michael Halliday, working in UC at the time (though in a different department), talking about his new 'scale-and-category' approach to grammar, and fell in love with it. That's where I first met Geoff Leech, who was working with him, and discovered that some linguists could do a lot more than just linguistics – in Geoff's case, play a fine classical piano. And that's where I learned all about Chomsky – someone who had never been mentioned (as far as I can recall) in my undergraduate years. This was 1963. Chomsky's ground-breaking book, *Syntactic*

Structures, had been published in 1957, but had so far made little impact in the UK. We learned about it from Jim Sledd, an American linguist who had been invited to give a series of seminars on generative grammar. He took us through *Syntactic Structures*, and brought us up to date, as he had somehow acquired advance material related to what would appear in 1965 as *Aspects of the Theory of Syntax*. Reading Jim Sledd ought to be an obligatory experience for all neophyte linguists. His titles illustrate his style and character – such as 'The lexicographer's uneasy chair', an article on the *Third Webster's International Dictionary*. He had a sharply satirical sense of humour, and an approach to academia which reminded me best of the little boy in the story who observed that the emperor was wearing no clothes. He couldn't stand waffle, laziness of expression, or any kind of academic posturing – and it was in reacting to him that I realized that neither did I. I'm sure this nurtured an interest I would later have in linguistic lexicography – a concern for terminological definition which is too often lacking in the subject. At the same time, he was an excellent expositor and critic. He was no Chomskyan acolyte: at the end of the course we had a sense of both the strengths and the problems with the new approach. And he was excellent company. The grad students took to him straight away; we would show him round London, and he would join us for visits to Ronnie Scott's. It was a sad day when he went back home.

During those first months at the Survey, I had no real thought of becoming an editor, a writer, a lecturer, or anything so ambitious. I was just very pleased to be being a researcher. I loved bathing in a warm pool of data, and had no intention of doing anything else. But it was not long before the real world started to intervene. What are you up to? What have you found out? Come and tell us about it. Can you write us an article about it? The more I learned about linguistics, the more it became apparent that there were many others who wanted to know about it – and many many more who *needed* to know about it, because without a linguistic perspective their views on language were at best ill-informed, at worst harmfully misleading. Deep down, somewhere, a missionary spirit was growing, awaiting only the opportunity to be released. In due course, it would get me into all kinds of enjoyable trouble.

Chapter 9

Worlds within worlds

The opportunities arrived sooner than anyone might have expected. I was part of the academic world, sure enough, but had yet to discover the many other worlds which lurked within it. By early 1963 these came tumbling into view, all beckoning enticingly. The first was a world which would later involve a significant part of my life, and provide some of the best stories – English language teaching, or ELT, as it is universally called. The Survey office would often be phoned by people wanting help with their English, and these requests were passed on to anyone who had time to help. I worked for a term, an hour a week, with a Dutch lady who was worried about her tenses. I diagnosed what seemed to me to be severe adverbial deficiency, and we spent some happy hours exploring the way the English tense system worked. To explain. A present-tense form does not by itself express such meanings as future time or habitual action, but relies greatly on accompanying adverbial expressions of time and frequency, as in 'I'm leaving *tomorrow*' or 'I visit London *once a month*'. Many English-teaching courses, however, fail to draw sufficient attention to this point, giving the impression that the present tense does the job all by itself – in some books, suggesting that this form has a dozen or more 'meanings'. No wonder foreign learners get confused – and my Dutch lady was no exception. I felt that she'd be greatly helped if I devised some exercises which focused on adverbials and played down these so-called 'meanings', and so it turned out. A couple of years later, I would write a general article on the point for the *Journal of Linguistics*, called 'Specification and English tenses'. Here, as so often, the motivation for a theoretical study came from an applied conundrum.

One thing led to another. I suspect there was a 'Crystal will do it' assumption in the outer office. Otherwise, how did I end up working with a central European gentleman who was writing up his PhD thesis on Germanic sound-changes, and who wanted its English expression checked, word by word, before he sent it in? It's not a task which would bring out the volunteer in most people, after all. I expected it to be dull work, but it turned out that he wanted reasons for every little change, and that made it interesting, as often I had to go hunting for the answers. There is nothing more infuriating (and at the same time motivating) than to have your linguistic intuition challenged with a 'why is it so?' I well earned the extra few pounds these jobs brought in. And he got his doctorate, too, which was a relief. It would have been rather embarrassing if the thesis had been referred back on linguistic (rather than on philological) grounds.

For a month during the summer there was the University of London Summer School, held then at Queen Elizabeth College, a rather pleasant campus between Kensington and Notting Hill. This was a different kind of teaching. RQ was directing the school, and I was taken on as one of the grammar tutors, so for the first time found myself having to devise my own teaching course – a minimalist one, for my classes met only a few times, but enough to lay the foundation for the more ambitious courses which I would soon have to compile. ELT summer schools are great fun. Some fifty, a hundred, sometimes more students from a wide range of countries come together with a common aim – to improve their English. They are from all kinds of backgrounds and display every conceivable personality. Later I would teach courses on such schools all over the UK, and in different countries, and they were always the same. The students are there to learn, and also to have a good time. Visits are arranged for them to local tourist spots, theatres, and organizations (such as the BBC or a newspaper office), and the teachers often go with them. Within a week you're good friends with many of the students, and within a month you're the best of friends. Then they are gone, and only rarely do you ever meet again. It is an intense, high-living, and thoroughly immersing escapist month. Whatever is going on in the real world is someone else's business. You forget to read the daily newspaper. The cold war might have become hot and cold again, and you would never know. Was there a Great Train Robbery in the summer of 1963? So they say.

Being a grammar tutor didn't mean totally ignoring pronunciation and vocabulary, but it did give a focus to the work. And there is plenty to focus on. If you count up all the points about grammar in the index to a major work, such as *A Comprehensive Grammar of the English Language*, you find that it contains about 3,500 general observations. That's 'how much grammar' there is in English. Or, if you prefer a measure by weight (in a book of 1,800 pages), just over 2 kilos. Any of these points can present a problem to the learner, as indeed to a native speaker, but the ones which cause the biggest difficulties emerge very quickly and repeatedly in an ELT class, and you soon develop a sense of what 'the issues' are – problems with tenses, articles, word order, irregular verbs . . . My interest in prosody came in handy, too, as English intonation seemed to attract more student angst than almost any other topic. The problem, it transpired, lay more in the textbooks than in the language. Having been told, by one book, that the low rising tone in English could express a variety of meanings from 'friendly and warm' to 'warning and grim', one student asked me how she would ever be able to master the difference, in such a crazy language. 'Try looking friendly, when you want to be friendly,' I suggested, 'and grim when you want to be grim.' The point evidently hadn't occurred to her before. And indeed, in looking through the various textbooks on intonation, it was remarkable how many of the problems arose because the authors were presenting the subject without any reference to accompanying facial expression at all. I made a mental note to add a section on the semantics of intonation to my PhD thesis.

Because the students are from everywhere, in a summer school, there can sometimes be problems of a social or political kind. Imagine running a class in which there is an Israeli and an Arab during one of the Middle East wars. Or someone from India and Pakistan, during one of their crises. The course organizers have to be specially sensitive to issues of group dynamics, in such situations. Then there are the major cultural differences between the students. A male student from a country in which women are not well respected might carry his attitudes into the classroom. Racist and elitist attitudes might be encountered – racism is not solely the prerogative of whites, after all, and some countries have a much more sharply defined class system than the UK. It's not your business to change students' beliefs and practices, when you're a language teacher, but equally they mustn't impose theirs on people with a different background either. Often you end up as an international mediator, and you soon learn that there is much more to language teaching than language teaching.

There was one nice moment, in that summer school, when I was doing a grammar exercise with my group. In walks RQ. He had warned us he would be going the rounds, to see how we were all getting on, and as this was my first time as a tutor I expect he was particularly keen to see what sort of a mess I was making of it. He sits down at the back. I feel the imp of wickedness rising inside me, and realize I can do nothing to stop it. 'Late again, Mr Quirk,' I remonstrate, 'you'll never learn all about the English language that way.' I explain paternally to my mystified class, 'Mr Quirk is from the Isle of Man, you see, and is attuned to the Manx language. Lately he has been having especial difficulties with English grammar.' The point was lost on the students, who hadn't even heard of Manx or the Isle of Man. But having dared to launch myself into this course of action, I suddenly realized that it was good clean fun, so I had him change present tenses into past tenses, and add the right adverbials, and take his turn with all the other students. To give him credit, he played his part with good grace, and didn't make a single mistake – but he stuck it out for only five minutes before muttering something about having to get on. As he left the room, I heard the word 'Welsh', but didn't quite catch the noun it was qualifying. That's probably the last time I get invited on to this summer school, I reflected, as I carried on with my class. Then it dawned on me that my students were looking at me with awe. And after the class, the news spread. I was the teacher to whom the Summer School Director went, when he wanted to improve his English! My stock rose enormously, and the remainder of my classes were oversubscribed.

I was introduced to another pedagogical world, during the summer term of 1963. A request had arrived at the Survey asking for someone to teach an evening course on English at one of the technical colleges, in Dagenham, just outside London. It was for business managers, and they wanted a course on communication with particular reference to language. 'Who knows anything about business management?' We all remained silent. We were interrogated further. My experience of the business world, you will recall, was a half-day a week as a bacon boner in Liverpool Littlewoods for a year or so, and six weeks as a sickly bar-steward on the Holyhead–Dublin ferries; also there had been a month as a temporary copy typist at Foster Wheeler's engineering HQ in London during one of the summer vacations. However, this beat the others, and made me eminently qualified, so I was assigned the job. It was only two sessions, each three hours long, and I reckoned it wouldn't take me long to prepare. That was my first mistake.

I wandered into the library to find out what business managers were worrying about, and found myself faced with a wall of books. I called in at the local labour exchange, and came away with a mound of leaflets and brochures. Everybody and his dog seemed to have made policy statements about the importance of communication in the business world. Plainly it was going to have to be immersion time. For a week I lived inside the world of industrial negotiations, effective decision-making, mass media, advertising campaigns, and works information, and got to know the jargon. The only way to get out of this alive, I reckoned, was to stand on shoulders, so I made sure that every general point in my talks was illustrated by a situation from the business world, and every quotation was from a well-known industrialist, economist, or relevant politician. That way, I thought, I'd be able to make palatable to a business mentality the very same theoretical issues which I had found so unpalatable myself three years before, such as the nature of the communication 'circuit' between sender and receiver (out of Saussure), and help the class grasp those general notions which are indeed of great relevance to their work, such as the importance of feedback or the difference between connotation and denotation.

I suppose it must have worked, as I'm still here. And it's interesting to think how it must have worked. For I found the typescript recently, as I was digging through some old files trying to remind myself of what happened in the 1960s. It was, indeed, a typescript – seventy-one pages of it. I remember typing the whole thing out on my old Olivetti, then reading it to the class, word by word. Not the best way to introduce a big topic to a general audience, but it was my first time, and I didn't know the material sufficiently to rely on notes, or to dispense with them altogether. It horrifies me to think of doing it that way now. I would never dream of reading a talk to a general audience, and I try to avoid notes whenever possible. I firmly believe in the analogy between lecturing and acting, as I said earlier, and just as actors could never succeed if they stayed clutching their script, so lecturers should also prepare well enough to be able to dispense with their paper crutch – or, these days, their PowerPoint – when the context and subject-matter permits, of course. For a general talk to a neophyte audience, who want to enjoy their encounter with a subject as a prerequisite for being persuaded about it, then spontaneity is the order of the day. Obviously, when the topic is highly specialized or involves intricate statement, or if the contribution is one which is to be published, then reading may well be the most desirable option. But then it's necessary to remember the adage: it's not what you say, but the way that you say it. If the text is in front of you, the best you can do is to act it out, putting as much feeling as possible into the words. That must be how I survived, on those two evenings back in 1963, as I worked my way through those seventy-one pages. I was surprised to find myself being warmly thanked afterwards; several people said they'd enjoyed the occasion; and I was invited back the following year, so they can't just have been being kind. Yet I still can't help thinking I must have put those poor guys at least a little through purgatory, as I struggled to find my métier.

But I did find it, that year. I discovered, through those various pedagogical settings, that I liked teaching. I found I enjoyed the drama of audience contact, and the challenge of working out the best way of getting a message across. It's a coin with two sides, of course. On one side there is the delight which comes from knowing you've done a good job, sensing that an audience is totally yours, and seeing them smile and nod. On the other, there is the desperation which comes from knowing you've done a bad job, sensing that you've lost them, and seeing them frown and nod (in a different sense). At the same time, I found I revelled in the drama of the intellectual (and often emotional) encounter, as people engaged, questioned, disagreed, disparaged. To teach is, indeed, to learn. There is nothing better than a lively question-and-answer session after a talk, and nothing more disappointing than a situation where a talk has a silent sequel, or when the organizers haven't left time for a meeting of minds. A lecture or talk is simply the first part of a potential conversation; and if the second part is denied, for whatever reason, it remains only half the thing it might have been. It's funny how organizers always ask, 'Will you take questions?' It shouldn't be a necessary request. Part of the problem, I think, is the widespread sense of 'lecture', meaning 'speak at', often antagonistic in tone. 'I gave them a good lecture' can mean a telling-off, with no reply expected. These days, I avoid the term whenever I can. 'Will you come and give us a lecture?' No, I reply, but I'll be happy to come and give a talk – as long as there's time for questions. Seems much more customer-friendly, somehow.

The drama of audience contact? Of course. You never know exactly how an audience is going to react, or what extraneous circumstances are going to interfere with everyone's concentration. That's part of the fun. I suppose I have had my share of interesting moments, as any other lecturer has. I have been in competition with passing traffic, passing lawn mowers, Concorde's daily flights (Reading University was on the flight path), an orchestra in an adjacent room, a parade of angry vociferous striking miners, and an exploding overhead light bulb (just as I mentioned the name of Chomsky in a lecture once, I kid you not). I have had people walk out, fall asleep, faint, fall off their chairs, have an epileptic fit, dance, use mobile phones, listen to the radio, copulate . . . Oh yes, I've seen it all. (Excuse me, did you say 'copulate'?) Yes. At least, that's what it sounded like.

It was a hot summer afternoon in a large lecture room at the University of Reading – the Friday three o'clock hour, when all student attention was on the forthcoming weekend. I was working my way through the vocal effects in the English prosodic system, as part of a phonetics course. I

LINGUIST AS DANCER

In the early 1970s, I was teaching on another summer school, at the south end of Copacabana beach, in Rio de Janeiro. I know it sounds like an unlikely place for a course on English grammar, but that's how it was. And I know you're thinking, Copacabana, eh, well that's all right, being a linguist, then. But I did have to teach grammar for two solid hours on that particular afternoon, and it was in the 90s, and the air-conditioning was full on and very noisy, and because it wasn't working very well the windows were open too, so let me tell you it was not all ice-cream and caipirinhas.

I was well into the intricacies of the noun phrase, when I noticed that there was some audience twitching going on. The students had heard what it took me a minute or so more to hear, above the traffic. A drum beat. A whole samba school of drum beats. In the distance, but coming nearer. It was Carnival the following weekend, you see, and some of the samba bands were out and about getting in some practice (see plate 9.3). And here was one of the best, some twenty musicians and dancers, gyrating slowly towards my lecture. There was no point in going on. My audience was Brazilian through and through, and their pulses were genetically programmed to follow a samba beat. They looked at me appealingly. I gave in. 'Which band is it?' I sighed.

They were at the windows in a flash, all dancing, and I was given a tutorial on which part of Rio the band was from and what the name of the song was. Due deference was shown to my professorial role, and I was placed mid-window. The band reached us, and we gave it a special cheer. Not expecting such a sizeable audience, they stopped and did an impromptu show. I mean show. The leading female dancer, dressed – if that is the right term – in three feathers, came up to the window, and homed in on the least Brazilian-looking spectator. I had never seen feathers gyrate before. I was advised to gyrate back. I remember saying, 'I don't know how to gyrate. I'm from Wales', or words to that effect. 'I show you,' said one of the male students, and I abandoned my window spot to him. Fortunately the band moved on before I was offered the chance to demonstrate my gyratory skills, and the class reconvened.

Even noun phrases lose their fascination, after such an interlude.

don't know, maybe it was something I said – one of the tones of voice, perhaps – but it evidently turned two of my listeners on. They were sitting in the very back row. The lecture room had raked seating, so I could see only their upper halves. About half way into the lecture, those upper halves started to disappear, down below the level of the desk. I saw them go, and thought they were looking for something. They were. Within a minute or so, there emerged from beneath the desks a series of unison breathy back vowels, interspersed with glottal stops and creaky voice, all uttered on a rhythmical series of falling intonation patterns with increasingly higher onsets, crescendo, accelerando, and a widening pitch-range – I give the technical prosodic description now, as indeed I did then. It was a phonetics lecture, after all, at the point where I was illustrating different tones of voice in different social situations. So, I reasoned, I might as well make use of this new material. It was not something I had previously encountered in my forays into surreptitious recording, after all, and it was important to stay learnedly cool, faced with fifty or so smirking students, all of whom were enjoying the moment enormously. Actually, the class probably learned more phonetics terminology that day than at any other time. Well, I say, the class. All bar two of them, whose upper forms emerged once again, smugly grinning albeit somewhat dishevelled, a few minutes later.

And an audience listening to the radio, during a lecture? Ah yes, but that was entirely understandable. This was a day course for speech therapists, at Chelmsford in Essex. The venue was a lecture room in the local hospital. It was a hot day – not quite as hot as in Rio, but hot enough for the audience to want the windows open. The good news was that this brought some cool air into the room. The bad news was that this air came wafting in from the adjacent arena, which happened to be the county cricket ground. And Essex were playing at home. It was all right to begin with, as play didn't start until mid-morning. But when it did start, my points were regularly punctuated by gentle clapping and the occasional 'How was he!!!' Some members of the audience turned out to be cricket enthusiasts, as well as speech therapists. You could tell who they were by the way they positioned themselves around the open window, where you could just about see the ground. I'm not sure how much clinical linguistics went in that morning; but there was even less during the afternoon. During the lunch hour they must have discovered that the match – a rather critical one, it turned out – was being broadcast on local radio during the afternoon. I learned this only later, after wondering why there was a sound resembling a permanent commentary counterpointing my afternoon session. The reason was obvious. It *was* a commentary, a sports one, proceeding from a portable radio judiciously located just outside the window. Everything, however, can be turned to advantage, and if my cricketing listeners learned nothing else that day it was how to do a grammatical analysis of 'How's that!'

But this is to leap years ahead. Back in 1963, I was the least in the kingdom of lecturers, trying hard to master the art – for it is, so much, an art, a verbal art, part of the domain of rhetoric, now regrettably rarely taught. And I was least in the kingdom of writers, too. But that too would quickly change, for RQ encouraged all of us research assistants to write, as soon as we felt we had something to say. My very first article was for a newspaper, the *Liverpool Daily Post*. In April 1963, while on a visit to Liverpool, I'd read an article by a local headteacher called 'Eternal vigilance will keep English intact'. It was a typical purist, prescriptive piece, imagining that television had caused the language to deteriorate, trying to impose the writer's own likes and dislikes about usage on to everyone else, and arguing that we must preserve the tongue that Shakespeare spoke. It is the kind of article which still appears regularly, and which has been part of our epistolary literature for more than two hundred and fifty years, ever since prescriptivism became a routine part of our language pedagogy. It is not difficult to refute such articles (though refutation rarely persuades). Many of the instances of supposed contemporary deterioration in usage, which are often blamed on radio and television, can be found as issues in the eighteenth century, long before broadcasting had been invented, and many examples of supposed 'new usages' can be shown to have ancient *Oxford English Dictionary* pedigrees. There is something particularly satisfying when you point out to someone who is condemning a modern usage as awful, and wishing for a return to the standards of Shakespeare, that Shakespeare employed that usage himself! Never end a sentence with a preposition? 'To be or not to be . . . and fly to others that we know not of.' I would spend hundreds of hours in later years, using every available medium, attacking the ignorance and prejudice which underpins such purism – for at its most intolerant, purism can do real harm, sharing in its disrespect for others' usage some of the features of racism – but this was the first time I had attempted to do so in print. I wrote a piece, sent it in, and blow me down the *Post* accepted it, without alteration. I was, as they say in the 'Pool, dead chuffed.

My first venture at academic writing, however, immediately got me into trouble. It was an unusual sort of article, as it was written for *le maître phonétique* ('The Phonetic Master'). Now, the thing you have to appreciate about the 'm.f.', as this abbreviation indicates, is that it was written entirely in phonetic transcription (see plate 1.4). The journal had an illustrious history, dating from 1889, and had become a brilliant way of maintaining an interest in 'hands-on' phonetics. Writers were encouraged to use a transcription which reflected their own accents, and you could indeed catch their voices in the way they wrote. My curious mix of Welsh,

Liverpool, and London proved to be especially interesting to transcribe. When I submitted my piece, the editor (Gimson) went through it with the kind of toothcomb that only phoneticians use, and pointed to various inconsistencies. But my accent was indeed inconsistent. Sometimes I would say *example* with a short 'a' and sometimes it would come out with a long 'ah'. Sometimes I said *controversy* with the stress on the second syllable, and sometimes with it on the first. The inconsistency has increased, rather than decreased, over the years. And I am by no means alone. Increased social mobility and opportunities for travel means that 'mixed' accents are everywhere now, in various stages of transitional development – and with transition inevitably comes inconsistency. You don't notice it until you have to write it down, as the policy of m.f. demanded that you did.

The article was called 'A perspective for paralanguage'. I liked the word 'perspective', and would go on to use it, mantra-like, in subsequent publications. 'Paralanguage' was the name I had chosen for a range of vocal effects we had encountered in the Survey transcripts – effects which did not play as central a role in conveying grammatical structure as did intonation and stress. They included such tones of voice as whispered speech and husky speech and all the effects produced when you speak while laughing or giggling. Because these effects are at the 'edge' of language, I called them 'para-linguistic', adopting a term which had been used by a number of scholars previously, but giving it a narrower definition (excluding facial expressions and bodily gestures) and presenting a classification which reflected the kind of vocal effects we had been describing in the Survey materials, some of which hadn't been discussed in the previous literature. There hadn't been an article on this topic in m.f., apparently, and Gim asked me to do a general expository piece, characterizing the field as a whole.

I wrote the piece early in mid-1963, after I'd done some background reading for my thesis, got RQ to read it through, and sent it in. After a bit of editorial tweaking, it was accepted, and appeared later that year. It was largely a review of what the leading US scholars in the field had been saying about paralanguage. I'd not been working on the subject for long, but the corpus-based approach certainly seemed to identify pretty basic weaknesses in the work that had been done hitherto. Pioneering and insightful as that work had been, it lacked breadth of illustration and phonetic detail. I really could not understand what some of the vocal effects were, from the information given in the US articles, and the picture seemed partial and vague at crucial places. So my article, as I thought, began by bowing dutifully to previous scholarship, in the form of such great names as Kenneth Pike, Charles Hockett, George Trager, and

Henry Lee Smith, then being critical. Just mildly so. I pointed out that their coverage of this field was inadequate, incomplete, ambiguous, a distortion . . . and that we needed a new approach (which a forthcoming book – see below – would provide).

Well, I thought it was mild. It was certainly mild by the standards of vituperation encountered in the Marlborough Seminar. But academics are sensitive souls, and there is a law governing the intensity of their response: the reaction to criticism displayed by senior academics is in inverse proportion to the juniority of their critics. There was none more junior than me. And there were few more senior than the above-named. So I was savaged. Trager, it was, who went for me. I read my piece again now with some disbelief. George L. Trager, one of the leading linguists of his generation. 'Trager and Smith' – a book which appeared in 1951, when I was ten – was so well known in the business that it had become a catch-phrase. And here's me talking about inadequacies and ambiguities. He took me to task: a left to the body ('selective quotation'), a right to the body ('misleading implications'), and an uppercut ('serious errors'). I was about to retire hurt, give up linguistics and take up a nice safe job, like deep-sea diving, when Gimson said, 'Of course you'll reply,' in a falling tone, telling, not asking. I didn't know about replies. Replies were things one gave to questions, not blitzes. He showed me some precedents. I penned a short reply, a mixture of mollification and sod-offication. Errors? What errors? Just because I have a difference of opinion, it doesn't count as an 'error', surely. And he has misunderstood my approach totally. Such bravado. Later, the Marlborough Seminar nodded approvingly, and muttered between pints about 'earning spurs', and suchlike.

The importance of publication, for the aspiring academic, was a major lesson learned during that Survey year. Everyone spent all their spare time writing, or so it seemed. As soon as RQ sensed that there was an area of potential significance in the way the transcriptional side of the Survey was developing, he suggested we write it up. As a book? Yes, as a book. We would explain the theoretical basis of the approach, present the description, and illustrate the more unusual effects using acoustic pictures of the voice (spectrograms). I would take responsibility for the literature review, the description, and the acoustics; RQ would write up the general approach and put the whole thing in context. He had the experience and contacts to get a publisher interested, and through that I had my first encounter with the world of contracts and deadlines. In the event, the book was published in 1964 by Mouton at The Hague, under the title of *Systems of Prosodic and Paralinguistic Features in English*. It was No. 39 in the same blue-covered softback series as had published Chomsky's first book. Our topic, even with a vivid imagination, was not quite as world-shattering in its linguistics as the earlier book had been, but it was a prestigious location. Much later, Mouton's editorial standards would deteriorate, and the series would fold. But at the time, that publisher was riding the crest of the Chomsky wave, and its books were being widely publicized. We benefited from that, and a year later I suddenly found myself with an unexpected and only half-deserved reputation. RQ had, quite deliberately, put my name first as co-author. Alphabetical order, he insisted, when I demurred. But it wasn't that, of course. He knew very well that a first name in an authorship list achieves a subtle aura of additional prominence. Often, when more than two, the 'other authors' can even be reduced to anonymity under the designation '*et al*'. Not for the first time, he had given me a push in the right direction.

Nor, that year, would it be the last. One of the regular topics in the staff common room was career moves. At the time, people moved about quite a bit. The 1960s was one of those rare periods, a time of university expansion. There were jobs, tenured posts, and it was assumed that I would in due course apply for one of them. Every Friday lunch-time, I would join the phonetics gang in the common room. I was, after all, qualified in their business – even in the most tiny of ways – and I got to know them all during that year, including the ones who had never taught me, and the head of department, Dennis Fry. If joviality was a criterion for becoming head of department, then Fry was overqualified; but he would have had strong competition from most of the others. Those lunch-times were famous for their conviviality and jollity (two words which I always knew would come in useful one day: see p. 42). Although in fact most of them would spend their entire careers at UC (other phonetics departments to move to being conspicuous by their absence), they were avid readers of the academic job columns. And it was Gim in fact who pointed out to me one day that there was an assistant lectureship coming up in the newly established Linguistics Department at the University of North Wales, in Bangor. Knowing my Welsh interest, and the fact that the job wanted someone with a broad range of interests, including phonetics, he thought I should apply.

Dilemma. Dare I apply? I had been working at the Survey for only six months. What sort of repayment to RQ would that be, if I were to leave now? I felt immensely loyal to the man, for having kept my job open when I'd been ill, and for all the guidance I'd had from him. But the phoneticians were adamant that this would be a sensible move. So I plucked up courage, and knocked on RQ's door, clutching a copy of the job ad. I timorously asked him for advice. What should I do? He read through the ad.

'It's ideal for you,' he said. 'Apply.'

'But what if I get it?'

'What do you mean?'

All my concerns came gushing out. The bottom line was that I felt I would be leaving him in the lurch.

'What about "loyalty"?'

'Loyalty to what?'

'Well, to UC . . . to you.'

He was unequivocal. I shouldn't allow myself to be influenced by the spurious concept of loyalty to an institution.

'The institution has no feelings. It doesn't care whether you are here or not. Individuals might care, but not the institution. Forget it.'

'So what about you, then?'

'Don't be ridiculous.'

He then bent my ear for five minutes on how I had already done more than he had hoped for in appointing me, and that I would be rewarding him just as much by going for and getting this job. I understand the point now, having been proud to see my own research students move on, but at the time it was a revelation.

'You mean, you really wouldn't mind if I was appointed?'

'I'd be delighted.'

I left the room walking on air.

I applied, and in due course was called for an interview. It was a funny feeling, arriving in Bangor, looking for a job. Bangor was where you went to the shops that didn't exist in Holyhead. It was a special day out, not a place to work. I'd never been in the university before. It had always been the grey, imposing, rather off-putting, castle-like structure at the top of the town. I found my way to the Linguistics Department, where I met the head of department, Frank Palmer, for the first time. He showed me round the tiny department and I met some of the staff – an opportunity for an informal chat that is often just as important as the 'real' interview following. The formal interview took place in 'top coll' – Bangor was a constituent 'college' of the University of Wales, and the main building was at the top of the hill, hence the nickname. There were two of us on the short-list. I recall very little about the interview. It was chaired by the principal, Charles Evans (the Everest mountaineer), and the panel included the professor of forestry, whom I remember because he asked me what the relevance of linguistics was to forestry. I cannot think what answer I gave, or even imagine what it might have been, for in all honesty I can see none. (A joke about Chomskyan tree structures would probably not have gone down well.) Maybe that was what he was wanting to hear.

We were both asked to wait outside, then I was called back in. I was offered the job: assistant lecturer in linguistics. I accepted it on the spot.

And then, notwithstanding RQ's protestations, felt guilty as hell, and worked my socks off during the summer of 1963, getting as much Survey transcription done as possible, before the time came to move. How to get up there? Fortunately, I was still in touch with one of my UC friends, Marge Nellis, who had been in my year – and also been one of the high points of my stay in the Llangwyfan sanatorium, turning up as a visitor there one day. She was going out with Walter Greaves, ex-president of the student union, and he agreed to drive me up to Bangor in a hired UC van. And that's what happened. One day, in late September, we met up at the house in Leytonstone, loaded the van, and headed north. Half a day later, I found myself living in Wales again.

Chapter 10
Becoming professional

But where to live? I was all right for the first term, as after my interview visit the accommodation people had told me of a room available in the Catholic Chaplaincy, then at 40 College Road in Upper Bangor. It was a large terraced house, with several rooms that were rented out to post-graduates to help raise some income. Evidently the income from a junior member of staff was just as good as anyone else's, and as it was an ideal spot – just two minutes' walk from the department – I was pleased to be there. I hadn't lived in a setting of this kind before, or anything remotely like it, but I had already had a little contact with the university chaplaincy world in London, and had always been impressed by the chaplains and the activities they organized. They fostered an intelligent, critical apperception of belief, and enabled anyone who chose to be involved the opportunity to develop a maturity of insight analogous to the intellectual growth being achieved through their degree. It is unfortunately all too usual for people with a religious background to grow intellectually in their academic subject but not in the nature of the spirituality they have inherited. They may achieve a first in the former, yet remain at a teenage level in the latter. A regular chaplaincy involvement can restore the balance.

I found this out at Bangor, in fact, which was my first serious encounter with the chaplaincy world. It was a congenial atmosphere, with some merry residents from abroad, and a most wonderful chaplain – a lovable, eccentric, Opus Dei priest, Michael Richards. A lawyer by training, and a razor-sharp intellect, he hid it all under a self-effacing manner, carrying himself everywhere with an absented air and a shy smile, eyebrows gleefully twitching above a pair of rimless spectacles. He didn't say much, but his observations were invariably insightful and to the point. He was an expert at fishing for support for the chaplaincy and its work, and I was soon hooked. One of the lecturers was offering a course on theology, another on church history, and there were talks and seminars on all kinds of things. I went to most events simply because I was 'on the spot', living upstairs. It was also the shortest distance I ever had to travel to get to Sunday Mass – two flights of stairs.

I found my own background, in linguistics, to be of some interest. This was 1963. The Second Vatican Council had begun its sessions the previous October, and the issue of what liturgical language to use was a big talking point. If the liturgy was to be in the vernacular, then what kind of English should it be? Should people use *thou* or *you*, for example? The general view was that it had to be one or the other; but my stylistics background had taught me that the best answer was 'it all depends'. Black-and-white solutions are never valid in language analysis. Sometimes the choice is unimportant; sometimes it is critical. The *thy* that might appear in the sentence *I know thy name* has a very different status from the one which appears in *Hallowed be thy name*. The latter is an idiomatic unit, hallowed indeed by tradition, which we tamper with at our peril. And when we take the whole range of grammatical structures into account, with all the variations in word order which English makes possible, and the huge stylistic and rhythmical range of English vocabulary, it is plain that developing a new vernacular liturgical style is a lengthy and complicated business. It requires two kinds of expertise to be successful: theological, to elucidate and validate the content of the texts in relation to the language (e.g. Latin) from which they are translated, and linguistic, to determine the choices available in English (all international dialects of English, note) and the stylistic effect they convey. The whole affair wasn't handled particularly well at the time – plenty of theologians, but linguists conspicuous by their absence – and several decades on, the consequences of this lack of sophisticated linguistic thinking are still with us. Some of the language solutions which were adopted – notwithstanding various revisions in the interim – still attract criticism. And the debate continues to raise temperatures in the 2000s.

I had to write about it, of course. It's the only way I know of getting on top of a subject – write it up. Looking at a blank screen – it used to be a blank sheet of paper – concentrates the mind wonderfully. You can think about a topic and talk about it until the cows come home, but only when you put fingers to keyboard – or pen to paper – can you give a subject a properly judicious treatment and become genuinely self-critical. Anyway, having given a paper at a conference where I had met a few Dominicans, I learned of their plans for a periodical, *New Blackfriars*; they asked for a contribution, and 'A liturgical language in a linguistic perspective' (I did like that word *perspective*) duly appeared in its first issue. The article had an unforeseen and not entirely welcome consequence. A couple of years later, at Reading, I found myself working for the Vatican.

Well, sort of. The International Committee on English in the Liturgy, based in Washington, had carried out an exercise in getting public reaction to the new English vernacular texts of the Mass, printing alternative versions of selected passages on facing pages and asking people to express their preferences. They had received several thousand responses, from all over the world, and they didn't know what to do with them. I wrote to the Secretariat in April 1966 suggesting that they should analyse the data in a linguistically informed way. They knew a mug when they read one. A few weeks later, all the responses arrived in my office, along with a small grant for clerical (in the lay sense) help. I did what I could, trying to identify trends and counting alternatives. It was a lengthy and tedious process, made easier by the assistance of Paul Fletcher, who was a postgraduate at the time. But it wasn't very meaningful: the attitudes expressed were as many and as various as the people who sent them in. Some ticked the boxes they were supposed to; some didn't. Some underlined parts for special attention; some wrote marginalia; some wrote mini-essays – harangues, often, would be a better word. It occupied me on and off for nearly two years. I wrote a report, drawing attention to trends and suggesting how the questionnaire might be better handled next time, and got a nice thankyou from Gerry Sigler, the Executive Secretary. I'm not sure how useful it was to them, but I got a lot out of it, for it was a real hands-on introduction to the complexities of language attitudes.

It was difficult to keep your mouth shut about religious language in the mid-1960s, because it was such a hot topic. In March 1963 the then Bishop of Woolwich, John Robinson, had published an article in *The Observer* called 'Our image of God must go', in which prepositions seemed to be the main problem (is God 'up there' or 'in here'?). From a linguistic point of view, the situation seemed altogether more complex, so I started working up an alternative perspective which reflected the linguistic realities I knew, ruminated about it to a couple of people, and ended up leading a seminar on it. Another hot topic was A. J. Ayer's view that religious language was essentially meaningless – a gross oversimplification of linguistic realities, it seemed to me, but a view which was over a generation old, and still widely promulgated. Another seminar was the outcome, memorable for my fear upon realizing that some of the Philosophy

Department staff had turned up to listen, and my relief when it transpired that they were generally sympathetic to what I was saying. A third topic really did keep my mouth open. An investigator called A. Q. Morton had decided on statistical grounds (such as the frequency of use of the Greek conjunction for 'and') that Saint Paul couldn't have written most of his epistles. The stylistic analysis was – to a linguist – naive in the extreme, and I went into the matter in some detail in another seminar. But this time something else happened – something totally unexpected and altogether exciting: my first radio programme.

The Pauline controversy had received quite a bit of publicity, and the BBC Third Programme wanted to do something. A Pauline specialist in the Department of Biblical Studies, just down the road from the chaplaincy, had been approached, and he knew of my interest. The result was two joint talks, recorded from the local BBC studios, which went out in early 1965. This taught me a couple of things and confirmed a couple more. What it taught me was the extraordinary reach of radio – something that still exists, even in these days of television and the Internet. In one week I think I got more correspondence than I had received in my entire academic life – people agreeing and disagreeing, offering extra thoughts and references, but almost without exception expressing an interest in the linguistic perspective I had been advocating. It confirmed my belief that the general public – or, at least, that segment of it tuned in to the Third Programme – was genuinely fascinated by language, and wanted to learn more. This was a new kind of general public from the kind I had encountered before: these were not usage purists, worried only about split infinitives and wanting to stop language change. For the most part they had not heard about linguistics, and wanted to know what it could offer.

The linguistic world had been listening too. I got letters from many of the leading linguists of the day, such as Barbara Strang, John Lyons, Pit Corder, John Sinclair, and Angus McIntosh, as well as theologians such as Kenneth Grayston and the Abbot of Downside. Some wrote in great detail, as often critical as supportive, but always constructively so. I was delighted to have had such an audience, but wondered at the time why the programmes had generated such an active academic response. I remember raising the question with some of them, years later. One said he wasn't surprised: 'I hadn't heard a linguist talking about linguistics on prime time radio before.' Could that have been so? Were there no radio programmes by linguists before 1965? I spent a few hours in BBC Radio Archives once, and looked for examples, but it was like looking for an auditory needle in a haystack, and I gave up, without finding anything.

The experience confirmed my early instinct. Radio was King. I was at the other end of the microphone now, and it engendered in me a feeling of awe which – several thousand radio contributions later – I have never lost. To begin with, it was the ambience – the studio set-up, the professionalism, the teamwork, the sense of occasion – especially noticeable on walking into a building full of historical resonances, such as Broadcasting House or Bush House in London. Even the Bangor studio had its history, for that was where a great deal of national broadcasting originated in the Second World War. But the ambience was only a part of it. The heartbeat moment is when you are sitting alone in a studio and the green light comes on and you know that whatever you say is going to be heard by – anyone, anywhere. Today, thanks to ISDN technology and an investment in a reporter's box, I have a studio in a corner of my home. The ambience isn't there, but the heartbeat moment is still the same. Back in 1965, I treasured that moment, and wanted more of them.

Without realizing it, I was slowly gathering a reputation in what many years later would be called theolinguistics. I found myself talking about aspects of the subject at first one conference, then another. The possible insights that might emerge from a systematic approach to language study seemed to attract everyone I came into contact with. Other places invited me to give talks on the relationship between language and religion. That meant trying to get my thoughts organized about what the links were. There turned out to be dozens. Apart from the ones that had been in the news, I remember investigating the (at the time) newly popular phenomenon of speaking in tongues (glossolalia), and also getting to grips with some of the problems involved in bible translation (how do you say 'give us this day our daily bread' when your culture survives on daily rice?). And then, at one of these conferences, I met Tom Burns. At the end of the conference I found I had agreed to write a book for his 'Faith and Fact' series, published by Burns and Oates.

The prospect didn't scare me, even though I was only 22. On the contrary. After all, I had been taught how to write a book, by Randolph Quirk, the year before. The basic principle is very simple, and years later it would be affirmed by Jack Osborne, production manager at the Edinburgh-based publishing house of W. & R. Chambers, when I was wondering how to put my first general reference encyclopedia together. Jack was hugely experienced in producing books of all shapes and sizes, so on my first visit to Chambers I asked him: 'How do you write an encyclopedia?' He looked quizzically at me, pulled down a mock-up of the book from a shelf – 1,500 pages of blank paper in hardback covers, produced to show how heavy the book would be – and opened it at the first page. 'All ye have to do', he said in his strong Scots accent, 'is start at the top there and write small.' Then he added: 'And don't stop until you're finished.' It was a salutary lesson. I have never written any other way. I cannot write a book in random bits, and later solder the bits together. I know writers who have written the last page of their book first, or a middle chapter. I can't. I have to start at page one. And then it isn't a question of 'don't stop' – I can't stop. The task ceases to be under conscious control. I write until there is no more to be written. Then I stop.

That is how it was with *Linguistics, Language and Religion*, eventually published in 1965 by Burns and Oates in Britain, and later by Hawthorn Books in the USA. It was my first single-authored book, and the first linguistics book (as far as I know) to receive an official papal Imprimatur ('let it be published') and Nihil Obstat ('nothing stands in the way') – and still, as far as I know, the only one. It is nice to know you're writing nothing heretical – though the linguistic view of the world it reflected (based largely on Michael Halliday's approach) would certainly have seemed so to old-world generative linguists. I began writing early in 1964 and wrote up all my notes on everything I had encountered in my language and religion talks over the preceding year. There was a brief introduction to the history of linguistics and language study, then individual chapters on various religious topics. The final chapter, on the language of logical positivism, took longest to write, and was long – not least because, having given it to Dewi Z. Philips (from the Bangor Philosophy Department) to read, I had to take on board his many insightful criticisms. The contract had said a book of no more than two hundred pages, but I was not then an expert in judging book length from typescript. The book had a natural length, if the topic was to be properly covered. Its physical length was not the issue. Surely the kind publisher would see that?

The kind publisher did not see that. When I sent the typescript in, it transpired that it was far too long for a book in a series where all the items were more or less the same length. I would have to cut it. Something would have to go. In fact, said the publisher, who now seemed less kind, twenty per cent would have to go.

Twenty per cent?

I read my carefully honed text, and it had indeed been carefully honed. There was very little fat within a chapter. Quirk had seen to that. From his reading of my first efforts in writing, I had seen how redundant words in a sentence were ruthlessly excised, and repetition – no matter how elegantly varied – eliminated. Everything had to count. And so I had no choice but to cut chapters. Out went the Bishop of Woolwich, and a great deal more. You might think this would teach me a lesson. It didn't. Most of my books have been too long. The only difference is that I have learned to cut before sending the book to press. I have to admit that the cutting generally makes for a better book. If only bloggers did the same thing. But then, there is no one looking over your shoulder when you're writing a blog.

The book took longer to finish than I had expected. After all, I had already done most of the thinking, and I knew I had a facility in putting it down on paper. I had bought a little typewriter, an Olivetti 22, so the technology was in place. The deadline was the end of the summer, and I thought that would be plenty of time – but I missed it by several weeks. By no means the first author to miss a deadline – Douglas Adams once said that one of the nicest sounds is the noise a deadline makes as it whooshes by – I nonetheless felt very guilty about it, and resolved never to miss one again (a resolution which, on the whole, I have lived up to). But I had a good excuse – several, in fact. There was much more teaching to do in the department than I had expected. I was finding new linguistic worlds to explore. I was trying (not very successfully) to get on with my PhD. I was learning (successfully) to drive. I moved house. Oh, and I got married.

My relationship with my Seafield judy had lapsed, by common consent, after the leaving of Liverpool, but during my second year at university, feeling lonely one day, I wrote out of the blue to Molly again, and after a stunned silence she replied. I started making visits to Liverpool whenever I could. Heswall, in the Wirral, was a regular port of call, for she was training to be a children's nurse, and that was one of her placements. In Bangor I started out on the mortgage trail, and found a semi in Bryn Eithinog, not too far from the university. £3,500. That would be the deposit on a wheely bin now. We decided to get married, and that meant regular bus trips to Merseyside along the North Wales coast – one of them on 22 November 1963. How do I know? Doesn't everyone over sixty know where they were when Kennedy was shot? We were married in Molly's parish church in Fairfield, just off the Prescot Road, on 1 April 1964. I can't remember why that particular date was chosen, but I do remember being the butt of innumerable family jokes.

So there was a lot going on, domestically, in 1964. Steven was born just before Christmas, and Michael Richards baptised him early in the New Year, scaring everybody silly after the service when he asked to hold him. As Molly passed him over, he remarked that he'd never held a baby before. Too late to take him back, or to give tuition, we could only watch in horror as he casually took Steven by the left ankle, letting him dangle like the partner of an acrobat on a trapeze. He seemed quite puzzled by the reaction around him (the priest, that is, not the baby). Steven, for his part, was equable throughout.

Fathers sometimes moan about the impact of a child on their professional lives, but not me. I was in the very fortunate position of having a wife who was a qualified children's nurse, and by all accounts an extremely good one. (Just how good I would see for myself five years later.) Not for me the panic that comes when a new baby goes down with a cold or a rash and you start imagining desperate measures. Or rather, I *would* panic, but then be firmly told off. After having done a stint on prems (the premature baby unit) and their problems at the Royal Liverpool Children's Hospital, dealing with the minor ailments of a full-term bouncer was, to Molly, a doddle. And I gradually learned to calm down. The family wasn't the cause of my missed deadline.

It was the teaching that did for me. Some background about the department, first. The Department of Linguistics had been set up by Frank Palmer in 1961, the first specialist department in the country, and he had done a great job building up a small but dedicated team. There were joint degrees with other departments, and Frank's aim was to introduce a single-subject degree in linguistics, which would be the first of its kind. When I joined in September 1963 I found a department in two halves: the departmental office, the phonetics laboratory, and some lecturers' rooms were in an old building called Tyn Rodyn, at the bottom of the hill on which the university stood; the remaining lecturers were in rooms in another old building called Vron, at the top of the hill. I had a small room on the first floor in Vron, rather dark and dingy, but perfectly functional. Vron is long gone now – along with the ghost that the ELT lecturer Ken Owen swore he had seen – but Tyn Rodyn is still there, opposite the students' union, though with a different function today. Getting between the two halves of the department, often several times a day, kept us all – staff and students alike – fit.

I found I had five new colleagues, in addition to Frank – Peter Barnes, Ron Brasington, Peter Matthews, Ken Owen, and Alan Thomas – and there was Emlyn the technician, who kept all the specialist equipment working in the phonetics laboratory and the tape recorders in a small language laboratory. It didn't take long to get to know them. There was the equivalent to the UC 'seminar' in the pub at the end of College Road, the Belle Vue, where Miss Hughes – a small, round Welsh lady of great joviality – exercised a maternal discipline on everyone who crossed her threshhold, whether professors or students. In fact, she called virtually everyone professor – *athro* in Welsh can mean either 'professor' or 'teacher' – a habit which caused foreign students not a little confusion. It was a much more intimate world than the university in London. For a start, there were more 'at homes', so that I got to know the 'departmental wives' and – in the case of Frank, Peter Barnes, and Ken – the 'departmental children' too. Frank used to have regular departmental gatherings at his house, for staff and students – a most effective way of fostering a sense of belonging and mutual respect in everyone involved, and a gesture which was always much appreciated by students from abroad. I was so impressed that I copied the practice when we started the language pathology course in Reading, some years later.

There was interdepartmental intimacy too. Because of the joint degree system (linguistics with English, linguistics with French, and so on) – and also, partly because of the Belle Vue – I got to know many members of other departments. And I now know that friendships formed as junior departmental colleagues can last a lifetime. I kept annually in touch with two of them – Richard Bailey, from the English Department, and Brian Mastin, from Biblical Studies. Then in 2002, the travel wheel led me to Newcastle's English Department, where I met Richard again, and to Cambridge, where I met Brian. There was some debate as to who had aged least. I won. (Well, this is my story, and I'm telling it.)

Talking about departmental children: I encountered one after just a few days. It was in an office shared by Peter Barnes, who was our phonetician, and Alan Thomas, who was running the Welsh Dialect Survey. Peter had brought his little boy, Michael – aged about three – into the office. On the wall was a huge map of Wales, reaching almost down to the floor, and on it Alan had pinned little yellow flags showing where various dialect features of Welsh were to be found. Alan and Peter were deep in conversation when I arrived, and had not noticed what I saw straight away – that in South Wales, which was little-boy-height, Michael was engrossed in taking the yellow flags out from one location and sticking them randomly in another. For a few moments, the accuracy of South Welsh dialectological description lay in a tiny pair of hands. I drew my colleagues' attention to the point. Welsh like I had never heard before issued from Alan's lips. Little Michael received some oral and manual plosives from his father. But the future of Welsh dialectology was safe. (At least I think so. I often wonder whether there might not have been other – unnoticed – occasions . . .)

I mentioned students from abroad. This is what nearly did for me. We were dealing with several different kinds of student. There were British undergraduates following a first degree in one or other of the joint courses. There were British undergraduates taking a course or two in linguistics as a 'minor' option within their 'major' subject. There were British postgraduates following a course in Teaching English as a Foreign Language (TEFL) leading to a Diploma or an MA (see plate 2.1). And there were foreign postgraduates – from all over the world – doing the same thing. The numbers weren't large – in the dozens, only – but the fact that the different groups were at different levels of familiarity with the subject, wanted to go into it to different depths, and were intending to use it for different purposes meant that they couldn't all be taught in the same way. For some lecturers, that had one inevitable consequence – duplication. I ended up teaching some of my courses two or three times over. The teaching hours per week grew and grew. And just when I thought they couldn't get any higher, the South Americans landed.

I wasn't party to the negotiations, so I'm not sure how it happened. It was a decade when the British Council was seriously expanding its English-teaching operations in several parts of the world. Many teachers were being sent to Britain to be trained in the new techniques of applied linguistics, and whole-year TEFL courses were booming. Bangor had already developed quite a reputation for its expertise in this area – being one of the first universities to offer such courses. And, doubtless because of this reputation, in the second term of my first year there arrived in Bangor a – what is the appropriate collective noun for a host of South American teachers? – an allegria (Portuguese, 'happiness') of characters from various Latin American countries, to be given an intensive term of learning about all aspects of linguistics. It was a bold – and by all accounts successful – experiment, but it was certainly intensive, both for them and for us. None of the usual courses would fit this ten-week schedule, so a whole new range of introductions to linguistics, phonetics, grammar, semantics, and so on, had to be devised. As the new 'assistant lecturer' (as the grade was called in those days) I was deputed to live up to my title and 'assist', by giving them courses in – well, everything except the teaching methodology side. I obeyed, with a sinking heart. It brought my teaching hours up to thirty-three a week. (The university average at the time was about twelve.)

I got to know that group very well, and had the pleasure of meeting some of them repeatedly in later years, on various visits to South America. Linguistically – though I moaned to anyone who would listen about how I was being brought to an early grave through overwork – it did me the world of good. It meant I had to work up proper teaching courses in all aspects of the subject. As others have often said, the best way to learn a subject is to teach it. I nearly taught myself into the ground, that term; but, at the end of it, for the first time, I felt I really did have a grasp of linguistics as a whole. From the questions which came my way – and they were many, for these teachers were the best – I learned which linguistic notions were easy and which posed special difficulty. My colleagues helped me out when I had to dip my toe into their pools. For instance, Peter Barnes generously let me use his phonetic ear-training exercises, to save me having to work out my own. And I began to compile a mental list of things not to do, such as avoiding rude words in phonetics classes.

LINGUIST AS FOUL-MOUTH

An ear-training class can have its awkward moments. The aim, as I had found out myself some years before, is to train the ability to identify sounds and discriminate them. It is an essential skill in English-language teaching, where one of the tasks is to get students to distinguish English vowels, consonants, stress patterns, intonation contours, and so on, so that they can understand the contrasts which are used in English. Hearing the difference between /l/ and /r/, for instance, is quite difficult for some oriental learners. So, not knowing which particular contrasts were the ones which would cause greatest difficulty for Spanish- or Portuguese-speaking students, I opted for a general approach.

I would start at the front of the mouth, with consonants such as /p/ and /b/, then add /t/ and /d/, and put these alongside some of the maximally distinct vowels, such as /a/ and /u/. I would compose some 'nonsense words', such as /bapu/, /pata/, and /puta/, and I would say these slowly and distinctly, several times, while they wrote what they heard down in their newly learned phonetic transcription. I noticed during the first lesson that there was some disturbance among the group, but put it down to the novelty of the situation. Then, a day later, I got an anonymous note. 'Dear Dave, please in your phonetics class do not use the following sequences of sounds . . .' – and they listed three or four of my nonsense words. I had apparently being saying, ten times over, slowly and deliberately, some of the most obscene words in South American Spanish.

The 1964 intake of students proved to be a mad lot. I still have a menu from the departmental Christmas party held at a local restaurant. It was a feast of linguistics-inspired puns. The starters consisted of Velarized Pâté Maison and Amplitudes of Smoked Salmon, followed by Suprasegmentals of Chicken and a host of other technical treats. There was a leak of the end-of-year examination published on the back. Intriguing questions on quadrilabials (sounds made using four lips) were mixed with observations about the striking looks of the predominantly female South American contingent. The opening question would be a real puzzle to any linguistic historian:

> Write down ALL the Turkish you know. Unless you are very dull you will require at least one line of the paper not provided.

The department had had a thing about Turkish that year. Two of the students were from Turkey, and they had acted as information providers ('informants' we used to call them) for morphology practicals. Most had found it a very difficult language to get to grips with.

What (you may be thinking) is a morphology practical? It is a technique for teaching students how to do linguistics. It's an attempt to replicate, in the classroom, the real task facing someone who encounters an unfamiliar language for the first time and has to make sense of it. First, you find someone willing to act as an informant – usually a foreign student studying at the university – and their job is to provide data on their language for the class, which consists of maybe ten students and the lecturer. The rules are that they are allowed to understand English but not speak it: they must use only their own language. So you start by asking what various objects are in their language and writing down the words in phonetic transcription, then repeating the words back to the informant and asking whether they sound all right. Slowly you build up a little dictionary, and then you move on to making the words more complex – turning a singular into a plural, turning a present tense into a past tense, and so on. This is where morphology comes in. Morphology, in linguistics, is the study of the structure of words – just as, in botany, it is the structure of plants. The aim is to work out, from the informant's data, how the words are made up.

It is like doing a huge jigsaw puzzle, but without a picture. You know there has to be a system, but you also know there will be lots of irregular forms. The jigsaw will not have straight edges all the way round, and there will be alternative pieces that fit in a particular slot. Consider English. Most nouns have a straightforward plural: *cat* becomes *cats*. *Dog* becomes *dogs*. *Horse* becomes *horses*. 'Add an *-s*' seems to be the rule. But listen carefully. The endings are not exactly the same when you speak them aloud. The ending on *horse* sounds like the word is, whereas the ending on *cats* is just an *s* sound. And the ending of *dogs* is more like a *z* sound. Why is that? If you were doing a morphology practical on English you would have to work it out. You'd find that you can't just 'add an *-s*' if the word already ends in an *-s* (as in *horse*). The language makes you add a vowel, to separate the two *s*'s. And the choice of endings on *cats* and *dogs* depends on the character of the final consonant in those words – no vibration of the vocal cords in t + s, vibration of the vocal cords in *g* + *z*. Splendid. You think you are getting somewhere. Then you encounter *mice*, *geese*, and *sheep*, and words which don't seem to have any plurals, such as *police*, and words which don't seem to have any singulars, such as *billiards*. It will take you quite a while to complete the English morphological jigsaw puzzle.

The Bangor students had sweated on Turkish for ten hours during the first term, and got into some terrible tangles trying to sort out what was going on – thanks mainly to the way the vowels in Turkish words 'harmonize' with each other. You can't have a word in Turkish with the sound structure of *horses*, which has a back vowel in the root of the word (the *or*) and a front vowel in the suffix (the *es*). Both vowels have to be the same type. This doesn't happen in English – apart from when very young children are trying out words for the first time. So it took the students a while to get to grips with Turkish word-endings – of which there are quite a few, including quite a number of irregular forms. And by the time of the Christmas party, they felt they were sinking rather than swimming.

But a term later, and all was well. That is the way with language practicals. It's hard slog for a while, and then suddenly things become clear. After twenty hours working on a new language, it's surprising how much you have learned – certainly enough to carry on a basic conversation in the language. You've cracked the phonological code – the pronunciation system – and worked out the main features of grammar, and learned a few hundred words. Not enough, perhaps, to say that one had 'learned the language'. But enough to mean that, parachuted suddenly into the relevant country, you would survive. And if language practicals do nothing else, they teach you not to be scared of foreign languages. No matter how alien they sound or look, at the end of the day they are just sounds and letters, roots and affixes, and orderings of words. Vocabulary, of course, is the nuisance. That's what takes most of the time and memory, as I said in Chapter 1. And it's this limitation in vocabulary that makes it impossible to give a sensible answer to the question linguists are always asked: 'How many languages do you speak?' Thanks to language practicals, I could ask for a beer in a few dozen languages. But carry on a conversation about politics in them? Never.

I spent two years at Bangor, and it gave me a foundation as a professional linguist and applied linguist. Being professional also meant joining the relevant professional linguistic associations – the long-standing Philological Society of Great Britain, and the newly formed Linguistics Association of Great Britain. I'm not quite sure how it happened, but I came away from my first meeting of the LAGB with the position of assistant secretary to Christopher Ball, who had taken on the job as secretary. People made jokes about 'crystal balls'. Apart from anything else, that meant I had to go to all the meetings. But that was a good thing, for a young lecturer in a subject, as it meant I met all the leading linguists of the day, heard some stunning papers, gave a couple of papers myself, and generally felt part of the whole business. It was a decade when new departments were being planned all over the country, and the scope of the proposed *Journal of Linguistics* was being debated. It was an exciting time. The membership of the Association grew steadily. Linguistically orientated research projects were bobbing up here and there. Nobody quite knew what was going on. The LAGB wanted to know. They felt a survey would be a good thing. That word 'assistant' caught someone's attention. I ended up organizing the first surveys of linguistic research in the UK, sending out questionnaires, collating the results, and producing annual reports. I graduated to secretary in 1965, and held the post for five years.

I had expected to be travelling to LAGB meetings from Bangor. But the linguistic gods had other plans. I ended up making the journeys from Reading.

Chapter 11
The sexy subject

I had expected to stay in Bangor for a few years. For me it was a great place to be. Holyhead was a short distance away, and I was able to renew contacts with various aunts, uncles, and cousins. My Welsh was steadily improving, thanks to Alan Thomas, who in the process introduced me to every pub in east Anglesey. I learned to drive, coping with Bangor hill-starts that would prepare you for getting a car up Everest if you had to. I couldn't afford a car of my own, but the house in Bryn Eithinog did have a garage. Several of the linguistics postgraduates were quite senior people, and they sometimes needed a place to leave their car while they went on vacation travels; in lieu of rent, I got the use of the car. As a result, in those two years little Steven saw the inside of more cars than most garage mechanics, and experienced more of Snowdonia than the average mountaineer.

Yes, it was only for two years. In the Linguistics Department, things had not gone entirely according to plan. The vision which had attracted Frank Palmer to Bangor – to establish the first single-subject linguistics undergraduate degree course in the country – hadn't materialized, and the prospect of it happening seemed less likely as time went by. Meanwhile, the University of Reading had expressed an interest in starting just such a course, and was prepared to establish a whole new department of linguistics in order to do it, including a phonetics laboratory. It was to be called a Department of Linguistic Science. Frank was head-hunted, and decided to move. He was able to appoint four new members of staff at Reading. Were any of us interested in coming with him? he asked one day. I nearly got trampled in the rush!

Three of us travelled down to Reading to be interviewed – our theoretical linguist Peter Matthews, our phonetician Peter Barnes, and me – travelling in Peter B.'s slightly creaky but efficient Ford Cortina. The journey down was memorable for two reasons. Somewhere along the A5 (no motorways in those days), Peter B. wanted a break and asked me to take over. Peter M. didn't drive. I pointed out that the ink on my new driving licence had hardly had time to dry, and did he really want to put the future department at such a risk? It was my first long drive at the wheel of a car, and nearly my last. Peter M. took the opportunity – by way of passing the time – to launch into a detailed critique of my system of intonation analysis. Well, it beats pub cricket. My defence was not of the best, I have to say, thanks to (a) the unfamiliar gears on the Cortina and (b) the unfamiliar bends around Birmingham. And unfamiliar T-junctions. I recall making what I thought was a very telling point about high rising tones in response to Peter M., and being about to develop it at length, when Peter B., using precisely the high rising tone I had just been talking about, but accompanied by what can only be described as a hysterical falsetto, drew my attention to the brick wall at the T-junction approaching his beloved Cortina at forty miles an hour!

But we survived the journey, intonation system and Cortina intact, and the next day made our way up to the new university campus in Whiteknights Park. I fell in love with it straight away. A long avenue led to a cluster of modern buildings in spacious grounds. I glimpsed halls of residence behind tall trees, and the original park mansion, where the staff club was housed (see plate 2.2). I was shown the wing where the new department would be, on the ground floor of the Faculty of Letters building. The offices were a huge contrast with the tiny dark rooms in the old houses in Bangor. There was even a purpose-built seminar room. And the space proposed for the new phonetics lab was enormous, six times what we had had before. It all felt right. I was in no doubt. If they wanted me, I most certainly wanted it. And once there, I couldn't imagine anything less than an academic earthquake would ever make me want to leave it.

The interview wasn't just a formality. I was asked searching questions about how I thought a degree course in linguistics should develop and what my contribution might be. Having taught virtually an entire linguistics course in a single term – thanks to my close encounter with the South American kind – I had no difficulty with that. And this time, there were no forestry questions. They offered me the job on the spot, and it was on the lecturer scale. That was a promotion. My cup brimmethed over.

The next few months are a blur. The three-year registration for my PhD at London was due to end in 1965, and I had to get it finished before we moved. I guessed (rightly, as it turned out) that there would be no time to work on it in the opening months at Reading. The little Olivetti went into overdrive. Carbon copies (remember those?) of chapters lay all over the sitting-room. Steven, now with mobile feet and grasping hands, couldn't believe his luck. If frequency and perceptibility of parental input to a child is a determinant of language emergence, then by rights Steven's first words should have been DON'T TOUCH.

There was hardly any time to go house-hunting in Reading. In an intense weekend I found a little detached semi-bungalow in Upavon Drive, a tiny cul-de-sac alongside the A4 as it leaves the town centre. The neighbours had complementary tastes in children. On one side lived an elderly spinster with a pathological dislike of anything that toddled; on the other, the matron of the local maternity hospital. We endeared ourselves to the latter, but not the former, when Susie arrived, a month after we moved in.

To a linguist, the arrival of children is a twofold gift (see plate 6.1). The parental part of the linguist revels in the birth, as any mother or father would. The linguistic part salivates in anticipation of the rich research opportunity that has suddenly landed on the doorstep. To this day, when an academic friend has a baby, I cannot resist the urge to send 'Congratulations on the birth of fresh data'. And in the mid-1960s, any child language data could not but be fresh. The study of child language acquisition – as it would one day come to be called – had hardly begun. It was very hard to find real examples of what children actually did. I began to make recordings and to transcribe them. Anything Susie vocalized would be taken down and later used as evidence. And Steven too, steadily acquiring a 200-word vocabulary as he approached his second birthday. They provided a real-life perspective for the language acquisition course which was one of the first special options to be taught in the new department. It was a course which we felt would be of real interest to the students who were beginning to sniff around the unfamiliar university subject of 'linguistics'.

I cannot think of a more intriguing, challenging, fascinating, rewarding branch of language study than the study of language development in children. It is a commonplace for parents to react with amazement to the speed and ingenuity with which their children establish their personalities and develop their abilities, but few are aware of just how remarkable the whole language learning process is. In a nutshell: language is the most complex piece of behaviour a child will ever learn. *Languages*, in the case of two-thirds of the human race – for most children grow up in a multilingual environment and learn two or more at a time. Languages typically have dozens of sounds, hundreds of sound combinations, thousands of grammatical constructions, and tens of thousands of words in everyday use, and most people are unaware of the way they are acquired. Consider how much linguistic detail there is in this sentence, used by Susie when she was approaching age three: 'The mouse is very cross cos his hat felled down in the water.' Note her awareness of how we can intensify meaning (through the use of *very*). Her sense of causality (*cos*). Her knowledge of how we form past tenses by adding *-ed* – something she has worked out for herself, for no adult would ever have said *felled* in her hearing. And, though you can't see it in this transcription, she had every vowel and consonant right, and produced the thirteen-word two-part sentence with perfect stress, rhythm, and intonation. All this from a child who had been alive for less than a thousand days. How on earth did she do it? How on earth do they all do it? And why, sometimes, are they not able to do it? That is the task facing researchers in child language acquisition.

The establishment of a new department – the first in the country with the name 'linguistic science' in the title – made a huge impact in the university and beyond. It was like the arrival of a mysteriously gorgeous stranger in a small town: nobody was very sure what exactly the newcomer was doing there, but everyone wanted a date. Linguistics, we quickly realized, was a sexy subject. As the student numbers grew, other departments in the university became increasingly curious about the kind of thing that linguists did. It was an exciting time. Joint degree courses – such as linguistics with English or linguistics with French – brought departments together in fresh ways, and fostered new courses and approaches. The joint degree with the French Department, for example, led to a new course on the structure of the French language. The link with English prompted a new course on the study of style. We found ourselves approached by people from sociology, psychology, and education, all involved in language from their individual points of view and interested in the perspective that linguistics could provide. It felt a bit like walking through a fairground, with each stallholder inviting you to 'have a go'. And the difficulty, for me at least, was that every stall was hugely enticing.

The reading and writing stall was one. The School of Education had a centre devoted to the teaching of literacy – the Reading Reading Centre, as some (confusingly) called it. Betty Root and her colleagues there were especially interested in the need to relate the teaching of reading to the linguistic level achieved by children by the time they arrived in primary school, and they were keen to hear about work in child language. I found myself regularly talking to groups of teachers, and visiting school classrooms to see what actually went on. I was horrified to see the artificiality of the language used in the most popular reading schemes of the day. I suppose I must have encountered Janet and John in my own early reading, but I had forgotten them. Now I met them again, and found them linguistically bizarre, presenting young readers with a kind of English which was unnecessarily difficult and often unreal. *A tall red jug stood next*. What sort of sentence was that, for heaven's sake! The best readers were coping with virtually everything they saw on the page; but it was easy to see that most of the children were not. The reading centre tutors were sure there must be ways of improving their lot. So was I. But it would take me nearly a decade of involvement in the educational world before I dared to do something about it.

The clinical stall was another. Soon after I arrived in Reading, the phone rang. It was Kevin Murphy, the audiologist at the Royal Berkshire Hospital. They'd heard we had arrived and wondered if we could help with a problem? It transpired that one of their patients was a little girl called Gillie, who had a serious language delay, and they were having trouble identifying exactly what her problems were. I went down the hill to the Audiology Unit and watched through a one-way window as Gillie worked with one of the speech therapists. It was enthralling. This was a brave new world indeed, for me, and what amazing people were in it! I had a welter of first impressions – the caring, meticulous, purposeful teamwork on the part of the audiology staff . . . the struggle Gillie was facing as she tried to express herself . . . the anxious expressions on her parents' faces as they willed her to do well.

I made notes of the way she was talking, and her sentences quickly fell into a pattern. In terms of normal child language acquisition, it was easy to see that she was at a stage of grammatical development some two years behind her peers. After listening to her for half an hour, it was clear to me that she was using a very small range of sentence patterns. It was possible to identify what types of construction she could manage and what she couldn't. After she and her parents had left, I started to give a brief account of her problem to the staff who had been involved, referring to subjects and objects and word order and clauses and . . . realized that I had lost my listeners. I asked the speech therapist whether she had ever done any grammar. Only in secondary school, she replied, and she'd never got on with it. Kevin was the same. Had they ever studied child language acquisition? They shook their heads. These things evidently weren't a routine part of speech therapy or audiology training. No wonder they were at a loss.

I promised I would sketch out a simple summary of the main stages of grammatical development in normal children, and show on this primitive chart exactly where Gillie's development lay. Once they could see where she was, in relation to where she ought to be, then it would give the speech therapist something to work towards. They were delighted. And I went back to the department buzzing with the prospect of being able to do something useful. I did my chart and made a couple of suggestions for the next therapy session. If I'd got it right, Gillie should respond well to them. I had. She did. Everyone was thrilled, and mostly me.

As I watched that second session, I had a feeling it would not be my last. And sure enough, as I was leaving, Kevin mentioned that they had another patient who had a different problem he thought I'd be interested in. If I had a spare few minutes . . .? And so I found myself using the same chart for a second child, and then for a third. I was totally hooked. I visited the unit as often as I could, over the next few years, and saw as many different types of patient as I could. The unit was attached to the ENT (ear, nose, and throat) department, and so it wasn't long before I was able to see patients with hearing loss, various kinds of paralysis, and anatomical deficiencies such as cleft palate. Adults too. I met my first deaf signers there. And my first brain-damaged patients, with the language loss known as aphasia.

As my knowledge of language disorders increased, so did my reputation among the local speech therapists. They asked me for seminars on aspects of linguistics. We had training days. There were joint clinical sessions, where everyone would get together to discuss a patient. The School of Education was planning a diploma course in the teaching of speech therapy, and the Linguistics Department was asked to contribute to it. That was how I met Sister Marie, who figured in my Prologue – she was one of its first students. News of these initiatives travelled further afield. I went to talk to groups in Oxfordshire and Hampshire. In Oxford I met Catherine Renfrew, one of the most experienced speech therapists around, whose assessment procedures were widely used in children's clinics. Remember that name: she appears again in this story. Within a year of that first phone call from Kevin Murphy, it was plain that a 'clinical linguistics' was going to play a large part in my life. Just how large a part I could not possibly have imagined.

Back up the hill in the university, I had meanwhile discovered that some of the other stallholders were already very well informed about linguistics. Whitney Bolton was one, an American who had become a professor in the English Department. He had a head which buzzed with possible collaborative projects. One came to fruition, in the form of an anthology of historical essays about the English language. The other one didn't. It was a great idea, nonetheless – to compile a Dictionary of English-Speaking Peoples.

It was the perfect moment, late 1966, with many countries of the British Empire (such as Ghana, Nigeria, and Singapore) having become independent during the previous decade, and developing new varieties of

English to express their individuality as new nations. The big dictionaries had not yet engaged with these developments, and even long-standing dialects, such as Australian and Canadian English, were receiving only limited treatment. Lexicography projects were already being planned which would one day produce excellent dictionaries for these regions. But at the time, hardly anything had appeared. So Whitney and I thought it was a good moment to bring together the first fruits of these projects into a single dictionary. He would look after the USA and those parts of the world where American English was strong (such as in the Philippines). I would look after the rest. Cassells, in the form of John Buchanan Brown, showed publisher interest, and commissioned a pilot survey.

I wrote to linguists in every country where there was a significant English-speaking population, and asked them what was going on. It turned out that new local vocabularies were growing up everywhere. Several leading lexicographers, such as Walter Avis and William Mackie, came on board as consultant editors. Some sent in preliminary word-lists, to show where they were up to. The lists were already very long, and likely to get a lot longer. When individual dictionaries later appeared for some of these countries, it was possible to see just how much longer. The *Dictionary of Jamaican English*, for example, would contain some fifteen thousand local usages. After completing the pilot survey, it was clear that this was going to be a huge enterprise. It would take at least seven years. We did some preliminary costings. John Buchanan Brown's face went pale. The project quietly died.

LINGUIST AS LEXICOGRAPHER

I don't know what it is about dictionaries. They fascinate me. I have a huge collection, including some quite rare ones. And I have tried to write one myself, on four occasions – but only once with any success.

The principle is clear. Never, never, never, never, never start a dictionary project unless you are prepared to devote a serious number of years to it. I learned that lesson the hard way, by starting one, and then realizing, usually after reaching AB–, just how time-consuming it was going to be. The Dictionary of English-Speaking Peoples was one of three abandoned dictionary projects during the late 1960s and early 1970s.

I spent much of one summer, with a research assistant, compiling a dictionary of colloquial English. I was struck by the way everyday informal vocabulary, such as *bolshy* and *thingummyjig*, was missing from most dictionaries, and began to compile a list of absent items.

When the list reached a thousand, I realized it was a lifetime job. I gave up, and passed the collection on to Longman. I made a promise to myself never to start a dictionary project again.

I broke that promise a few years later by agreeing to compile a dictionary of speech pathology terms on behalf of the UK's College of Speech Therapists. That project came to a sticky end too – not because of the number of terms, this time, but because of the way the terms were being used differently by the various disciplines involved in the diagnosis and treatment of speech disorders (medicine, psychology, education, linguistics). An apparently simple term like *articulation disorder* had over twenty alternatives – *articulatory defect, abnormality of articulation, misarticulation, dyslalia*, and so on. And the meanings often altered subtly. It was plain that only an interdisciplinary project would provide a solution. I made a promise to myself never to start a dictionary project again.

I broke that promise too. During a visit to Toronto in 1971, Hal Gleason had shown me his collection of slips documenting the way linguistic terminology had evolved. He had begun to go through major texts (such as Bloomfield), to extract all the terms and definitions. It was an impressive start, but he was dubious about ever finishing it. Back in the UK, I tried to persuade the British linguistic societies to take the job on, but they weren't in a position to do so. And eventually I decided to have a go myself. I stuck a pin in an alphabet, began with letter *P*, wrote the entries on *palate* and *palatal*, and then couldn't stop. *A First Dictionary of Linguistics and Phonetics* was finally published in 1980.

Why 'first'? I insisted on this being part of the title because I was conscious of the need for the job to be done properly, on solid historical principles. I dropped my insistence when, five years later, preparing the second edition, I realized that the prospect of a historical linguistics dictionary was as far away as ever. Twenty-five years on, with the book now in its sixth edition, nothing has changed.

That was six months of wasted work. Or was it wasted? Yes, in the sense that there was no product at the end of it. But very much No, in other ways. It taught me a lot about the realities of world English, and I was able to use some of the material in later writing. It helped to promote local enthusiasm for dictionary compilation, for lexicographers in small countries did not always find it easy to gain support for their efforts and were able to cite DESP as an indication of why their work was important. And it gave me a reputation (without realizing it) for cheek.

A Linguistic Circle had been formed in Oxford, and we used to drive over for the meetings, held in Lincoln College. They asked me to give a paper, and as it was right in the middle of the DESP pilot survey, I decided to talk about that. I made my case with customary enthusiasm, drawing especial attention to the lack of work in this area and the regrettable weaknesses in existing dictionaries. I noticed that someone in the second row was getting pucely agitated. And when it came to question time he exploded. No experience! Inadequate planning!! Totally wrong to take material from existing dictionaries!!! Did I not know what was already going on in lexicography? It will never get off the ground!!!! He went on for five minutes or more. 'Who was the man who got so angry?' I asked the Circle organizer afterwards. 'Ah,' he said, 'that was Robert Burchfield.' The editor of the *Oxford English Dictionary*.

I suppose, if I'd realized he was in the audience, I wouldn't have been so critical about other dictionaries with quite such panache! He was correct about the inexperience, of course, and subsequent events proved him right about our project. But he was wrong about what was already going on in lexicography, for the *OED* then had only a very limited coverage of world varieties of English; its tradition, starting with the original editor, James Murray, had been to present a highly 'Britocentric' view of English vocabulary. And Burchfield was certainly wrong to condemn the practice of taking material (with acknowledgement) from existing dictionaries, for all dictionaries borrow in this way (including the *OED* itself). Anyway, I wasn't intending to rely on other dictionaries, in most cases, but to work with new projects. There was a 'lively exchange of views', as they say, before I retired bruised to Reading – and then learned later that the exchange hadn't done me any harm. Apparently Burchfield wasn't the most popular of personalities in Oxford, and the story of a young whippersnapper 'taking him on' evidently received some nods of high-table approval – notwithstanding the fact that I had simply walked into trouble rather than gone looking for it.

Might that inadvertent encounter have had some influence on Burchfield's thinking? In her 2007 memoir on the history of the *OED*, *Treasure-House of the Language*, Charlotte Brewer, having read the memoranda that circulated within Oxford University Press at the time, thinks the DESP proposal 'may have planted (or nurtured) a seed in Burchfield's mind that grew and prospered'. I would be delighted if that were the case. It would be another positive outcome for a project to which several people devoted a great deal of time. Mind you, the idea has still not lost its relevance, even forty years on. As English continues to grow in foreign-language settings, such as Spain and Germany, localized vocabulary steadily increases. In Colombia, for instance, I talked not long ago to a group of

ELT practitioners, one of whom was enthusing about a rasca-rasca which had taken place in a verbena. It didn't occur to him that I might have no idea what he was talking about. So I asked. It turned out that these are words associated with the Barranquilla carnival. A rasca-rasca is an onomatopoeic word for the sound produced by the guacharaca, a scraping musical instrument played in accordion songs. People evidently dance fast and close along with rasca-rasca songs. And they do it in a carnival meeting-place where dancing and drinking are the norm – a verbena. There are still no dictionaries of the words being used in English that reflect local culture in this way. Nowhere to look this sort of thing up. We still need a DESP.

This mention of English language teaching brings me back to another enticing stall in the language fairground which, with its promise of getting to see the world, few linguists have ever been able to resist. The demand for linguistically inspired ELT courses was steadily increasing, and our new department was ready to offer a Diploma and an MA to anyone interested in the applications of linguistics, especially teachers from abroad. David Wilkins was appointed to develop that side of things. An ex-British Council man, he was in an ideal position to act as an interface between the academic and professional worlds.

The British Council. I had vaguely come across it in Bangor, through the South American students, but I had no clear idea what it was. Now I know. It is the most marvellous organization, whose presence is universally acknowledged abroad, but which is hardly known among the general mass of the population in the UK. It is perhaps best described as the cultural dimension of the Foreign and Commonwealth Office. Its responsibilities are wide-ranging, for science, technology, education, the arts – and the English language. Its centres around the world devote a large part of their time to the teaching and examining of English. Founded in 1934, it rapidly developed a presence in many countries, numbering 109 today. During the 1960s it devoted large resources to providing scholarships to teachers and others to study English in the UK, either for a whole year or (as we have seen) for a part of a year – and also in the form of summer schools, usually a three- or four-week stay in July or August in one of the main British cities. Abroad, English Language Officers were trained to work in several countries, advising on how English teaching could be promoted. And, as only a small number of people could be given scholarships to the UK, lecturers from British universities were brought out to help develop an English-teaching presence all over the world – hence my close encounter with the gyratory sambaista in Rio.

That was just one of a series of visits abroad, which began quite soon after we arrived in Reading. I remember a meeting with a group of senior British Council managers. We sat around a table in the Linguistics Department seminar room and discussed the global ELT situation. Could we provide visiting expertise? South America was going to be a particular focus. We thought we might just be interested. And as a result Peter Barnes and I went out at the beginning of 1967 to provide input for the first international summer school – international, because it brought together teachers and teacher-trainers from several South American countries.

The conference was held in the Hotel Paneiras, halfway up the Corcovado mountain in Rio de Janeiro – that's the one with the huge thirty-metre-high statue of Christ the Redeemer at the top. The views over the city were staggering – and indeed it was a visit still remembered for its staggering, thanks to the discovery of caipirinha at a club called Le Kilt (honestly), late-night active participation in local samba schools, and the subsequent long walks back up to the hotel, a struggling 465 metres above sea level. There were other discoveries too: that American embassy hospitality was pretty darned fine, that dawn coming up on Copacabana must be one of the finest sights in the world, and that crippling sunburn is the inevitable outcome if British newbies play volleyball on a Rio beach dressed only in a T-shirt and shorts.

I'm still in touch with a few of the people I met then, though contact with most was lost, due to a silly cultural linguistic difference. I would get letters with the address of the sender written on the envelope and not on the notepaper inside. Not used to this, I would jettison the envelope without thinking, so when I tried to reply I suddenly realized I had no knowledge of where to send it. Thus do growing friendships inadvertently die.

But some were renewed through subsequent visits. The success of that first summer school – and it *was* a linguistic success (despite the impression conveyed above), for Peter and I did actually work quite hard, in between our cultural explorations – led to several others. The Reading connection stayed strong. The British Council had fostered a scheme to teach English in the 'culturas' – independent teaching institutions in Latin America. It became known as the ACU project, from the initials of Argentina, Chile, and Uruguay, and it kept some of my Reading colleagues very busy. I never spent as much time in South America as others did – Peter would later spend a whole year there with his family – but I did go back half-a-dozen times over the next few years, mainly to Brazil, with courses in Rio, São Paulo, and Recife, and also to the other countries in the south. As a result, I have one of the best vinyl collections of Carnival songs in Britain, and my ability to name all the instruments in a batucada (the accompanying percussion band) used to be second to none. I even became quite adept at playing the quica, that remarkable pitch-altering drum whose distinctive 'kweek-kweek' sound is made by rubbing a stick fixed in the centre of the drumskin. A group gave me one as a present, but my skills have died through lack of opportunity. Not much call for quica-players in Holyhead.

Why was there always a revolution going on, during those visits in the south? Or an armed uprising? The British Council never seemed unduly concerned about such things. But I did get a bit of a shock when I arrived in Montevideo at the height of the Tupamaros urban guerrilla movement, and found myself travelling with the British Council representative on a different route to his office every day, to avoid being kidnapped. I was given strict instructions about varying my movements and not going out on my own. Apparently the revolutionaries were just as interested in juicy visiting academics as they were in local politicians. They weren't joking. I was there in April 1970. A few months later, an American agronomy lecturer was held for several months, and they even managed to kidnap the British ambassador, who was eventually released in exchange for £42,000. I often wonder what the British Council would have offered in exchange for me. About £3.50, I imagine.

LINGUIST AS REVOLUTIONARY

Chile was also in some turbulence, in early 1970, preparing for the election that would bring the leftist Salvador Allende to power in September that year. When I arrived, courtesy of the British Council, I had no idea anything out of the ordinary was going on. I was due to lecture at the university about linguistics and language teaching, and I was very impressed to see a large hall absolutely packed. 'The level of English is not good,' said my host, 'so we have arranged for a translation.'

I assumed he meant simultaneous, but it turned out to be sequential. Up on stage came an interpreter, who stood next to me. We agreed I should speak a sentence at a time, and I would keep them quite short. I produced my first sentence. I can't remember exactly what it was – something quite basic and succinct like 'I am delighted to be here in your splendid university to talk about linguistics, the science of language.' The interpreter took over. I had very little Spanish in those days, and he spoke at a huge rate of knots, so I couldn't understand anything apart from the word 'linguistica', but he seemed to be saying twice as much as I had said. Then he stopped, and a huge cheer came from the floor. I looked at my interpreter, totally puzzled. All I'd said was that linguistics was a science. Why should that have been so enthusiastically received? His face was uninformative, as he waited for my next sentence. I stumbled on, receiving several more cheers at unexpected intervals, and got another huge round of applause at the end.

Later, my British Council host told me what had happened. Apparently most of the audience were supporters of the socialists, communists, and other left-wing groups forming the People's Unity Party – as was my interpreter, and evidently my first sentence had been translated as something like: 'The illustrious professor from England, who supports our campaign for the election of Señor Allende, is expressing his solidarity with us by visiting this splendid university to talk about linguistics, the science of language.' My political support was reaffirmed several times during my lecture, hence the applause. And I left the university a local hero – though probably thereafter labelled as a known risk in the CIA database.

But they were intensive, those cultural summer schools. They started early and finished late. They included general lectures as well as practical classes with small groups on pronunciation and grammar. And it was usually a two-dimensional experience, with literature alongside language. For me, that was one of the bonuses: you never knew who you'd be working with on the literary side, and it was usually someone you'd always wanted to meet. There were shared sessions, too, where we would explore some domain of language from both a linguistic and a literary point of view – a piece of Shakespeare, for instance, or a contemporary play. To make everything come alive, classroom analysis would be counterpointed by a performance. As a consequence, alongside critic-novelist Christopher Bigsby, I've played most of the parts in Harold Pinter's *The Birthday Party* – and I don't just mean the male ones. It's an unnerving experience, though, realizing that you're being closely scrutinized by a novelist while in full linguistic flow. Are you going to turn up as a character in his next book? One of the itinerant linguists in eastern Europe must have been the model for Dr Petworth in Malcolm Bradbury's novel *Rates of Exchange*. I hope it wasn't me. He wouldn't say, when I asked him.

It wasn't as if I needed convincing that literature and language were two sides of a wafer-thin coin; but those British Council courses affirmed it over and over. Repeatedly I was enthralled by having my language analyses illuminated by my literary counterpart's observations, and excited to discover that he found my analyses illuminating in return. For my part, I could see patterns in the texts we were using, but couldn't always see why they were there. He showed how they contributed to the development of

University College London

Plate 1.1 Randolph Quirk (p. 83). From David Crystal, *The Cambridge Encyclopedia of the English Language* (CUP 2003), with permission.

Plate 1.2 A. C. Gimson (p. 84). From Susan Ramsaram (ed.), *Studies in the Pronunciation of English: a commemorative volume in honour of A F Gimson* (Routledge 1990).

Plate 1.3 J. D. O'Connor (p. 84). From Jack Windsor Lewis (ed.), *Studies in General and English Phonetics: essays in honour of J D O'Connor* (Routledge 1995).

Plate 1.4 The contents page of the 1964 issue of *le maître phonétique* (p. 116), showing the way phonetic transcription was used. Despite the French headings, most of the articles were in English.

lə

mɛːtrə fɔnetik

ɔrgan də l asɔsjɑsjɔ̃ fɔnetik ɛ̃tɛrnasjɔnal, 1964

tablə de matjɛːr

Plate 1.5 The Survey of English Usage office, in the early 1970s. This photograph was taken long after I left, but the activities continued much as before. The researchers on the right are using a tape-repeater system as I did, to listen over and over to short pieces of speech (p. 95). © Survey of English Usage, UCL. Reproduced with permission.

Bangor

Plate 2.1 A group of Bangor staff and postgraduate students outside the Antelope Inn in Menai Bridge in 1964 (p. 130). Apart from me (front left), it shows linguists Frank Palmer (centre) and Peter Matthews (to his left), phonetician Peter Barnes (just behind them), and ELT methodologist Ken Owen (in front).

Reading

Plate 2.2 Arrival, 1965 (p. 137). New buildings now fill much of the area behind me.

Plate 2.3 The abstract composition produced by a group of Reading art students in 1969, representing what they heard in one of my lectures (p. 15).

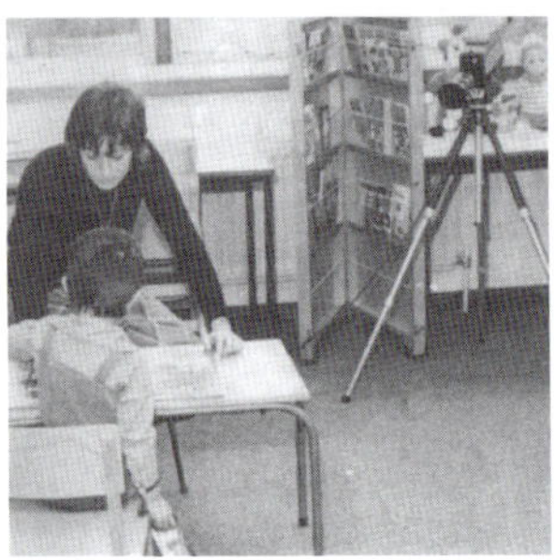

Plate 2.4 The Reading special assessment clinic in 1980 (p. 184). Speech therapist Catherine Evans is videoed while working with a language-delayed child.

Plate 2.5 On the other side of the window, we can see them, but they cannot see us. The one-way window is on my right. The other members of the clinical team, and a group of students, are out of shot behind me. For the whole group to see what is going on, the video monitor is essential.

Reading (continued)

Plate 3.1 Lecturing at an in-service day for speech therapists in the late 1970s. An early version of one of my clinical linguistic profiles (p. 181) is on the screen.

Plate 3.2 Presenting Randolph Quirk (p. 83) for the honorary degree of DLitt to the Reading University Chancellor, Lord Sherfield, in 1982.

Plate 3.3 In 1982 I edited a collection of papers as a Festschrift in honour of Frank Palmer's sixtieth birthday: *Linguistic Controversies*. The picture shows some of those who gathered to celebrate the occasion (from left to right): John Trim, Marion Trim, Peter Roach, Frank Palmer (p. 120), Jean Palmer, me, Hilary Crystal, Hazel Bell, Wilf Jones, Margaret Davison.

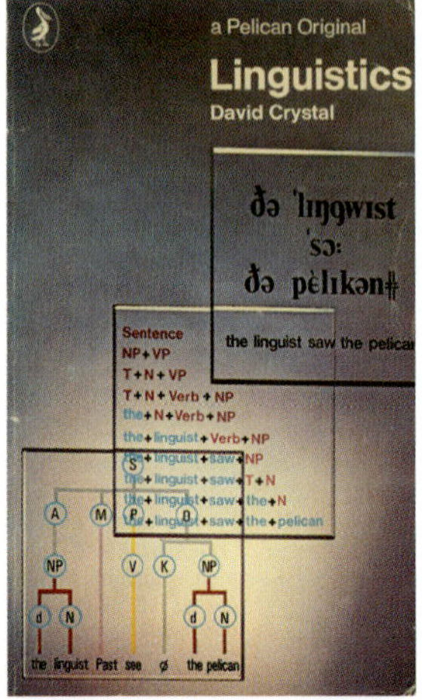

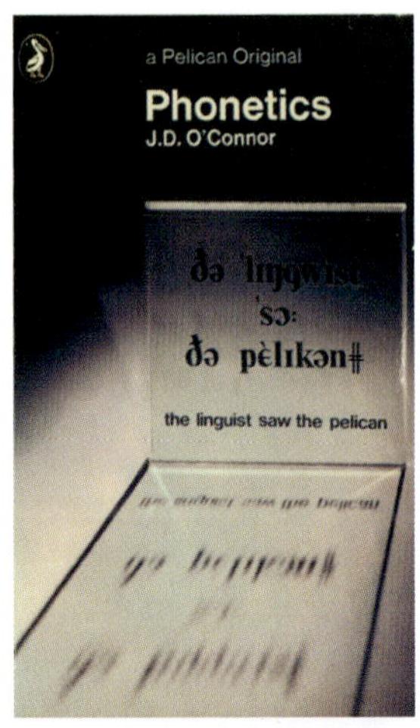

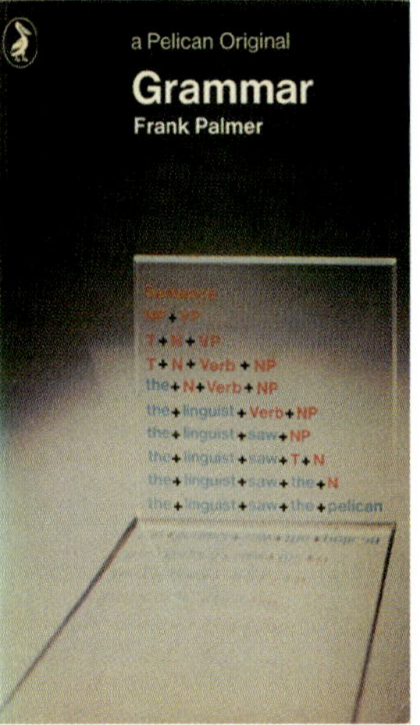

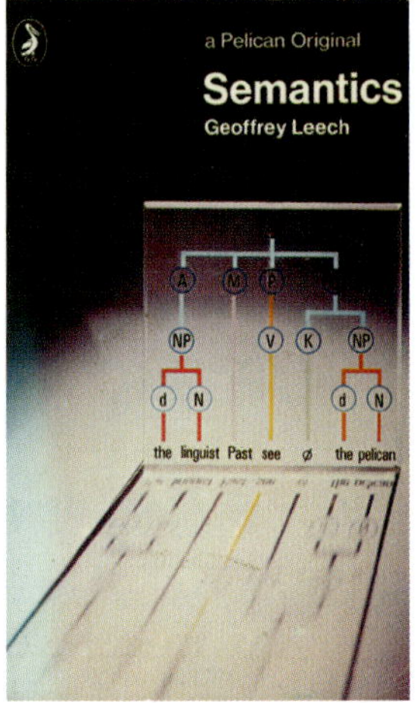

Plates 4.1–4.4 The first four titles in the Pelican Linguistics series, showing the unifying design theme (p. 156).

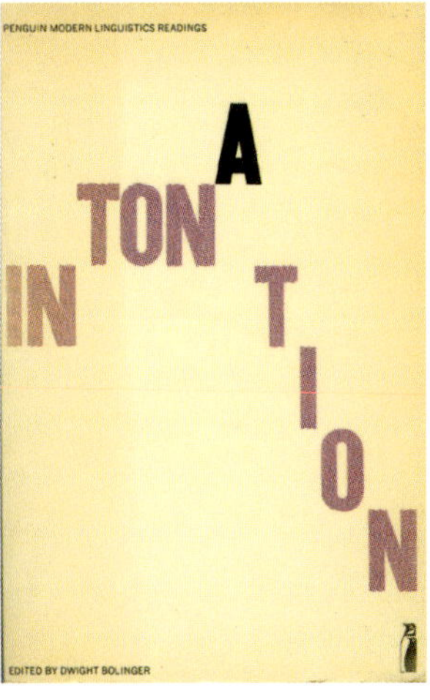

Plate 4.5 One of the most striking designs in the Penguin Modern Linguistics series (p. 159): Dwight Bolinger's *Intonation*.

Plate 4.6 The invitation to the Penguin Education farewell party, with the views of the organizers made perfectly clear (p. 160).

Plate 5.1 Working on the Index to *A Comprehensive Grammar of the English Language* in 1984 (p. 210). From left to right: Jan Svartvik, me, Sidney Greenbaum, Geoffrey Leech, Randolph Quirk.

Plate 5.2 Checking a proof page in 2000 with Hilary during a publicity shoot for *Words on Words*, our compilation of quotations on language and languages (p. 257). Between us we read or re-read some 1,500 texts in our year's 'licence to read'.

Plate 5.3 The Linglex advisory panel (p. 264) at one of its meetings in 2000. Membership of the committee changed often over the years. On this occasion there were: (back row, standing left to right) linguists Rod Bolitho, Paul Meara, Peter Trudgill and Philip Schofield, lexicographers Patrick Gillard and Stella O'Shea; (middle row, standing) linguist Katie Wales, lexicographer Emma Campbell, me; (front row, seated) lexicographer Adam Gadsby, linguists Geoffrey Leech, Gillian Brown, and Randolph Quirk, and editorial director Della Summers. The meetings were held in the Longman offices at 5 Bentinck Street, in Mayfair, London. The address will be known to students of espionage. This was where Anthony Blunt and Guy Burgess lived. During the Second World War, the 'Bentinck Street Set' included Kim Philby and Donald Maclean, and it was after an orgy here that Maclean laid himself open to Soviet blackmail by being photographed *in flagrante delicto*. After all that, our lexicography meetings must have seemed a bit of an anti-climax to any passing ghost.

Family known . . .

Plate 6.1 Looking after the data (p. 138) – sorry, children – in 1968. Molly, holding Timmy, with Sue and Steve.

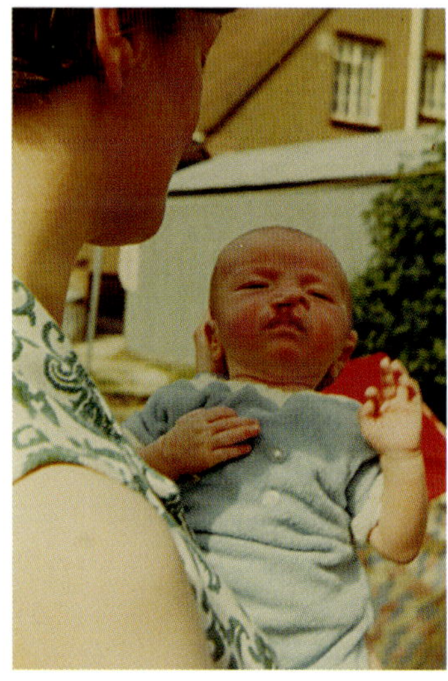

Plate 6.2 Timmy before his cleft lip operation . . . (p. 162).

Plate 6.3 . . . and after, age 3 – an excellent repair. Older children with unrepaired clefts are still common in many parts of the developing world. The organizations which work towards providing them with corrective surgery deserve every support.

Plate 6.4 The data grown up: a birthday gathering in London in 2006. Left to right: Steven, Sue, me, Hilary, Lucy, Ben.

. . . and discovered

Plates 7.1–7.2 The missing person from 1942 – restored (pp. 21, 39, 232).

Plate 7.3 My father in the early 1990s.

Plate 7.4 The first conversation in 1991 (p. 232). New sister-in-law Licia is just in the shot.

Plate 7.5 Accumulating brothers (p. 230): Michael (top left), Jonathan (top right), Zvi (bottom left).

Family: old worlds and new

Plate 8.1 Exploring roots: at the Vilnius Yiddish Institute, with Dovid Katz (p. 233) and his staff.

Plate 8.2 Hirsh Pekelis, standing in front of the mass graves outside Ukmerge (p. 233), tells the story of his town.

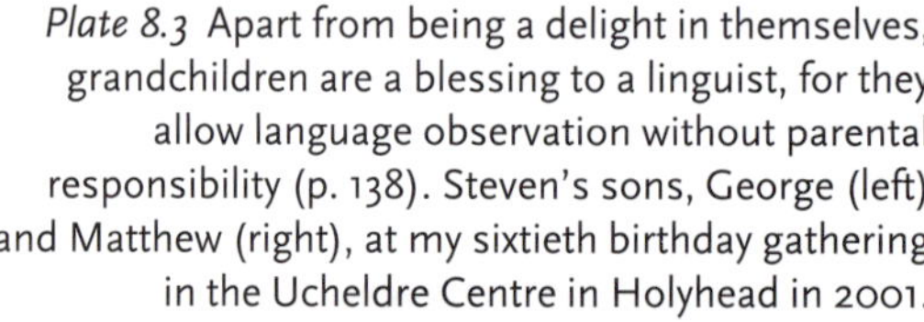

Plate 8.3 Apart from being a delight in themselves, grandchildren are a blessing to a linguist, for they allow language observation without parental responsibility (p. 138). Steven's sons, George (left) and Matthew (right), at my sixtieth birthday gathering in the Ucheldre Centre in Holyhead in 2001.

Plate 8.4 Mateo, growing up trilingually in Amsterdam (p. 271), brings home to me how little we know about the process of language acquisition in multilingual settings. Here he is in 2006 with Lucy and musician father, Vicente, from Venezuela.

Lecturing around

Plate 9.1 Addressing a conference of logopedists (speech therapists) in Rimini, Italy, in 1980 (p. 193). I travelled to Padua to lecture during the same visit, but not without some anxiety on the part of the Rimini organizer. I'm not sure why, but apparently there was a risk of my being kidnapped on the way!

Plate 9.2 A significant lecture, at the Barcelona Forum in 2004. President Pasqual Maragall (centre behind the desk) listens intently. The Barcelona House of Languages was the outcome (p. 247).

Plate 9.3 In between lectures, in Rio de Janeiro in 2000. A renewal of acquaintance with one of the samba schools, Salgueiro, which I first visited in the 1960s (p. 114).

Plate 9.4 In Mexico City airport on the way home after lecturing at the British Council (p. 145) 'Best of British' conference in 2007. Benjamin Zephaniah and I experiment with a wrist-pressure technique which we had been told would eliminate jet-lag. (It didn't.)

Favourite jackets

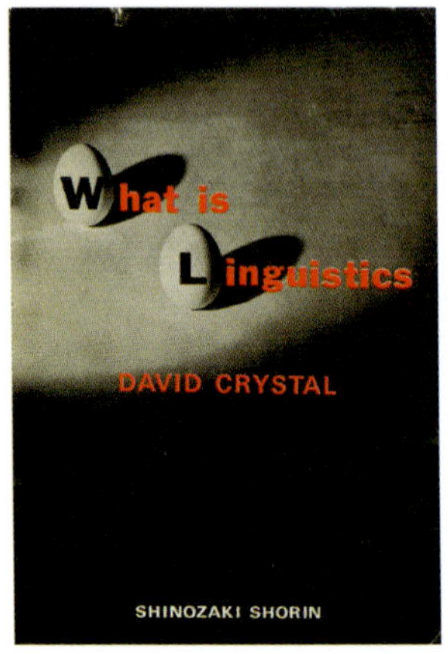

Plate 10.1 The Japanese edition of *What is Linguistics?* (p. 153). I have never understood the significance of the eggs.

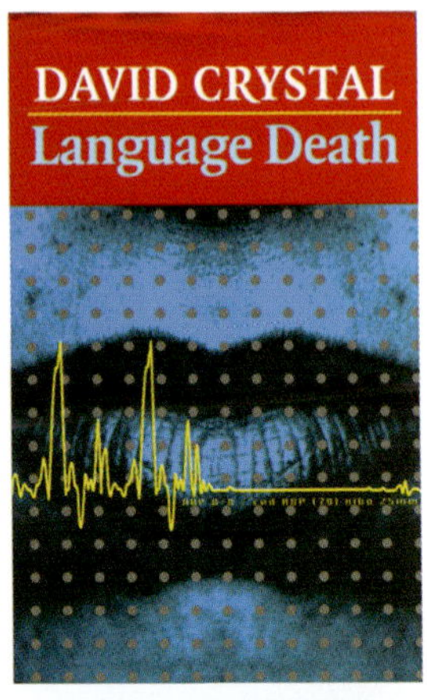

Plate 10.2 A brilliant idea to visualize hope for endangered languages (p. 244). The life pulse flatlines – but perhaps picks up again.

Plate 10.3 The jacket of *CEEL* (p. 214) was constructed physically, not computationally, with a sculpted head and cut-out cards. The images were projected on to the head and cards from slide projectors mounted on towers of milk-crates.

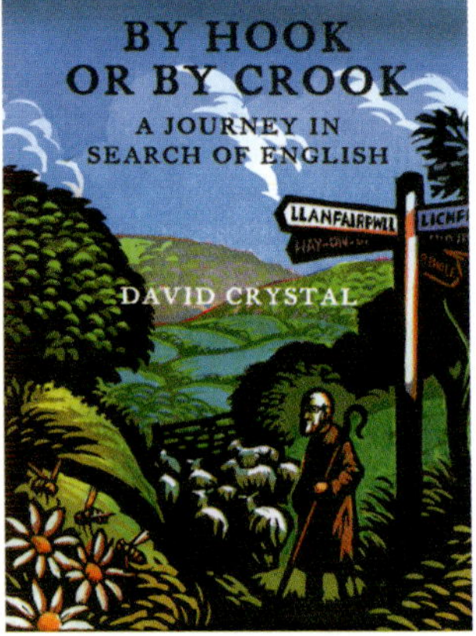

Plate 10.4 I had not actually thought of myself as a language shepherd until this book (p. 269).

Plate 10.5 The Cambridge encyclopedia family, as it appeared in the late 1990s (p. 225). The picture of John Wayne on the front of the *Biographical* has been doctored. He was originally carrying a very prominent rifle!

Cambridge visits

Plate 11.1 Paris. Book signing of *CEL* (p. 214) at the Salon du Livre in 1987. On the next table was William Golding – who got fed up after five minutes and left the hall to find a drink, leaving behind an enormous queue of puzzled but Gallically philosophical book-holders. The organizers suggested that they join my queue instead – but for some obscure reason an encyclopedia of language didn't prove to be as attractive as *The Lord of the Flies*.

Plate 11.2 Sydney. The things one has to do, sometimes, to satisfy a newspaper photographer eager for a fresh angle. The letter-tiles say 'English language'.

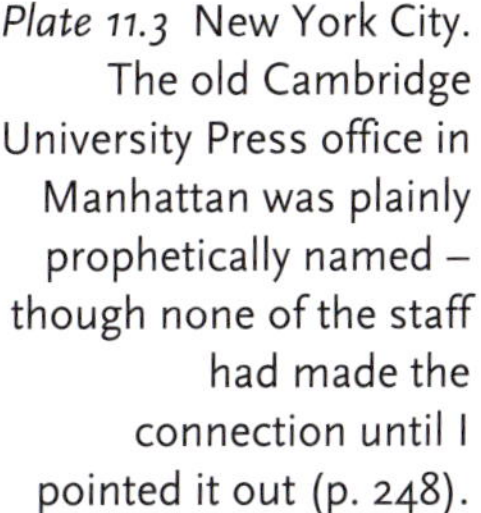

Plate 11.3 New York City. The old Cambridge University Press office in Manhattan was plainly prophetically named – though none of the staff had made the connection until I pointed it out (p. 248).

Plate 11.4 Melbourne. A CUP party for the launch of *CEEL* (p. 248) in 1997, with everyone in the organization wearing a *CEEL* T-shirt showing an extract from the book – the longest cliché in the world. While I was giving a talk to the company, the CEO Kim Harris (front right) took himself off to hospital with a suspected heart attack. I can't think what it was I'd said!

Dying languages

Plate 12.1 Meeting Ailton Krenak (p. 246), whose activism for his endangered Brazilian tribe was being followed by Czech film-maker Michael Havas (left). We shared the stage at the film festival in Uherské Hradiste in July 2007.

Plate 12.2 The cast of *Living On* (p. 246), during rehearsal for the performance at the School of Oriental and African Studies in April 2007, supporting a week devoted to endangered languages. Left to right: Joseph Marcell, me, Karl Kelly, Simon Manyonda, director Robert Wolstenholme, Ben Crystal, Emma Swinn. In front: (standing) Nick Oshikanlu, (crouching) Rhoda Ofori-Attah, Scott Ainslie.

Plate 12.3 Chairing the opening meeting of the scientific advisory committee for the House of Languages (p. 248) in Barcelona, July 2006. President Maragall is to my left; Juan Clos, Mayor of Barcelona at the time, is next to him, and Antoni Mir Fullana, director of the House of Languages, is on his left.

Plate 13.1 Making the documentary *The Way That We Say It* for BBC Wales in June 2005, as part of the BBC Voices project (p. 264). The location is the boardwalk by Cardiff Bay. Co-presenter Jane Harvey and I travelled around Wales in a Porsche collecting material on local accents and dialects. Life can be hard, sometimes.

Plate 13.2 A British Council lecturer stands in a doorway in Schreyvogelgasse, Vienna – the same doorway where, in *The Third Man* (p. 252), Harry Lime is first seen by Holly Martins. The British Council office in Vienna is just a few blocks away.

Plate 13.3 Revisiting the 1960s. Schloss Nymphenburg in Munich, the location for some of the most striking scenes in *Last Year at Marienbad* (p. 71). It was winter-time, so the statues are boarded up. But it was sunny, so all the shadows are real – unlike in the film.

Shakespeare days

Plate 14.1 Day 1 working on *Shakespeare's Words* (p. 268). Ben and I in the grounds of the Ettington Park Hotel, near Stratford-upon-Avon in July 1999. Just 21,262 entries to go!

Plate 14.2 A book in progress – sorting out the order of topics and pages for the *Shakespeare Miscellany*, with Sushi the cat doing his best to disrupt proceedings.

Plate 14.3 Jobs done. Signing copies of *Shakespeare's Words* and the *Shakespeare Miscellany* at the Hay Festival in 2005.

Shakespeare days (continued)

Plate 15.1 Never work with animals. . . An unknown dog arrives on stage during rehearsal for a midnight reading of Shakespeare's sonnets at the Uherské Hradiste film festival, July 2007.

Plate 15.2 Hilary and I visit Shakespeare's Globe in 1997, while investigating locations for the proposed World of Language (p. 247). The Globe was still under construction – hence the hard hats for everyone, no exceptions.

Plate 15.3 Rehearsing a production in original pronunciation (p. 267) at Shakespeare's Globe in August 2005. The play is *Troilus and Cressida*.

Business world

Plate 16.1 With Ian Saunders in the Holyhead office of Crystal Reference Systems, 2006. The picture is a poster for the later-to-be-assassinated *Find Out* website (p. 262).

Plate 16.2 Some of the Holyhead team in 2006 (p. 260). Left to right: accountant Rob Phillips, technical officer Tony McNicholl, taxonomist Jan Thomas, editor Ann Rowlands. The latest editions of the Penguin family of encyclopedias are on Ann's desk. The calendar on the wall was there to remind everyone about forthcoming major sporting events, whose results would need to be included in the database.

Plate 16.3 Keeping an ear on what the man on the telly is saying. The occasion was the launch of iSense (p. 261) by Ad Pepper at the Online Marketing show in Düsseldorf in 2008.

a character, identified a significant narrative moment, related to the author's life and times, and much more. On the other hand, while he could see purpose in the texts we were using, he couldn't always see the linguistic techniques the author had used to achieve it. Or, if he sensed what they were, he usually couldn't describe them in a precise way. A linguistic apparatus is an enormously valuable part of a literary critic's toolkit.

If there was anything which solidified the lang/lit friendships of those days it was unity in the face of adversity. For what did the poet say? 'He today who sheds his blood with me shall be my brother'? We shed, all right. Metaphorical blood, trying to persuade the local Council office to increase the inadequate (we argued) vs. generous (they argued) per diem allowance. Weight, when we stopped running, after the dawning realization that the log across the path, on which we had just stepped, had moved, and that we had unconsciously strayed into anaconda territory. More weight, after the predictable bouts of stomach trouble. And still more weight, after a weekend boat trip around Isla Bella, off the coast of São Paulo, where the encounter with the Atlantic swell made us so sea-sick that I ended up in hospital on a saline drip.

But this is to jump ahead. I actually earned my British Council spurs (if that is the right expression) in Wales, during the late 1960s, thanks to an Anglo-Soviet exchange initiative. The idea was that a group of British teachers of Russian would spend a month in the Soviet Union while a group of Soviet teachers of English would spend a similar period in the UK. It was a great idea, which in its small way will have helped to improve the atmosphere at the heart of the 'cold war'. Anyway, whoever thought the idea up decided that the best place for the Russian teachers to go to improve their command of the English language was – South Wales. The summer schools were held, first in Cardiff, then in Swansea, for several years, and I was a regular teacher on them. One of the first tasks, of course, was to eradicate the natural confusion of these poor teachers, thinking they were coming to England and then being told by some local people, in no uncertain tones (these were the early days of Welsh language activism), that English was the language of the devil.

They were a curious group, in many ways. They came from all over the Soviet Union, and taught at all educational levels. They were all very competent in English – the learning of English, surprisingly, managed to stay alive and strong in Russia throughout the communist era – all, that is, except one. Each year there was one person who stood out, rather, because of his poor command of English. This person we dubbed the commissar, and clearly he was there to keep an eye on the group as a whole, to make sure no one did anything out of line and to protect the members from bad influences. One evening, I recall, the group was sitting happily watching the television when something on it upset him. He stood up, made a comment in Russian, and went to his room. Within five minutes the room was empty. Another time, one of the more daring members, observing a cartoon character on screen, joked 'He looks like Mr Khrushchev.' The atmosphere froze. The commissar looked blackly at him. Next day the personality of the joker had noticeably altered: he hardly said another word that week.

There was a barely hidden agenda of confrontation between the British teachers and administrators on the summer school and the Soviet visitors. On the Swansea courses, the school was held in a hall of residence near the university, and in the foyer was a table-tennis table. This became a centre of cold-war conflict. It was constantly in use, and it was a matter of national pride to win. Fortunately, the academic director of the summer school was Ken Whibley, a lecturer in Russian from Bangor, and he wielded a mean bat. So did I: during the Liverpool years a schoolfriend, Simon Hayes, had owned a table-tennis table, and for a group of us it was a post-homework pastime for years. So at Swansea we usually won. And then, at the summer school party, we usually lost.

Each year, the group arrived armed with small gifts – this is the Russian way – and a huge supply of Russian food and vodka for the party, held towards the end of the course. I remember very little of those parties, but they always took the same form. There would be some kind of entertainment provided. The staff would perform a sketch. Some Russians might sing or play. And the vodka would flow. They would press glasses upon us. We, not wishing to be impolite, would accept them. And to begin with it was all very pleasant. They would teach us how to drink vodka the Russian way, knocking it back, glass after glass. Then it would begin to get less pleasant. The salty Russian fishy dishes would begin to chemically interact with the vodka. They probably enjoyed the sight of each of us going down like flies. No fibre, these capitalists. You would think we would learn not to get sucked into a downward spiral – but in fact it is extremely difficult not to be. I probably exaggerate in thinking of it as a communist plot to show our moral inferiority. Several of the visitors genuinely wanted to give us a good time, by way of a thankyou for our work with them. And either they could hold their vodka better than us, being more used to it, or they were not drinking it as much as us. I suspect the answer is a bit of both.

I remember the end to one such evening. I desperately needed some fresh air. I staggered outside. The fresh air hit me like a steamroller. I could no longer stand up. I thought I might be sick. I needed somewhere safe to lay my head. I saw a hedge. A lovely, welcoming hedge. I fell forward towards the hedge. My head hit the soft soil. I lay there, with my eyes closed, waiting for my dizziness to subside. I opened my eyes – and saw another pair of eyes staring bleakly into mine. They were the eyes of the British Council officer, who had arrived in the hedge just a few moments before.

Chapter 12
Meeting needs

With the new linguistics courses at Reading, the demand for introductory material was becoming increasingly urgent. All of us needed further reading to support our lectures, but there were few books that were both accessible and (even more important) enthusing. I wasn't going to fall into the trap of getting my new-to-the-subject students reading Ogden and Richards, *et al*. Why were there no motivating introductions to linguistics, to phonetics, to stylistics, to grammar, to semantics, to language acquisition – to *anything*? It wasn't good when students (or prospective students) came up and asked for something easy to read on my subject, and I couldn't help them. There were nice introductions to psychology, sociology, and other subjects around. Why not linguistics? We moaned for a year, then realized that the solution was literally on our doorstep.

In the mid-1960s, publishers had begun to realize that Something Was Up, as far as linguistics was concerned. All the leading houses had sensed the potential of the new subject, especially in ELT, and they wanted introductory material. With relatively few professional linguists about, and only a tiny number of them willing or able to write at this level, the news that there was a linguist who not only had a hobby-horse about the need for introductory texts but had actually written one (albeit in a somewhat marginal domain, religion) travelled around the publishing stands at the various conferences. It was not long before commissioning editors were prowling the Reading departmental corridors and knocking on doors.

An editor from the London firm of Edward Arnold was one of the first. I sounded off to her about the need, and evidently with conviction, for a few days later I got a phone call asking me to come up to town to discuss possibilities. It was my first experience of what is euphemistically called a publisher's 'lunch'. I arrived at their office in Maddox Street, and was ushered upstairs to meet the managing director, Anthony Hamilton. As a very young and inexperienced writer, I was highly impressed by the warmth of his reception, the table in his office laid ready for lunch, and most of all by the size of his wine cabinet, which he opened with a flourish that would have been the envy of any sommelier.

I made my way unsteadily towards Paddington in the late Friday afternoon, having apparently agreed to write an introductory book for schools. Then there was one of those moments. Trouble on the trains. A strike or go-slow, I forget which. I had several hours to wait before the next train to Reading. So I found myself a corner, got out a pad, and started to write. I must have been unconsciously waiting for this moment. It was like releasing water from a blocked drain. I'd finished a draft of the first chapter by the time the 9.05 train left. Then the project obsessed me, as so many later would do, and when that happens there is nothing you can do but finish it as quickly as possible so that you can get on with something else. The family looked on curiously. Steven, now aged three, decided he would write a book as well, and covered several sheets of drawing paper with hieroglyphs. I sent a draft of the book off to Arnold's on the Monday, along with a thankyou note for the wine. It became *What is Linguistics?*

I think it was that weekend which convinced me that my first love was writing. I was never happier than when sitting in front of a keyboard. A day passed without something written was a wasted day – whether it was a review, an article, a radio script, or a bit of a book. It still is. I was rarely proactive. My fault was that I couldn't say no – and there were so many ideas and opportunities around not to say no to. The publishing reps continued to visit, and there were more lunches. Lots of brilliant ideas came up. Only a tiny number came to fruition. The problem with a publisher's lunch is that it's easy to agree to anything. Then, in the cold sober light of the next day, you realize that the project is not for you. You start with the best of intentions, of course, but lack of time, knowledge, or interest overtakes you, and you give up. My files were soon full of abandoned opening chapters. But even these non-books were useful, for they were giving me a sense of the kinds of topic that publishers were interested in. And if I couldn't write them, then I knew a colleague who could. The idea grew. Might there be a publisher interested in a series of introductory books on linguistics?

It would mean changing roles, from author to editor. But that didn't seem such a bad thing. The projects with Whitney Bolton had taught me a bit about editing. And I had begun to do some editorial work for the new Linguistics Association periodical, *The Journal of Linguistics*. The founding editor had been John Lyons in 1965, and when he decided to give up the role, Frank Palmer took over, and Peter Matthews and I became his assistant editors. Although the changeover didn't actually take place until 1970, we found ourselves receiving papers for our first issue as early as 1968. Two years ahead? Nothing unusual in that. There's invariably quite a long time-lag between submitting an article to an academic journal and seeing it in print.

Why is it such a long process? Because there are so many steps involved. First you read the submission, and if it seems publishable you send it out for review to people who know the field. It's called a 'peer review', and it usually takes a while, because the chances are that your chosen reviewers are on a field-trip to Peru or Hong Kong. You then collate the comments that come back, transmit them to the author, and ask for a revision. That takes another while, because by this time the author is probably in Nigeria, and doesn't have a copy of the paper to hand. In due course a revised version comes through (assuming the author accepts the criticisms and wants to resubmit). You read it and decide whether to accept it. Any of these stages might become a mini-saga. Two reviewers might disagree violently about whether an article is publishable. The author might disagree even more violently with the judgement of the reviewers. It can take a year or more before everyone is satisfied. At the end of the day, the editor makes the final decision, and lives with the result. It is a hugely important, responsible, and demanding exercise. And yet journal editing is given hardly any credit when boards evaluate the quality of a university department. Scandalous.

After all that is over, the real editorial work begins. You become a copy-editor, looking out for ambiguity, inconsistency, unnecessary repetition, and all the other faults which interfere with clear writing. You have to knock the paper into stylistic shape, so that it follows the expository method normal in academic publishing – an abstract, introduction, method, results, discussion, conclusion, references. Hammer rather than knock, sometimes. I've edited three academic journals in my time – *The Journal of Child Language*, *Linguistics Abstracts*, and *Child Language Teaching and Therapy* – and I can count on the fingers of a couple of hands the papers that didn't display basic inconsistencies. 'See Smith (1932)' the author says on page 6, so you go to the list of references and find there is no 'Smith (1932)'. Or there is a 'Smith (1933)'. Is this the intended reference? You have to go back to the author and check. There can be dozens of points like this. It can take ages to sort out, especially if the author has gone on another field-trip somewhere along the Amazon.

Then you have to make the paper conform to the journal house style established by the publisher. In the case of the *Journal of Linguistics*, this was Cambridge University Press, and that meant assimilating the pre-publication style-sheets that would one day appear as the CUP editorial bible, Judith Butcher's *Copy-editing*. Now you enter a world of abbreviations, capitalization, hyphenation, italics, inverted commas, footnotes, formulae, tables, and a host of other presentational issues. Is it *judgement* or *judgment*? *Medieval* or *mediaeval*? *Analyze* or *analyse*? *Flower-pot*, *flowerpot*, or *flower pot*? With linguistics, extra tasks emerge. How are examples from languages to be laid out on the page? How are they to be transliterated, if they use a non-Roman alphabet? None of us were trained to do all this. We had to learn. Fortunately, the in-house editors and typesetters at Cambridge were patient and persevering, and we gradually assimilated their experience.

So that's that, then? The paper has been edited and copy-edited, and sent off to press. Job done? Ah no, there is the little matter of the proofs. These arrive a few weeks later. The editor gets a copy. So does the author. The publisher wants no changes at all, for each change costs. The editor also hopes there will be nothing to change, apart from the occasional typesetting error, for each change is time-consuming. The author, however, wants to change everything! Well, some do, at least. I remember one paper where the author's proof came back with dozens of changes on each page. The writer had changed his mind about all sorts of things. It would have been cheaper to typeset the paper all over again. He didn't get his way. All authors have to learn a basic truth: proofs aren't drafts.

Finally, after the first proofs go back, duly corrected, and the second proofs go back, checked again, the job is over. That's a satisfying moment. You are, for a few months, ahead of the game. You have read, in an unbelievably thorough way, the papers that are going to form the talking-points in your subject in the immediate future. And when the issue appears, you can take deserved pleasure from its crisp, elegant look – though always prepared for the application of Crystal's Law (something I formulated to myself very early on: when you randomly open a new book or journal, you will immediately see an uncorrected typo). It would be time to relax – if you had the time. But of course you haven't got time. The next issue of the journal is already on your mind. And the one after that. A journal typically appears several times a year. There are always piles of papers on an editor's desk-side table: newly submitted papers (this week's post) in one pile; papers sent out to reviewers in a second; the contents of the next issue in a third; the proofs of the current issue in a fourth; maybe even correspondence about the previous issue in a fifth. No wonder editors want to move on. I edited each of my journals for a dozen years or so, and that was too long – but it took me several years to find a replacement. I actually think it's bad for an editor to stay with a journal for more than a decade: journals need to be regularly refreshed from the top, if they are to avoid becoming too idiosyncratically focused. Apart from that, if you didn't take a break from journal editing, you would, I am convinced, go slowly crazy.

But all this was good basic training. And so, when a lady Penguin knocked on my door, in the middle of 1968, and suggested some editing, I wasn't phased by her proposal. Julia Vellacott it was, who told me that the people at Penguin had been pondering long and hard about the lack of introductory books in the linguistics field. The Pelican imprint, she thought, was the obvious home for them. I visited Harmondsworth and met Dieter Pevsner, in charge of the list at the time. Would I be willing to act as a general editor and put together a proposal for a series? It was like the answer to a prayer.

The proposal was the easy bit. After all, it meant no more than attaching book ideas to all the basic courses in linguistics that we were teaching at Reading – phonetics, grammar, and so on, plus a general introduction. The difficult bit was persuading colleagues to take time out from their busy course-planning and teaching schedules to write them (for new linguistics courses were proliferating in the late 1960s). I also realized that I could not act credibly as a series editor without taking on a writing role myself, and so here, as in several later series, I ended up with an authorial as well as an editorial involvement. But at least it meant, when I approached someone, that they could see I wasn't one of those editors who was intending to build a reputation out of someone else's labour.

It took a while, but eventually I found my writers, and the first two books duly came out in 1971 – my own *Linguistics* and Frank Palmer's *Grammar*. J. D. (Doc) O'Connor's *Phonetics* and George Turner's *Stylistics* followed in 1973; Geoffrey Leech's *Semantics* and Peter Trudgill's *Sociolinguistics* in 1974. It was my first experience of working with an in-house design team, and I was hugely impressed with their creativity. Penguin always had a fine reputation for cover design, and it was a delight to explore with them the possible ways of visualizing linguistic ideas. I told them how phonetics, grammar, and semantics were seen as 'levels' of language, all different and yet all simultaneously present in a single sentence and equally important. I explained how linguists tried to reflect the structure of language in their analyses. They came up with the idea of overlapping prisms (see plates 4.1–4.4). On the cover of *Linguistics* you see a sentence ('the linguist saw the pelican') analysed in three different ways – phonetically, grammatically, and semantically – but none is dominant. Then, on each of the specific books, you see the same sentence enlarged, but with an unclear reflection. (They had obviously noted my point that linguistic analyses are not always clear-cut!) The prisms, along with the same colour design, unified the books. It was satisfactory linguistics, and good marketing too. After all four books had appeared, I was told that many customers bought them together, thinking of them as a set.

Even more creative was another wing of the Penguin empire – Penguin Education. Martin Lightfoot, the managing director, wanted to build on the success he was having with his publishing programme in psychology, where the subject had been split up into several fields, each with its own academic editors, and everything under the general editorship of London University professor of psychology Brian Foss. Dozens of books were planned for that series, called the Penguin Science of Behaviour. With the Pelican series now moving ahead, I went over to Harmondsworth again, this time to meet Martin. As far as I can remember, the conversation went something like this:

> 'Could you do the same sort of thing with linguistics that we've done in psychology?'
>
> 'What do you mean, "the same sort of thing"?'
>
> 'A series of monographs, and a series of readings – anthologies of core texts.'
>
> 'How many?'
>
> 'Oh, no particular number . . . A hundred, maybe . . .?'

I gulped. Martin's list in psychology, sociology, and education had already passed that total. He was not joking.

I went home and got out a big sheet of paper. *Were* there a hundred topics in linguistics that could be treated in this way? I scoured my library for ideas and wrote everything down in a fit of personal brain-storming, then counted up. I had easily passed a hundred. But how to manage such a vast enterprise? This was too big for any one person to handle. The psychology series provided the answer: Brian Foss had brought together a team of a dozen psychologists to look after the various special areas of that subject. I would have to do the same. And not just people from the UK either.

Fortunately, I'd managed to meet many of the leading players in linguistics at the time, thanks to a ten-week visit to the USA. Bowling Green State University in Ohio had approached the Reading department early in

1968 asking if anyone would be interested in spending a quarter (that is, a term) in their English Department. Given the English connection, Frank asked me if I was interested. They were prepared to cover all costs for the lecturer and his family. We talked about it at home. The quarter ran from January to March 1969. Steven would be starting school later that year. If we were going to do any serious travelling, early 1969 would be a good time. And the salary BGSU was offering for a single quarter was almost as much as my entire year's salary in the UK. We thought it through. It was an offer I couldn't refuse. Yes, there was a baby due in May, but (s)he would be eight months old by the time we had to travel. Molly thought we would cope. I accepted.

Fast forward now to the visit. My BGSU teaching commitment turned out to be for only a couple of days each week. That meant I had the rest of the week to go travelling. Bowling Green is within easy reach of Ann Arbor, Chicago, Bloomington, Columbus, New York, Boston . . . all places where there were important linguistic centres and well-known linguists or phoneticians. Chomsky was King, and the talking-point everywhere. I fixed up a weekly visit, gave a few papers, and got well looked after. Another visit took me over to Fort Worth in Texas, where there was a group enthusiastically studying paralanguage, one of my first specialities. Another got me into Canada, to Toronto and Edmonton. As I flew home, I realized that I had met more famous linguists in a few weeks than most people would meet in a lifetime. Professionally, it was an invaluable secondment. And it gave me my contacts when I needed them. My Penguin Education advisory board ended up consisting of two Americans (Dwight Bolinger and Jim Sledd), a Canadian (Iain Stuart from Edmonton), and three Brits (Michael Halliday, John Lyons, and Frank Palmer). A powerful team, which gave me the confidence to start planning, knowing that they would not let any rubbish through.

LINGUIST AS TEASE

When the wind blows in the wrong direction, flights from Milan airport sometimes leave from Malpensa instead. The coach journey to Malpensa takes a couple of hours, and in 1972 I was on this bus, on my way home from the Bologna Linguistics Congress, sitting next to an American lady. It was early spring, but everything looked very wintry. On the way we passed a garden centre which had an English name: 'Green Ideas'. The collocation had a certain familiar ring to it. It was in the sentence – *the* sentence – which Chomsky had used in his first book, *Syntactic Structures*, to show how a sentence could be meaningless and yet grammatical: *Colorless green ideas sleep furiously*. Some linguists felt that it could be made meaningful, with a bit of ingenuity, so when my travelling companion commented upon it, I seized my chance. As far as I can recall, our conversation went something like this:

Lady: What a lovely name!
DC: Yes, but the ideas don't seem to be very green, at this time of year.
Lady: No. They'll come, though. It's such a lovely climate here.
DC: *(pushing his luck)* They're rather colourless green ideas, in fact.
Lady: *(laughing)* That's true.
DC: *(still pushing)* Everything's still sleeping, at this time of year.
Lady: It surely is.
DC: The colourless green ideas are sleeping, indeed.
Lady: Excuse me?
DC: I said the colourless green ideas are sleeping.
Lady: That's what I thought you said.
DC: *(going for broke)* Mind you, I expect there's a tremendous amount of activity taking place, just beneath the surface. The colourless green ideas are sleeping furiously, wouldn't you say?

There was no reply, but I got one of those 'What-are-you-some-kinda-nut-or-sumpin?' looks, and she didn't talk to me any more. That's what happens if you push a native speaker too far.

The series, accordingly, got off to a great start. We called it Penguin Modern Linguistics. Each book had the clever Penguin Education logo on the front: a junior penguin nestling alongside an adult parent. The anthologies came first – four out in 1972, and a couple more the following year (see plate 4.5). The first textbook to appear was in 1973 – Pit Corder's *Introducing Applied Linguistics*. And everything in the garden looked rosy. Then, disaster. What I didn't know was that in 1970, following the death of Penguin's founder, Allan Lane, Penguin had merged with Pearson Longman, in an operation technically called a reverse takeover. Soon after, Penguin became a subsidiary of Pearson, which is how things stand today. Things continued as before for a while, but the merger caused many internal problems, and a looming economic recession didn't help. Suddenly, in the middle of 1974, it was announced that Penguin Education was to close. And everything just stopped.

I couldn't believe it. I had a book of readings about to appear – Dennis Fry's *Acoustic Phonetics*, which had got to proof stage. And several other proposals were in the pipeline. But it was no use complaining. I had to cancel everything. Even the Pelican series shut down. I desperately tried to find alternative publishers for some of the books, but managed it only in a couple of cases. Fry's was eventually placed with Cambridge University Press.

There was a fine farewell party at the Young Vic in London. It was called 'The Last Great Penguin Education Party'. In a pastiche of James Joyce, the invitation was subtitled 'lots of fun at Pennyguins Wake'. The logo on the front showed the junior penguin lying dead on the ground alongside its parent, with a knife in its chest (see plate 4.6). 'How could Penguin kill off its own progeny?' was the underlying theme. Or, to put it in the Joycean terms of the party invitation: 'Twas its own murther dead it? Its one own lone procreator? Its penguinnish payrent? What a gnawful thing!', adding with dark suspicion, 'Nor was there no ahcomplease with this moider?' No accomplice? I don't recall seeing a Pearson Longman presence at the party.

You may have noticed, a few paragraphs ago, that I said 'I flew home'. The pronoun was singular. The family were not with me, despite all the hopeful planning. Indeed, there was a time when I nearly didn't go at all. Everything was to change in May 1968. On the 15th, to be precise. The baby arrived, as predicted. In the little maternity unit, near where we lived – you remember? The one whose matron lived next door? She let me in to see the birth. It wasn't a long process. Much shorter than Steven, who took all night. But when the baby appeared, the room went very quiet. You could see straight away. It was a boy. And he had a cleft lip. And there was something else. The silence was broken by Molly, the children's nurse, seeing what none of the rest of us saw. 'He's blue!'

He was indeed blue. Timmy had Fallot's tetralogy – a heart disorder, I learned a few days later, when the diagnosis was confirmed, named after a French physician. It involved four related anatomical abnormalities. One was a failure of the chambers of the heart to join properly. Another was a narrowing of one of the valves. That's why he was blue. There wasn't enough oxygen circulating around his body to give the skin its normal pinkness. Cyanosis, it was called. A 'blue baby' was the popular name.

The cleft lip – and palate too – was a parallel development. The tissues hadn't joined at the required stage in foetal development. Nobody could ever tell us why. When he cried, you could see a gaping hole in the roof of his mouth. Such children, Molly told me, were often informally described as having a 'muddle in the middle'. She had nursed several during her training in Liverpool. Now she would nurse one of her own.

She did it brilliantly. The first and most important task was to get some food down the little fellow. No breast vs. bottle issue here. Timmy could suck neither, with an upper lip splayed away to nothing. It had to be spoon, from the word go. But then, if you spoon in some milk, and you have a hole in the roof of your mouth, what are the chances of the milk going down your throat? At least 50–50 that it will go up into your nose and immediately out again. It can take ages to feed a cleft-palate infant. Add to this the fact that Timmy needed every lungful of oxygen he could get. When you eat, you don't breathe in – or if you do, food can go down into your lungs. For most of us, not breathing in is a temporary and usually unnoticed inconvenience. For a child like Timmy, it is an ever-present danger.

Molly became totally committed to keeping Timmy alive. It really was a daily task. One of those huge oxygen bottles was always by his bedside. You never knew when he was going to have – I soon learned the phrase – a cyanotic attack, when his oxygen levels would fall dangerously. Infections were common, and each one was a nightmare. Croup was the worst, because the inflammation narrowed his larynx and made breathing difficult. When things looked really serious, he would be whisked into the Royal Berkshire Hospital for special care. Steven and Susie saw little of Molly, during those days. If you're spending most of your days and nights keeping one child alive, there isn't much time left for the others.

It was obvious that the America trip was off for the whole family. But should I go alone? Molly had been doing some part-time children's nursing at local hospitals. That would have to stop. We could really do with the extra money that the BGSU appointment offered. I ought to go, we agreed. But what if . . .? And what if . . .? We had to make a final decision by the autumn. We would wait and see how Timmy was progressing.

As it turned out, he did very well. It was standard surgical practice in those days – as it still is – to close the lip and palate as early as possible, in a two-stage operation. A tricky decision, always, and an intricate surgical procedure – made even trickier, of course, if your patient has a heart condition. Operate early, and the surgeon has the difficult job of anticipating subsequent growth of the lip and palate. Both have to function well, and the lip especially has to look right. Operate late, and you reduce the chances of normal speech and hearing development. From a parental point of view, of course, the sooner it can be done, the better. Your baby begins to look like other babies. Feeding improves. Infections reduce. Breathing is easier. And along with better breathing comes better vocalization. It's difficult to coo and babble if you have a hole in the very articulatory organs you need to make those sounds. I knew the way vocalization developed in the first year. I'd spent ages recording Steven's and Susie's early sounds, and I'd made infant speech a focus of my ongoing work on intonation. Before Timmy's operation, the noises that came out of his mouth were like nothing I'd ever heard before. And even after the op, it was a long time before he was able to move his palate enough to make the sounds resemble normal speech.

The lip operation took place at Oxford, when he was just three months old – a bit later than we'd hoped, but we had to choose our moment, in between infections. The op was postponed more than once because he just wasn't well enough. But finally the surgeons performed one of their usual miracles. Timmy looked fantastic after his lip was closed (see plates 6.2–6.3). A year later, you'd hardly have known. Just the thinnest of scars. A magnificent job. We met the cleft palate team to discuss the future. I recognized the speech therapist straight away: it was Catherine Renfrew. She would work with him, and us, for the next three years. Under her guidance, I read everything I could about cleft palate and its management.

We were told that it wouldn't be advisable to do the second stage of the operation – the closure of the palate – until Timmy was around a year old. Although some children were being operated on earlier, the extra time would give him a chance to gain strength. The palate op was more complicated, and everyone was concerned about the heart condition. There was no chance of a heart operation for a long time, said the paediatrician. That wouldn't take place until he was three or so. So it did seem, after all, that there would be a lull, after the panic of the first few months had subsided. We decided I would go to the States as planned. Our mothers would come down and help out. The matron next door would be available. It would be OK.

So I went. And it was. But it wasn't fun. I was terribly homesick. No easy communication then – transatlantic phone calls were complicated matters and letters were pointless (for what was the use of reporting how Timmy was on the 10th, when everything might have changed by the time the letter arrived, a week later?). So I was really glad to get home. I bought genuine Texas cowboy and cowgirl outfits for Steven and Susie, and had two sets of toy revolvers in my luggage. Nobody at the airport batted an eyelid. Those were the days. Carrying a toy gun today would be risking a death sentence. When I went through New York in 2006 they even thought my beard looked suspicious.

The palate operation came and went, without incident. Timmy's speech began to improve. But the heart condition kept us busy. As he moved from being an infant to being a little boy, increased mobility brought increased breathlessness. Increased outside world brought increased infections. We still made regular use of the bedside oxygen. Speech therapy appointments meant routine hospital visits. Still, we developed as much of a normal life as we could. We went on holiday up to Holyhead. Timmy copied almost everything Steven and Susie did. No swimming for him, but plenty of slides and sandcastles. The two older children were brilliant with him. Frequent visits to parks and fairgrounds. Lots of television. Even today I could quote you long chunks of dialogue from *Trumpton* and *Camberwick Green*. I developed quite an affection for the firemen Pugh, Pugh, Barney McGrew, Cuthbert, Dibble, and Grub – as, indeed, did the British fire service, which for a while was nicknamed 'Trumpton'.

Timmy was scheduled to have his heart operation when he was three. But in May 1971 he wasn't well enough and it had to be postponed. There were further postponements. Eventually, in October, on the 21st to be precise, he had the long-awaited op. And it was a failure. He died early the next day. Even now, nearly forty years on, I can hardly bring myself to write about it. In fact I've only ever managed to talk about the events of that night once, and that was by distancing myself, turning them into fiction. In my play about dying languages, *Living On*, one of the characters describes the way her little girl died. That is how it was with Timmy too.

The next few months are a bit of a blur. I suppose it's a way of coping. I can't remember anything about the appearance of the various Penguin books. I imagine there was a launch event. It's gone from my memory. We had moved house, up to Tilehurst in Reading, some time before, and were in the middle of building an extension when all this happened – ironically, we needed the space for an extra bedroom. I can't remember anything about how it was finished. We went back to work as soon as we could – Molly took up part-time nursing again. I carried on with my teaching. But I found I was unable to write anything which required continuous time and concentration. I managed the occasional short article or review, and kept up with my editing, but that was it. People who have looked carefully at my writing career sometimes ask me why no new books by me appeared between 1971 and 1974. That is why.

Chapter 13

Choices and consequences

One of the choices facing linguists, at some point in their career, is whether to take a 'pure' or an 'applied' direction, or somehow to strike a balance between the two. The terms are more appropriate to such subjects as mathematics and chemistry, but they do indicate two very different reasons for studying language. The 'pure' reason is what brought me, and I imagine most linguists, into the subject: the intrinsic fascination of language. I want to find out how language works, how it evolved and diversified, how it varies within society, how the brain represents it, how children learn it (or fail to), how languages differ, how we speak, and write, and sign . . . There are a thousand such questions awaiting exploration, and several thousand windows of exploration provided by the languages of the world, each with a unique structure and history, and expressing a unique vision of what it means to be human. Even the smallest features of pronunciation, grammar, and vocabulary contain intricacies which can easily occupy an intellectual lifetime. All this is the study of language as an end in itself. And that is what linguists usually mean by 'linguistics'. They don't use the adjective 'pure', unless they have a contrast with 'applied' at the back of their minds.

That contrast brings up the second reason for studying language: as a means to an end. The term 'applied' has many interpretations, in this connection, but for me it is the way the theories, methods, and findings of linguistics can be used to help solve problems in some other walk of life where language is a priority. And where *isn't* language a priority? I never cease to be amazed at the domains where a linguistic insight or two turns out to be helpful. In the first half of the twentieth century, it was just foreign language teaching and learning (and ELT in particular) which attracted the interest of those wanting to apply their linguistics. I've already told that story, or at least, my encounter with it. In the second half of the century, many other areas of application emerged, and yet more continue to emerge in the new millennium. I'll tell their story shortly.

Linguistics or applied linguistics? I was already feeling torn, as the 1970s arrived, especially as these two directions had become more distinct in the previous decade. They were now institutionalized: the former through the Linguistics Association of Great Britain (LAGB), which had been meeting since 1959; the latter through the British Association of Applied Linguistics (BAAL), launched at a meeting in Reading in 1967. I very much identified with linguistics. As you know from earlier chapters, I had become secretary of the LAGB and assistant editor of its Journal. And the way my writing had gone in the 1960s was clearly in the direction of mainstream linguistics. My PhD thesis on intonation, seriously revised and adapted, had been accepted as the opening volume in a new series, the 'blue-backed' Cambridge Studies in Linguistics. A two-year investigation of language varieties with Derek Davy, the assistant director of the Quirk Survey, had come to the boil in *Investigating English Style*. The collaboration with Whitney Bolton had been a straightforward exercise in the history of linguistic ideas. Through an unplanned coincidence of publishing schedules, these three books all appeared in the same year, 1969. If there was ever a statement that I was going to be a linguist (as opposed to an applied linguist), that was it.

The point was picked up by the university. Frank Palmer put me forward for a readership – a serious step up in the academic hierarchy. I'd evidently written enough to warrant consideration. Indeed, I'd evidently written too much! At the readership panel, I was told quite firmly that my future academic career would be jeopardized if I continued to publish so much. No one was attacking the quality of the work. It was evidently my penchant for popularization (such as *What is Linguistics?*) which the panel found disturbing. But times change. And at a later promotions panel, in an increasingly cash-strapped and public-conscious academic world, it was precisely the books that had achieved the highest public profile for which I was especially commended. I got the readership, anyway, and kept my promise not to write any more popularizations for, ooh, a whole year. I signed the contract for my Penguin *Linguistics* in May 1970.

But while all this was happening, I was becoming an applied linguist without realizing it. When I look back now at the articles I wrote in the first decade of my academic career, I see that half of them were on applied topics or written for applied journals. Most of them related to just two themes: religious language and ELT. The first of these was really a continuation of the topics that had come up in Bangor. I carried on exploring these in Reading, finding others there who were interested in exploring the nature of 'God-talk' – theolinguistics. There weren't many within the formal university setting, I have to say – things would improve a bit when Antony Flew became professor of philosophy in 1973 – but outside there was plenty of interest from those involved in the university chaplaincies and in ecumenical groups around the town. At least, there was after things got going.

There was no Catholic chaplaincy at Reading when I arrived. Father Gregory, a monk from Douai Abbey, a few miles away along the Thames Valley, came over to say Sunday Mass at St Joseph's Church in Upper Redlands Road. Staff and students could meet in the church hall afterwards for a while, but apart from that there was nothing. It was a far cry from the intellectually inspiring and socially intimate atmosphere of the chaplaincy in Bangor, and I found myself missing that greatly. I tried to replicate the kinds of events that I had found so rewarding in Bangor, inviting small groups of students around to my house to discuss this and that, but it was awkward for everyone. There was only one solution: we had to get a proper chaplaincy off the ground. So a group of us, both town and gown, got together, set up a committee, and planned a campaign. An end-of-terrace house next to the church became available, and in 1967 a gift of £6,000 from a local philanthropist allowed us to purchase and refurbish it. Good news: the Abbot of Douai was prepared to let us have one of his monks as a chaplain. An ideal choice in many ways, for the man's youth, enthusiasm, and intelligent approach to chaplaincy work endeared him to staff and students alike. Bad news: not only was he very young, he was also very handsome. He married a postgraduate from the French Department a couple of years later.

By that time, though, we had made great progress. I visited the Bishop of Portsmouth, Derek Worlock, and made the case for diocesan support for running costs. He was sympathetic, helped with the funding, and (following the loss of our first chaplain) found us another who was not quite so young or handsome but hugely experienced and charismatic – John Maguire, a Salesian, who had been chaplain to the University of East Africa in Uganda. The chaplaincy quickly became a reality, vibrant and popular. We established a programme of visiting lectures – people like literary critic Terry Eagleton and psychiatrist Jack Dominion were doing the rounds at the time. I went to as many of these talks as I could, and found (as in Bangor) that my linguistic background attracted disproportionate attention. Everyone was interested in language, and curious about what this new thing called linguistics might be. And it was that which kept my interest in religious language alive.

On the ELT side, curiosity had turned into curriculum. The postgraduate courses in Reading, and the summer schools both in the UK and abroad, had motivated a regular focusing on the problems encountered by foreign learners of English. I gave a lecture course each year on the structure of English grammar, and with many ELT professionals in the audience the associated question time always brought up teacher-related issues. I also had a monthly assignment to respond to English language reader queries for a German teacher magazine, *Praxis*, and that brought up similar questions to do with vocabulary and idiom. 'Would you have marked it wrong?', the column was called. Here's an example.

> The candidate wrote, 'The hotel was fully unknown to me'; the examiner corrected 'fully' to 'entirely'.

Would I have marked it wrong? Well . . . would you?

A gut reaction isn't enough. You have to be able to say why. *Fully* does sound odd, in this context – but why? You begin by exploring the meaning of the word: it means 'to the full, completely' – that is, without deficiency. So it tends to be used with words expressing something positive. We say things like *I was fully aware* . . ., *I fully recognized* . . ., and *It's fully grown*. It's not likely to be used with negative words. Compare *I was fully dressed by three o'clock*, which is totally acceptable, and *I was fully undressed by three o'clock*, which sounds odd. *Entirely* and *completely* are examples of more general words which don't have this restriction. So is *totally*, which I just used myself a sentence ago. The examiner was right.

If you're going to be a linguist, you have to be prepared to spend all day, if necessary, exploring a single issue of this kind, to work out why usage goes one way and not another. No, 'be prepared' is wrong. If you're a linguist, you have no choice in the matter. You won't be able to sleep until you've found the answer – or realized that there is no answer to be found (without engaging in a major piece of research). For sometimes, an apparently simple question turns out to hide unforeseen complications. It only takes someone to say, 'Actually I don't find *I was fully undressed by three o'clock* odd at all,' and you realize you're entering another dimension, a sociolinguistic one now. Why does that person accept it when I don't? Is it because we're different ages, different genders, belong to different social groups, come from different parts of the country, or from different countries . . . ?

This example illustrates the way linguistics and applied linguistics come together. You start with a problem – in this case, someone wanting to learn English well – and the solution involves a piece of linguistic analysis. You then feed this back to the enquirer, either directly (as in my *Praxis* column) or through an intermediary, such as a language teacher. The learner then makes progress. It was the same in the speech therapy clinic. There the problem was Gillie, also trying to learn English. The analysis that time derived from the linguistic study of child language. And the results were fed back to Gillie via her speech therapist. The professional terminology varies a bit: in the ELT case we talk about errors and evaluation and teaching; in the speech therapy case we talk about symptoms and diagnosis and treatment. But the three-part investigation is fundamentally the same. And it always starts with the identification of a problem.

In the second half of the 1960s, the problems asking for solutions were accumulating. Word-of-mouth is a terrible thing. Not only did the Audiology Unit visits bring invitations to talk to groups of speech therapists, the visits to the Reading (the subject, not the town) Centre brought invitations to talk to teacher groups involved in literacy. And not just teachers. The world of education has many other strands – teacher-trainers, local authority advisers, consultants, inspectors . . . – who mix and match in bewildering ways. One invitation leads to another – which is how I soon found myself at a weekend conference at the Abbey Hotel in Malvern talking to a group of Her Majesty's Inspectors of English. HMIs. All my stereotypes of school inspectors went out of the window during that weekend. I had never encountered such an amazing audience before: dedicated, enthusiastic, acutely intelligent, humorous . . . Roget hasn't enough adjectives. It was the first of many such conferences, and the making of many friendships. It brought me into contact with a world I had forgotten: the teaching of English as a mother tongue in schools.

It was a highly controversial time. The formal teaching of grammar, which I had found so boring in my own schooldays, had disappeared from the school curriculum in the mid-1960s. What was to be put in its place? Some linguists, under the leadership of Michael Halliday, were already supervising projects aiming to provide an alternative. One of the most influential projects would appear in 1971, called *Language in Use*. Educationists such as James Britton, Douglas Barnes, and Harold Rosen were exploring other approaches. The controversy focused on whether linguistics, or a linguistically inspired approach to English, was of any use in schools? Some thought yes; some no. A lot of the controversy was due to people having different ideas about what linguistics was. Some thought linguists were simply trying to get old-style grammar back into the classroom. Some thought it was an attempt to get Chomsky into the classroom. Some, having identified linguists with Henry Higgins, thought it was all to do with elocution and talking posh.

I was absolutely convinced that linguistics had a great deal to offer mother-tongue English-language teaching, but in the 1960s the arguments were all theoretical. I could affirm till the cows came home that the subject was relevant, that pupils would enjoy it, that it would actually improve their abilities in listening or speaking or reading or writing, but faced with the simple riposte 'Prove it', I was at a loss. To prove it you had to get into the classroom, work with teachers, devise materials together, and put the principles into practice. The Halliday group were beginning to do that, but hadn't yet published anything. And I'd hardly been into classrooms at all.

It was clear what had to be done. The ELT world had shown the way. Publish materials – textbooks, worksheets, tapes, anything which would help a teacher actually teach a class about helpful aspects of language on Monday morning at ten o'clock. I had to get in to schools and talk to teachers and find out about curricula, and lesson plans, and all the other practicalities which are part of everyday pedagogical life. But in the late 1960s and early 1970s nobody wanted to know. It was difficult to get into schools. The climate was wrong. Having got rid of old-style prescriptive grammar (for all the right reasons), people were scared of introducing anything which might reintroduce the artificiality and boredom which had accompanied it. In 1975 the government published a report on English teaching in schools (the Bullock Report). It didn't beat about the bush. 'Is there anyone here', it asked, 'who truly believes that it matters to anyone but a grammarian how you define a noun, or what the transformational rules are for forming the passive voice?' Me, me, me, I howled – but unheard, for I had no reputation in the educational world in those days, and was not called to give evidence. Anyway, even if I had been, it wouldn't have had much effect. Other linguists, such as John Sinclair, did submit written evidence, but you wouldn't have known from the final report.

However, even as Bullock was being published, the climate had begun to change. Work in child language acquisition had accumulated. So had psycholinguistic research into reading and writing. It was now possible to show that some grammatical constructions were easier to listen to, speak, read, or write compared with others. Try these, for instance. Which one is easier?

That the army should reach the coast by nightfall was essential.

It was essential that the army should reach the coast by nightfall.

Why is the second one so much easier? It's chiefly because, in the first example, the subject of the sentence is long and complex. English is a language which likes to have the 'weight' of a sentence after the verb. Three-quarters of the subjects of a sentence in speech are just one word. *I took the train. We saw the car. Everyone liked the concert.* Or two words. *The audience was delighted by the performance.* The longer the subject gets, the more difficult it is for our brain to process the clause. And if the subject goes on for too long, we can throw up our hands in disgust:

> The army, which had been travelling by night to avoid being detected by the enemy, and which, although well supplied with ammunition, had a serious shortage of weapons, apart from a few old-fashioned rifles . . .

Get on with it! What's going to happen to them? Give us the verb!

Beginners at reading of course don't encounter such monsters. But it is surprising how often traditional readers make the task of reading more difficult than it needs to be by using long subjects. Do you ever remember trying to read (or having your young children read) such an unbalanced sentence as this?

Daddy, Mummy, Jane, Peter and Pat are all here.

It's taken from Book 4 of one reading scheme – very early on. Beginner readers might be able to read it in a stilted, word-by-word way – but read it for meaning, with a nice rhythm? Hardly. Yet, with a bit of rewriting, it can be made much easier:

Here are Daddy, Mummy, Jane, Peter and Pat.

The proof of the pudding, of course, is in the reading. When teachers try out the alternatives, they are impressed to find that, indeed, children read the second sentence more fluently than the first, and remember its content more easily.

Slowly, examples like these were persuading people that an approach informed by linguistic thinking could be useful. At the same time, the Halliday project had shown how a notion of 'language in use' could be informative and enthusing in the classroom. I remember going to see a secondary school class studying the language of advertising, and they were all enjoying it, discussing such questions as: 'What were advertisers trying to do? How were they doing it? What words were they using? Should we be on our guard?' With newspapers and television commercials to draw upon, it was a lively and relevant session. It was developing the pupils' 'language awareness' – a term which was picked up post-Bullock and which became a watchword of the next decade. But there was something missing. As soon as everyone started to talk about advertising language, the lack of any precise terminology made the task difficult. Without a knowledge of even such basic terms as *noun* and *word order*, everyone started to waffle, talking about 'vivid' or 'effective' language. But what was it exactly that was making the language vivid or effective? Nobody could say. Gradually, the weaknesses in a grammarless world became apparent.

LINGUIST AS GRAMMARIAN

The terminology of grammar really had disappeared. Totally. I remember teaching a first-year group at Reading University a few years after formal grammar went out of schools. I always took as one of my examples the pseudo-rule that 'one should never end a sentence with a preposition'. I used it because I could guarantee that all the students would have been taught it. But one year, somewhere in the mid-1970s, I remember the students looking at each other in puzzlement when I brought it in.

I paused. 'What's the problem?' I asked. One student shyly put up her hand: 'Please,' she said, 'what's a preposition?' I must say it took me aback. I had thought that at least the basic terms would have somehow got into pupils' consciousness. I asked the class: 'How many of you don't know what a preposition is?' About three-quarters of the class put up their hands.

One student raised her hand, a mite tentatively: 'I think I know,' she said. 'Go on,' I prompted. And then I got the answer which will stay with me to the end of my days. 'Is it something to do with getting on a horse?' I could hardly speak. Eventually, I spluttered, 'What do you mean?' 'Well,' said the young lady, with perfect aplomb, 'I was always taught that there was a pre-position one should adopt before mounting.'

As a result, I found myself being invited more and more, during the early 1970s, to talk to teacher groups, to visit classrooms, and – eventually – to collaborate in publishing projects. The first was *Skylarks*, a language development programme for six- to nine-year-olds, written in association with primary headteacher Jeff Bevington. That came out in 1975. A few years later there was the *Databank* series, written in association with John Foster – more than thirty information books aimed at late juniors or a little above, on such topics as *Light, Dinosaurs, Castles*, and *Volcanoes*. These were really interesting to work on. John would provide the content of each book, with an initial text draft, and I would structure the language so that it conformed to good principles of acquisition – avoiding awkward subjects, for example. I also wanted sensible line-breaks. I didn't want hyphens at the end of a line breaking up words in a difficult way. And I wanted to ensure that the end of a line coincided with a break in the meaning. Compare these three versions, and you'll see what I mean. Which one is the easiest to read?

> It only takes about seven
> hours for a ship to go through the Canal.
>
> It only takes about seven hours for
> a ship to go through the Canal.
>
> It only takes about seven hours
> for a ship to go through the Canal.

People find the third one easiest, because there is a natural break between *hours* and *for*. So I insisted that our texts were not made all straight and even at the right-hand margin (printers call it 'justified' setting – as in the present book), but followed the ins and outs of the grammar ('ragged edge', or 'unjustified' setting). This wasn't something the typesetters were used to, of course, and it took ages to get the setting right. Indeed, the whole *Databank* exercise was time-consuming. People sometimes think that you can polish off a children's book in a week or two. Not so. Each book took us three months or more before we were both happy with it. Part of the trouble, in all collaborative exercises, is to find a time when the team can meet. School and university timetables rarely coincide. It would be easier these days. There was no email then.

All this was applied linguistics with a vengeance. And here, as always, the linguistics is never far away. As the *Databank* series began publishing, I realized that I needed more support for line-break decisions than my own intuition. It was important to prove that children find one type of line-break easier than another. The answer was provided by a year-long Social Science Research Council project, led by Bridie Raban from the School of Education at Reading. She and Adrienne Jack wrote a children's story specially for the project, 'Mr West and his monkey', and had it printed in the university's Typography Department with different line-breaks, as in this example:

Mr West lived in a house with a monkey.
One day, the monkey got up first.
He got up first before Mr West and
before the sun.

Mr West lived in a house with a monkey.
One day, the monkey got up first.
He got up first before Mr West
and before the sun.

Which one would children find easier to read? Bridie tape-recorded a contingent of 137 young primary schoolers reading the different versions, and logged the mistakes they made. Did they pause in the wrong place? Or leave out a word? Or repeat a word? Or go wrong in some other way? And did one version help them to read faster than the others, or with a better rhythm? It turned out that leaving the *and* on the first line was a real help: it gave a clue to the children that more of the sentence was to come, and 'carried them forward', as it were, into the next line. And we were able to draw similar conclusions about the other kinds of line-break in the story.

Fascinating stuff. And an excellent example of a research collaboration between linguistics and other subjects (education and typography, in this instance) with a clear application. That was how the 1970s went, for me. I started the decade off as a linguist, but ended it very firmly as an applied linguist. However, it wasn't just the educational applications that accounted for this. The speech therapy world had already sucked me in, first as an academic and then as a parent. After Timmy, I was emotionally totally committed to doing whatever I could to promote the growth of speech therapy as a profession. And not just speech therapy. Other professions were also involved in fostering good language development in children with special needs – teachers, educational psychologists, clinical psychologists, paediatricians, neurologists, nurses . . . A systematic awareness of language in general, and of child language in particular, seemed to be absent from the training of everyone.

Special needs . . . handicaps . . . disabilities. The terminology is dry and distant, and fails to convey the confusion, frustration, and anxiety, affecting both sufferers and their carers, that stem from an inability to communicate. Nor does it capture the pivotal role of language in becoming fully human. Whether it is a child who has problems in learning to understand, speak, read, or write, or an adult who has lost one or more of these skills, there is something fundamental about having no language. For linguists, it is the bottom line. All other language-based activities they investigate – learning a foreign language, translating, dictionary compiling, analysing literature, and so on – presuppose an intact biological linguistic ability. Having an efficient first language is the foundation on which everything else depends. If children lack this ability, a world of confusion and solitude awaits them. If adults lose this ability, they find themselves in an alien environment where everyday norms of personal expression and social interaction are disrupted. Speech therapists are lights in the linguistic darkness, introducing order and relief into these devastated worlds. The name varies – they are also called speech and language therapists or speech pathologists – but the expertise does not. Speech therapists hold the keys to the language gateway. But they have to be the right keys, if they are to open the gate.

The timing was perfect. The point about lack of training had already been noticed by a government committee established to enquire into the state of speech therapy in the UK. It was called *Speech Therapy Services*, and because it was chaired by Randolph Quirk (yes, the same), it came to be known as the 'Quirk Report'. One of its main recommendations was critical, from my point of view:

> the would-be practitioner of therapy, whether of speech or hearing, of reading or of writing must in future regard *language* as the central core of his basic discipline.

And what was the science of language called? Linguistics. I interpreted this to mean that the government would look favourably on speech therapy courses which were solidly based in that subject. And where better to launch such a course than in Reading?

In 1972 I wrote a paper for the *British Journal of Disorders of Communication*, the UK speech therapists' journal, called 'The case of linguistics: a prognosis', in which I outlined the way the two professions could come together. It proved influential. I was invited to join the Academic Board of the College of Speech Therapists to represent the subject. The chair was Jean Cooper, the director of one of the London speech therapy training schools, and it was she who gave me the tuition I needed about exactly what was involved in setting up a course. All sorts of people had to be persuaded that a linguistics-based degree was a good thing. The college's support was central, as its role was to monitor the professional side of all speech therapy courses. If it didn't think the course was viable, then there was nothing more to be said. And viability meant having sufficient clinical placements in the region to provide the students with their clinical training. It also meant having speech therapists on the university staff, which was an expensive matter for the university to decide. It meant establishing that the other contributing disciplines to a speech therapist's training were available – education, psychology, and medicine. Were the Education and Psychology Departments willing to collaborate in the new degree? And what was to be done about medicine? There was no medical school at Reading. We would have to persuade individual medics to teach on the course. Would they? *Could* they? And what about the basic anatomy, physiology, and neurology? Where would all that come from?

Nor could the Linguistics Department be taken for granted. Just because I was keen didn't mean everyone else would be. By the mid-1970s there were certainly some in the department who shared my enthusiasms and who were beginning to collaborate in research into language disorders – Paul Fletcher and Michael Garman in particular. The ELT side of the department had grown apace, so there would be a natural sympathy there for an analogous development – there are parallels between teaching and therapy which go beyond the fact that they both begin with the same letter. But not everyone in that department was an applied enthusiast. Frank Palmer and Peter Matthews, in particular, did not want to see too radical a shifting of emphasis within the department. And it would be radical. There would have to be a clinic within the department. A waiting area for patients. Apart from anything else, was there room? None of this had been anticipated when the department's location had been established in 1965.

I'm not quite sure now, looking back, how all the problems were solved, but they were. A letter to the Minister of State, Sir Keith Joseph, brought a strong message of support which helped persuade the university that speech therapy was an excellent opportunity for expansion (at a time when the spectres of cutbacks and economic recession were looming). Several consultants in the Royal Berkshire Hospital turned out to be strongly in favour of the idea. Local senior speech therapists in Berkshire and around were strongly supportive, and that helped assuage the college's worries about clinical placements. And the academic consciences were soothed by the way the research side of the work was progressing. The first linguistically based assessment procedure, known as LARSP (short for Language Assessment, Remediation, and Screening Procedure), was being trialled during 1974 and 1975. It focused only on grammar, and we had wanted to call it GRARSP, until we realized that people would start saying their patients had been 'grarsped', which was not perhaps the most elegant of professional acronyms. Having them 'larsped' was bad enough. Still, the book explaining the profiling procedure, *The Grammatical Analysis of Language Disability*, by myself, Fletcher, and Garman, came out in 1976. And that was the year we started the first degree course in linguistics and language pathology, with a speech therapist, Renata Whurr, appointed to look after the professional training.

I have much to thank Timmy for, during those years. Without a doubt he gave me a lot of the motivation and energy I needed to keep my act together. It wasn't all plain sailing, by any means. Some of the older speech therapists felt threatened by this new upstart linguistics, and were disinclined to support a subject which they felt would make them out-of-date. It took a great deal of patient argument to reduce that resistance. There were huge rows within the Linguistics Department. And have you ever tried telling an ENT surgeon what to do? Don't. There were three of them at the Royal Berks, and I needed them all to teach about ears, noses, and throats respectively, at the right level, at the right time, in the right place . . . It was like trying to rein in three unruly stallions.

Why the departmental rows? You have to appreciate that there is a conflict of interest between linguists and applied linguists sometimes. When you're putting linguistics across to a group of people who are new to the subject, the one thing you've got to do is simplify. But simplification goes against the grain of linguists who have spent their lives working with the minutiae of complexity. I also had to take a view about which theoretical approach to use to underpin a technique of grammatical analysis. The Chomskyan approach seemed unworkable, at this level. I had always felt most comfortable with a descriptive framework based on the sort of grammar I knew well from the Survey of English days – a grammar which Randolph Quirk and his associates had recently published. So the stage was set for some furious arguments about the relative merits of these approaches. There were staff seminars with tempers which would have put John McEnroe to shame. But one thing I knew. Any approach that could survive a Reading interrogation would stand up to anything later critics would throw at it.

Paul and Mike allowed me to dedicate the LARSP book to the memory of Timmy. It seemed right, even though dedications didn't seem to be very fashionable in the clinical linguistic world. And I had another thing to thank Timmy for too. A renewal of contact with a world of khaki, torn photographs, and childhood imaginings.

Chapter 14

Meetings and meetings

It was in the mid-1960s – I cannot discover the exact date – when I had my first near-meeting with my father. I suppose you could call it a close encounter of the first kind – adapting J. Allen Hyneck's classification of UFOs – a visual sighting within about five hundred feet or less. And it was linguistics which made it happen.

I was in Leeds, giving a visiting lecture to the Linguistics Department at the university. After the lecture, the professor, Terry Mitchell, drove me back to my hotel. As we turned into Clarendon Road, near the university, he commented, 'Funny name, yours. I have a doctor called Crystal.'

'Oh yes?' I said.

'Actually there are two of them – brothers . . . I wonder if you're related?' And then he slowed the car down. 'In fact we're passing their surgery now – over there. You can see their names on the brass plate.'

I looked. One was Dr B. L. Crystal, the other Dr S. C. Crystal. Number 25.

S. C. Crystal.

Samuel Cyril Crystal.

I was nine years old again.

'Is one of them called "Samuel Cyril"?' I asked.

'Well, I don't know about the Samuel, but certainly he's a Cyril,' replied Terry. 'And Boris the other, I think.'

There was a pause, then: 'How do you know that?'

I didn't know what to reply. I muttered something about having heard of a distant relative with that name, and he let the matter drop.

My hotel wasn't far away. Later that evening I walked back to Clarendon

Road and stood in front of the house. I walked up to the door. Did I dare to knock? What would I say? I rehearsed several conversation openings. 'Hello, I'm David.' No, it would need an element of explanation. 'Hello, sorry to trouble you, but I'm your son.' Hardly. 'Hello, you don't know me, but . . .' Nothing seemed right. Then, I reflected, it was a bit much to turn up unannounced. Bit of a cheek, really, I rationalized. And what if it was just a coincidence, and it wasn't him? I realized I was scared stiff. I completed the process of self-dissuasion in ten seconds flat, and scuttled back to my hotel, the door to number 25 left unknocked. (I later learned that nothing would have happened, if I had gone ahead. Number 25 was just the surgery. The family lived somewhere else.)

I learned years later that I was not the only one to have chickened out of a meeting. It was during a visit, in the late 1970s, to Cardiff, where I was giving a public lecture in St David's Hall. My uncle Hubert – Cyril's other brother – was living in Cardiff at the time, and he had seen the publicity. He knew who I was. So he came around to the stage door at the Hall with the intention of meeting me. But he couldn't go in. When we eventually met, and he told me this story, we compared our reasons. They were the same.

But in the 1960s I knew nothing of Hubert, or of any of the family apart from Cyril, and that was only a name on a set of divorce papers and a brass plate. I returned to Reading with an address, not thinking that it would ever be useful. I was wrong.

It was just after Timmy was born. The medical system took over, and Molly and I found ourselves part of a case-history exercise. Each department – cardiac, ENT, paediatrics – wanted to discover as much information as possible relating to the baby's condition, and this meant exploring his family history. Was there any history of these problems on Molly's mother's side? A quick check with her mother. No. And on her father's side? Another check. No. And on my mother's side? Again, no. And on my father's side?

Ah.

The hospital staff didn't seem particularly surprised to learn that I had no easy way of finding out. Asking my mother was out of the question, and she probably wouldn't have known anyway. The only alternative was a letter to Leeds. So, later that day, after much debate about whether it was the right thing to do, Molly – I had chickened out again – wrote a brief note to my father asking him whether he knew of anything.

A reply came a fortnight later, addressed to Mrs Crystal – Molly's handwriting was not clear enough, he said, to make out her first name. The letter was polite, brief, and to the point. He understood our anxiety, and knew of no family history, but he would look further into the matter and let us know. The final paragraph was interesting: 'I thought it better to let you have a brief note straight away so that you would not think I was amiss in acknowledging your letter. It will also give me time to digest your news of David, yourself and your family.' Then a 'Yours sincerely' and a formal signature: 'S. C. Crystal'.

This was real, physical evidence. A close encounter of the second kind. I was alive with expectation. He would let us know. He was intending to write again. And he was intending to digest the news. What did that mean? It suggested a subsequent action. A meeting, surely.

He didn't let us know. We never heard another word. And, in the chaos of looking after Timmy, we didn't follow it up. But I kept the letter, and often looked at it, wondering what its author looked like. I would find out, eventually, thanks to linguistics again.

But not for a few years. The first thing to do, after fateful 1971, was pick up the pieces, both domestically and academically. The devastation Molly felt would, we thought, be helped by having another child. You can imagine the nervousness which accompanied that pregnancy, but when Lucy was born, in 1973, she was as normal and beautiful a child as anyone could want. The extra bedroom found a use after all. My hope was that this would cure Molly of the deep depression she had been experiencing, and for a while it seemed as if it would.

On the academic side, my newfound commitment to the world of speech therapy demanded a greater concentration than ever before on child language studies. It was a subject that was just beginning to take off. Some anthologies of papers were now available. In 1972, American psychologist Roger Brown's hugely influential book, *A First Language: the Early Stages*, was in press. And the child language scholars of the world held an international seminar at Florence in September that year. This was an opportunity to really catch up on what was going on in that field, and to meet all the leading players, so I attended. Charles Ferguson was there too, with a proposal which he put to the business meeting. He felt the time was right to start a journal exclusively devoted to child language acquisition. Articles on the subject were currently scattered throughout a range of psychological, sociological, and linguistic journals. It was time to give the field a focus. Did anyone know a journal publisher? I realized that people were looking at me. Although only an assistant editor, my experience with the *Journal of Linguistics* and with the Penguin series it seems made me editorially pre-eminent in that room. I said I would make a case to Cambridge University Press.

So I did, and they welcomed the idea, and please could it start soon, and please would I edit it? I referred back to the seminar participants. Doubtless out of an instinct of self-preservation there were no other contenders for the job. But they all promised to help, and ten of the leading scholars joined a reading committee, and another twenty made up an advisory board. I wasn't going to be on my own. And Mike Garman agreed to be assistant editor, with Paul Fletcher joining him the following year. The first issue of the *Journal of Child Language* came out in May 1974. I stayed with it for twelve years.

By 1975 I was getting back into the swing of academic life. I even felt like writing books again. There was no question now: it was an applied linguist's life for me. I signalled the change of direction in two ways. I brought together all my articles on intonation and related tones of voice into a single book, *The English Tone of Voice*. I suppose it was a sort of closure. And I nailed my applied flag firmly to the mast with two books. *Advanced Conversational English*, working again with Derek Davy, aimed to make available informal conversation of high acoustic quality to ELT specialists. I described how we approached the task in an earlier chapter (p. 103). *Child Language, Learning and Linguistics* was a position statement in the direction of mother-tongue education. That appeared in 1976. Other projects were in the planning. But the outpouring was premature. Events transpired to make these the last books I would write for three years.

It's another moment I still can't talk or write about much. It seems that I, and everyone else, had not fully appreciated Molly's state of mind. At one level she had resumed her previous life. She had gone back to work as a children's nurse at local hospitals, and was much loved and respected. We had done the usual things families do – been on an exchange holiday in Switzerland, taken other holidays in Holyhead. There had been the usual church events, such as the children's first communions, and parental meetings in the primary schools. Steven had fallen in love with football, and Reading FC, which meant a regular visit to their old stadium in Elm Park. We had got involved in local parish activities, and joined a local book club. But at another deeper level, none of this was reaching her. There was a profound and encroaching sadness and introversion which I failed to respond to, probably because it had created a distance between us. She became increasingly depressed. It all ended, in May 1976, just after the anniversary of what would have been Timmy's eighth birthday, with an overdose. She was buried, alongside him, in Tilehurst churchyard.

The next few months are a blur. So much happened so quickly. Her mother came to help look after the children, and was a godsend. It gave me the opportunity to keep up with academic administrative tasks, which were at a critical phase. All the child language and speech therapy developments were coming to the boil at the same time. The journal had just begun. The new degree course was starting in October. The LARSP book was coming out, and we were in the middle of a series of in-service courses for therapists training people in the art of making patient grammatical profiles (see plate 3.1). Other members of staff, Paul and Mike especially, were immensely supportive in getting things done. But it was a pretty horrible time. And yet, out of all this chaos came a sudden and unexpected and wonderful outcome.

It started with one of those in-service courses. We'd been doing these for a couple of years at Castle Priory College in nearby Wallingford, developing our LARSP approach, and we were now putting these on for other counties, such as Oxfordshire and Hertfordshire. And it was at one of these courses, at the Lister Hospital in Stevenage, that I met Hilary. 'Whoever loved that loved not at first sight?' said the poet. I'm not sure whether I would have given any credit to Christopher Marlowe's words before that day. The phenomenon of love at first sight is a recurring theme in literature and art, from Plato to Kylie Minogue, but I think most people are naturally sceptical of it – until they experience it. All I can say is that it happened, we were married within the year, and more than thirty years later the mutual attraction is as strong as it was that day in Stevenage. It is a daily source of wonder.

And it nearly didn't happen. I almost missed getting to the Stevenage course. I had been on a short visit to Sweden – a conference up in Umeå, in the north of the country. Maybe it was the effects of the previous evening's visit to the coast to see the midnight sun, or an unrealistic self-assessment of just how much Swedish I knew, but on the plane down to Stockholm I missed a critical announcement. The plane was making some intermediate stops, and as it was an internal flight the announcements were being made only in Swedish. Basically, what the stewardess told us was that at our next stop, Sundsvall, anyone wanting to catch connections in Stockholm should change there to a direct flight. The flight I was on was going the long way round, making a couple more stops before reaching Stockholm. Unfortunately, I found out what she had said only after we had left Sundsvall. With the time for my British Airways connection rapidly approaching, I asked the stewardess whether I would make it. Her face told me it was unlikely. 'Didn't you hear the announcement?' Well, yes, I *heard* it, but evidently didn't catch . . . Her face said, 'Why didn't you ask? You are a prat,' but her voice said she would see what she could do.

She spoke to the captain, who spoke to Stockholm. Did I have any luggage? Only the cabin bag I had with me. It might just be possible. And so it proved to be. When we landed at Stockholm, I was ushered to the front of the plane. The door opened and I stood at the top of the steps. 'There it is,' said the stewardess, pointing to a plane a few hundred yards away on the tarmac, with its door still open. 'If you run, you'll catch it. They know you're coming.' So I ran, keeping an eye out for any approaching planes much in the manner (I like to think) of Steve McQueen at the end of *Bullitt*, and panted my way up the steps into the BA flight. They shut the door and started the engines just after I collapsed into my seat.

I doubt it would be possible now, health and safety concerns being the way they are. But Swedish pragmatism won that day. And as a result, I got back to Heathrow that evening, and to Stevenage that night, in time for our course first thing the next morning, in a lecture room in the basement of the Lister, where, in the back row, on my left as I faced the audience, there was a speech therapist in a red skirt . . .

I find it difficult to conceive now the scale of the task facing her, as she entered a household consisting of a boy almost twelve, a girl of ten, and another girl of three. We just soldiered on, I suppose, as one has to do, and hoped not to make too many mistakes. The Tilehurst house was full of the wrong memories now, so we moved as soon as we could. We found an old schoolhouse just outside Binfield, near Wokingham. It was a Victorian building, with a schoolroom and a headmistress's cottage adjoining. The previous owner had done most of the renovation already, and added an extension at the back with a couple of bedrooms in it. This suited Steven and Susie perfectly, as – with adolescence approaching – it gave them an independent existence away from the rest of the family, which grew by one with the arrival of Ben in 1977. It also gave them easy access to the back garden – of particular importance to Susie, who had begun to explore the animal kingdom with unprecedented intensity – as indeed she still does (p. 271). It was a time of rabbits, guinea pigs, hamsters, dogs, vet bills, more rabbits, cats, more vet bills, more rabbits . . .

The previous owner was Denys Pavitt, a film set designer – as we discovered as we got used to the house. That panelled dining room – lovely wood it was, until we realized that it wasn't all wood: most of the panels were doors, with paper covering the holes where the handles and locks once were, and painted to match. And what's the point in screwing a window into a wall, or bolting a toilet to the floor? You don't need to on a film set. But then, on a film set you may not actually need to open the window or use the toilet. We discovered these things as we saw the newly opened window fall away from the building and the newly sat-upon toilet move across the floor. On the plus side, it turned out that Denys had been production designer on the television series *Catweazle*, which had enthralled the older children (and me), and bits of the set were all over the house. If Catweazle were ever to return from his medieval time, it would be here.

LINGUIST AS (FAILED) SPEECH THERAPIST

You might think no child could be linguistically better off than to be born to a speech therapist mother and a linguist father who specializes in language acquisition. The perfect combination? Think again.

Poor Ben! We spent so much time giving him helpful linguistic stimuli that we ended up delaying his sentence development. We noticed when he was approaching his second birthday: he wasn't using the full range of two-word sentences that the LARSP chart insisted was normal for that age.

Hilary and I held a case conference. What could possibly be the problem? Then it dawned on us. We were doing all the hard work for him.

'What's that called?' we would say.

'Car,' Ben would reply, monosyllabically.

'Yes, it's a big red car . . .' expanded his parents enthusiastically, '. . . with big yellow wheels and a horn that goes beeeep . . .'

Ben found all this fascinating. Here were unending stories for free. No need to talk under these circumstances. Just keep listening. Once we realized, we back-pedalled. Stopped reinforcing quite so much. He caught up within a month. A salutary experience. We wrote it up for the College of Speech Therapists' *Bulletin* under the heading 'A cautionary tale'.

Still, there was no long-term harm. Ben lives by language now, in an acting, voicing, and writing world.

The old schoolroom made it an ideal house for parties. The new speech therapy course was off the ground, with six students, and serviced by a mix of full-time and part-time lecturers who didn't know each other, so it seemed to us it would be a good idea to hold a clinical linguistic Christmas party. The house was some way out into the countryside, but that didn't seem to bother anyone. It was a great success – not least for Steven, who discovered punch for the first time – and was repeated every year until we left Reading. It helped give the course a much-needed cohesion and identity.

As the course director, I realized I had to consolidate my knowledge of the clinical field as quickly as possible. I know of only one way to do that.

Teach it. And then write about it. So, just as with linguistics at Bangor, years before, I found myself on a fast learning curve, introducing the subject of language pathology to the new group and keeping a week or so ahead of them. I went to some of the classes being simultaneously taught in psychology, physiology, and medicine, and learned what they were teaching. Renata listened in to my new lectures, and gave me the benefit of her clinical experience. Once a week, I ran a seminar which did nothing else but talk about the relationships between the diverse subjects the students were studying. After a couple of years of this, I was ready to write it all up: the outcome was *An Introduction to Language Pathology*. There was one subject where I didn't need any extra training. I already knew it backwards. That was the course, for more advanced students, on cleft palate.

The best part of the new operation was the linguistics clinic. We had found a space on the ground floor of the building where our department was housed – a small complex consisting of a seminar room, an office, and a cloakroom, all usefully located next to the toilets – and turned it into a clinical domain. We knocked through the wall between the seminar room and the office, and installed a one-way window. We then kitted out the office as a therapy room, with toys, pictures, and all the other equipment needed for working with patients. A table and chairs were placed next to the window. A video camera on the floor transmitted pictures into the adjoining room (see plates 2.4–2.5). Another one on the ceiling allowed a view from above, so that observers could see exactly what was happening on the table.

And who were these observers? We were. Myself, or another member of the department; outside professionals such as a paediatrician and educational psychologist; often the child's teacher; students, parents, and (when adult patients began to arrive) spouses. It was a team approach. We weren't able, at that time, to cope with a routine speech service, but we could offer a special assessment for patients sent by the area's speech therapists. It was a bit like my visits to the Audiology Unit a few years before, but this time the children would come to us; and we were well equipped to receive them. The usual regime was to arrange two visits of half-an-hour or so a week apart. The first week would be an exploratory session. The child's therapist would elicit as much speech as she could, or (if there was no speech) establish the comprehension level at which the child was operating. The parents were usually there to help with interpreting obscure references. I would always spend time with them afterwards: they were such an important member of the team. We would record everything, and then analyse it from all linguistic points of view. What sounds were being used? What grammatical constructions? What words? What sort of conversation was the child having with the therapist? Did he speak to her spontaneously? Or did he only reply to questions? Or only echo what he heard? I say 'she' for the therapist and 'he' for the patient. Nine out of ten speech therapists were women. And three out of four children were boys.

The next week was spent analysing the recordings, and constructing linguistic profiles of the child's abilities. The aim was twofold: to make a detailed and accurate assessment of where the child was, in relation to normal scales of language acquisition. And then to work out, by comparing his performance with those scales, what the next steps in therapy ought to be. Here's an example of what I mean. Justin, aged six, was still talking like a two-year-old. He was saying such things as *Man jump*, *See car*, and *Red ball*. That's normal, at age two. But soon after, normal children start joining two-word sentences together, making three-word sentences such as *Me see ball* and *See red car*. We would choose some of these next steps as a target for therapy, and work out in advance with the therapist how to introduce them. Then, when the child arrived for the second visit, she would try to teach him these more advanced constructions. If we had got the analysis exactly right, she would usually be rewarded with immediate progress. If we hadn't, there would be signs of difficulty, and we would have to think again. It was an exciting session. We would see a child having difficulty with a sentence we all thought he should be coping with, and suddenly realize why. A quick discussion would lead to a new idea for therapy. We would phone through into the clinic room, and ask the therapist to try something new. A challenging role for her – and by no means easy, to therap knowing that on the other side of the window was a group of professionals (and students) scrutinizing your every move!

That example was an easy one, which didn't take long to work out. Most cases were far more complex, involving lengthy periods of transcription and analysis during the intervening week. The students were being trained to do these things, but their work had to be checked and corrected. It was immensely meticulous, hugely time-consuming, but enormously rewarding work. For there is no better reward than the sight of communicatively handicapped children making progress in language. Thanks to your analysis, they are able to say just that little bit more than they could before – such as putting an adjective in front of a noun to describe something, or stringing two sentences together to tell a story. You might think the idea of using an adjective before a noun is such a little thing. Why get so excited about that? Because it opens floodgates of expression. Now the children can talk about the world in so many more interesting ways. Colours, sizes, shapes, textures, feelings, and more all become available to them. Things are no longer just things, but blue, big, round, soft, pretty things. And this tiny new building-block of language will eventually take its place in a great skyscraper of expression. When we work with children's speech, we are building their communicative future.

As I came to realize just how much time it took to do a detailed linguistic analysis, I began to appreciate more than I ever had done before the real problems faced by therapists in their everyday clinics. We had just one patient a week, sometimes two – but never more. In the average local authority or hospital clinic, children were coming in for assessment or treatment every half hour or so. What chance had a therapist to do the kind of analysis required, especially if the case was complicated? There was a shortage of therapists. There were long waiting lists on the National Health Service. Might it be possible to help here?

I'd explored the possibilities a few years earlier. In 1970, following the fruitful collaboration with the Audiology Unit, the Reading Hospital/University Liaison Committee had set up a working party to investigate the possibility of a Child Communication Study Centre, which would combine clinical, teaching, and research roles. I chaired the group, and we were making great progress, with support from the then minister, Keith Joseph – until the government changed its mind. A 1971 paper on hospital facilities for children concluded that developments of this kind should be incorporated within Paediatric Departments in hospitals, and not in separate centres. The idea died. But it came to life again during a conference on speech therapy research organized by the Department of Health and Social Security in July 1975. I was in the audience and heard speaker after speaker complain about the difficulties in the way of doing research – lack of time, opportunity, and expertise. We were asked to think of solutions.

I lost no time in following this up. The next day I wrote a long letter to the senior civil servant involved, suggesting that the DHSS institute a category of 'clinical linguist' to focus research and a Language Analysis Centre to process recordings. My analogy was with the pathological laboratories. Imagine what would happen these days if GPs had to do all their pathology analysis themselves. The system would collapse. Today, GPs send off samples of blood, urine, or whatever to the path lab, and the results come back a few days later to be interpreted by the doctor. Why not, I argued, have the same thing for language? A speech therapist would make a recording and send it off to such a specialist centre, where it would be transcribed and analysed, and a report sent back for action. As the databank of reports grew, opportunities for research would grow too.

There was also a parallel with the idea of National Centres for Reading, which had been recommended by the Bullock Report the same year.

The College of Speech Therapists thought it was a great idea. The chair of its Council, Catherine Renfrew (the same), wrote a hugely supportive letter. A meeting was held at the DHSS at the end of the year. The civil servants were broadly in favour. The kind of informal arrangement we already had in place through our in-service LARSP courses had already put us in the position of offering an ad hoc advisory service, and made it clear that there was a place for some sort of 'centre of excellence' for routine investigations. However, the DHSS advisers foresaw major logistical issues in introducing such a scheme nationally, let alone economic complications (the UK was just coming out of a recessionary two years in 1975). And the research side needed further thought. I was asked to go away and come up with some costs for a scheme of centres and a protocol for a research enterprise. And if 1976 had gone according to plan, I suppose I would have done just that. But, as you know, it didn't.

The centres proposal faded out of view as the 1970s progressed. Public money was tight: another recession would develop in 1980–1. But the research idea never went away, and later, when things had settled down, I did work up an application for a research programme into the classification of language disorders, using the profile techniques that we had evolved. I went through all the patients we had seen in our clinic between 1979 and 1983, selected a group of thirty, and got funding from the Medical Research Council to give them an all-inclusive profiling. It was only an eighteen-month project, but the findings were extremely illuminating. They formed the input to most of the case studies I included in books and articles in this field in the 1980s. The data and analyses were eventually deposited in the Department of Speech and Hearing Sciences at University College, Cork (where Paul Fletcher had come to be based).

It was after one of those clinical sessions in the early 1980s that my policy of talking to the child's parents, after a session was over, brought an unexpected bonus. The child's father was just about to leave, when he turned to me in the doorway.

'Funny name, yours,' he said. (Where had I heard those words before?) 'I have a client called Crystal.'

He explained he was a London bank manager, and worked at a bank near Regent's Park.

'You're only the second person I've ever met called Crystal. I wonder if you're related?'

'What's his name?' I asked.

The manager couldn't exactly remember. He ruminated aloud.

'His name . . .? His name . . .? He's a doctor, that I know . . .'

The world stood still.

'Not Samuel Cyril Crystal, by any chance?' I stammered.

'Ah yes, that's it.' A pause. 'Oh, you know him, do you?'

'Yes.'

'And are you related, then?'

'Sort of.'

No time for chickens now. A moment of decision. I said this was someone with whom I'd lost touch.

'Would you mind passing on a note?'

The bank manager would be delighted. I scribbled a few words on a sheet of departmental notepaper, and stuffed them into an envelope. I can't remember exactly what I said. A greeting from Reading . . . it would be nice to meet . . . sorry that this is out of the blue . . . here's the address and phone number . . . Something like that.

I didn't have to wait long. A few days later there was a phone call. Hilary answered, and gave me the shock of my life when she told me who it was. I took the phone. I don't remember a word of the conversation, but we must have had one, for we agreed a date and a venue for afternoon tea: the lounge of the hotel on the corner of the roundabout opposite Lord's cricket ground. He lived just round the corner, it seemed, and had been in London (I later learned) since his retirement as a GP in 1977. I checked my diary. I was free. I had an appointment with the Queen that day, but I cancelled it. (Not really. But that was how I felt.)

And so we finally met. The sighting of life-forms: a close encounter of the third kind. Well, fourth, really, as this was more than sighting; this was communication between me and an . . . alien? I walked into the lounge. He was sitting there with his wife, Ray. A teddy-bear of a man (see plate 7.3). White wavy hair. Quite thick, rimmed glasses. His eyes smiled. A South Wales accent. And he called me 'boy'. He was an absolute delight. Not an alien at all.

His wife, Ray, on the other hand . . . She was very wary of me. The first thing she said was that this wasn't to be a long meeting, as Cyril hadn't been well – angina – and she was worried that this encounter would be too much for him. He waved away her concerns, but she was not to be put off. She fussed over Cyril like a mother. He was plainly her whole life.

We talked for an hour. There was a barrage of questions about me and my family. He didn't seem to recall the letter about Timmy. He asked how my mother was and what she was doing. He was especially interested, I suppose because of his medical background, in my clinical linguistic work, and he asked me about it in some detail. He wanted to know what books I had written, and hoped I would send him some. (I had anticipated that, and brought a couple with me.) He was delighted that I had done so well, and I was delighted that he was delighted.

We finished tea, and I walked with them back to their flat in Hanover Gate Mansions. They invited me up to see the place. We talked a little more. Then I left. I was to be sure to phone, so that we could arrange a visit to Wokingham to meet the family. Make it soon, he said. He seemed genuinely keen. I said I would call the next day.

I walked to Paddington to get the train home. I felt I was walking on air. As people passed, I had to restrain a desire to tell them, 'Oh yes, I have a father too! You're not the only ones with fathers . . .' When I got home, I gave as full an account as I could to Hilary. She asked me about him and his family – and I suddenly realized that I didn't know. I'd been so busy answering his questions – they had been thick and fast – that I hadn't thought to ask him anything in return. But it didn't matter. There would be plenty of time for that at the next meeting.

I phoned, as promised, the following afternoon. Ray answered. An icicle formed on the phone line. It was as she had feared. The meeting had been too much for him. He had had bad chest pains. He was in hospital. She had advised him against it, but he hadn't listened. It would not be a good idea to call again. No, he wouldn't be coming over to meet the family. Goodbye.

I felt numb. Then I felt guilty. Then I felt angry. Then I felt numb again. And then I thought, well, never mind. I've met him now. That's the big event over. I'll just get on with my life. A pity he never met the family. His loss. Still, it would have been nice . . . Forget it, Dave. Still, it would . . . No. Move on.

There would be a next meeting. But it would not take place for another ten years.

Chapter 15
Looking for remedies

As the 1970s approached their end, I found I was able to write properly again. Projects which had been on the back burner began bubbling away and slowly came to the boil. I finished off my language pathology course-book as well as the linguistics dictionary I'd been sporadically compiling. The work with LARSP had begun to spread, leading to an anthology of contributions from people who were using it in their clinics and class-rooms. The arrival of electronic typewriters helped in all this, as did the first word processors. I look back with disbelief now at the first draft I made of *The Grammatical Analysis of Language Disability*. It is eighty-four pages of lined foolscap paper, with every word written out in longhand. Today, with fingers virtually attached to a keyboard, I shake my head at the time it must have taken, and look at my erstwhile neat writing with awe.

Along with the writing, as ever, had come the editing. Edward Arnold, with its customary nose for developments, had noted the new perspectives emerging in speech therapy following the 1972 Quirk Report, and decided that the time was ripe for a series. Studies in Language Disability and Remediation was the result. Speech therapist Jean Cooper and I came together as editors, later to be joined by psychologist Maggie Snowling. The idea was to provide a unified approach to the investigation and treatment of language disability, bringing together speech therapists, linguists, teachers of the deaf, remedial teachers, educational psycholo-gists, audiologists, and anyone else involved in the subject. And indeed, the series did live up to its ambitious aims reasonably well, with its first books covering such diverse topics as aphasia, disadvantage, and dyslexia, as well as our own profiling work. The series obtained a second lease of life when Colin Whurr took it over a decade later. The distinctive red-and-black covers of Whurr Publishing would help to give the field of language disability an identity for nearly twenty years.

It suddenly seemed as if everyone wanted to get in on the act. Book series started to appear like spring flowers. And the phone started ringing. No sooner had the Edward Arnold series got under way than I had a call from publisher André Deutsch. I was seriously impressed. This was the man who had published Kerouac, Mailer, Updike, and many more. What would he want with me? It transpired that over the past twenty-five years he had been publishing books on language and languages as part of a series called the Language Library. The lexicographer Eric Partridge had started it in 1952, just after Deutsch had set up his publishing house, and had edited it by himself for fourteen years, before being joined by Professor Simeon Potter in the 1960s. (That was a name from my past: Potter had interviewed me for a place at Liverpool in 1959.) Between them, Partridge and Potter had published almost forty books on a bewildering variety of linguistic topics – spelling, etymology, dialects, translation, slang, the history of English, the language of authors such as Dickens and Shakespeare, and many other subjects of interest to a general readership. But Potter had died in 1976, leaving Partridge, who was by then eighty-two and not well, the only nominal editor. André urgently needed a replacement. One of his colleagues knew of my work with Penguin, which had by then come to an end. Might I be interested in taking on the Language Library?

I went up to London to the Deutsch office in Great Russell Street, and met him for lunch. I was taken with him immediately. I saw what journalist Frank Keating later aptly described as a 'mid-European leprechaun', and encountered a conversational wit and ranging imagination that made for one of the best lunches ever. I took over as 'working editor', keeping Partridge informed of developments by correspondence. But only three books appeared before I became sole editor. Partridge died in 1979. André insisted on a memorial book. I had no personal memories to speak of, having hardly met the man, but I visited several of his friends and collected stories for an anthology. Randolph Quirk and Anthony Burgess contributed beautifully crafted, poignant memoirs.

I edited the Language Library for the next thirty years, and by the time it ended I had commissioned and edited over fifty titles, including some absolutely marvellous books, such as Norman Blake on non-standard language in English literature, Whitney Bolton on George Orwell, Walter Redfern on puns, Geoffrey Hughes on swearing, Roger Shuy on legal language, and Katherine Perera on the development of children's written language. It was the best editorial experience ever. It was so wide-ranging in scope, and a pleasure to find so many authors willing and able to write at a general level – and a publisher willing to publish them. None of them became best-sellers, but they all did well, and filled a gap in the market, satisfying an appetite for accessible books on language which at the time was not otherwise being met. André himself had always been delighted with the Language Library. He told me it had actually been a great help to him financially, as he struggled to get his new firm off the ground. In the 1950s and 1960s, we must remember, there were no competing series on the subject of language, but considerable general interest. Until I started the Penguin series, I think the Language Library was unique in language publishing. Indeed, the people at Penguin told me they had the Language Library very much in their sights when they decided to launch Pelican linguistics.

It felt like a series that would run for ever. But times change. And in 1983, for reasons I never fully understood, André responded positively to a bid from Blackwell for the Library. He was torn, mind. He wrote me a letter in which he hoped that, rather than an outright purchase, there might be 'some kind of partnership so that we can have a continued relationship with the Language Library, to which I am emotionally attached – after all, it was started when the firm started'. In the event, a joint publishing deal was struck, but it lasted only a few years. Blackwell became sole publisher in 1988. They kept the series alive for another two decades, but there proved to be increasing problems with a publishing programme based on the uncertain notion of the 'interested general reader'. Student adoptions came increasingly to govern publishing policy, and other series began to eat into the Language Library's market. Blackwell called it a day in 2008.

I was sad to see it end. I had developed a real affection for the Library. To adapt a slogan of the time: it refreshed the parts other series never reached. It made me read topics at a depth that I wouldn't otherwise have achieved. Left to myself, would I have read so much on the language of Milton, Hardy, or Scott, or explored Chinese and Aboriginal languages in such detail? I doubt it. None of it was wasted, for it all helped to add breadth to the encyclopedias which I would eventually come to write. And many of these books have given me just as much pleasure to see in print as anything I have written myself.

Looking back now, I was plainly an editing addict. How else can I explain taking on two more series over the next few years? It certainly wasn't the money, for a tiny editorial royalty on each book doesn't put one into the Porsche league, by a long shot. I think it's partly the novelty of discovering a niche that needs to be filled, and the creative challenge of wondering whether one can fill it. It's partly the encounter with brilliant minds, and the intellectual intimacy which comes from a shared exploration of a fresh subject. It's also the delight of facilitation – that you've given someone an opportunity to publish – and the excitement of reading fresh and original material straight from the pen. I suppose, too, there is a vicarious element: these are all the books you would like to have written yourself!

Whatever the reasons, editing continued to play a large part in my life over the next decade. For Academic Press there was a short-lived (well, eight-book) series called Applied Language Studies, which hoped to bring together the various branches of applied linguistics in much the same way as the Language Disability series had aimed to do. It published only between 1981 and 1985 before policy changes within Academic brought it to a close. The concept and title were good, though, so I wasn't surprised to see it being picked up by Blackwell in 1988. Keith Johnson co-edited with me, and some fine books appeared, bringing together work from child language acquisition and computational linguistics, with a special focus on foreign language teaching and learning.

I was very happy at Reading as the 1980s dawned. On the speech therapy side, the degree course was attracting healthy numbers of students, and postgraduate interest in clinical linguistic work was growing too. LARSP had been taken up by practitioners in other parts of the world, such as Australia and South Africa. Thanks to Hilary's parents being available to childmind, we were able to get to the Australian Speech and Hearing Association conference in Perth in 1980, where the approach was being fanfared. The demand for materials led to *Profiling Linguistic Disability* in 1982, which extended the profile approach from grammar to the other main areas of language, phonology and semantics. And then I was approached by the editors of a German series, Disorders of Human Communication, to write a general account of the principles as well as the practice of applying linguistics to the analysis of language disability. I called it *Clinical Linguistics*, and in so doing seem to have named a field. The book went through several incarnations: both Edward Arnold and Colin Whurr reprinted it.

The clinical work also went in a second direction at that time. Teachers had begun to be interested. Under the 1944 Education Act, children with special educational needs had been categorized as 'disabled' in purely medical terms. Notions such as 'maladjusted' or 'educationally subnormal' were common, and 'treatment' was given through special schools. Baroness Warnock's Report in 1978, *Special Educational Needs*, changed all that. The 'SEN' of the title identified the need for an inclusive approach, with all children – in mainstream education as well as in special schools – sharing in the same educational goals of independence, enjoyment, and understanding. One in five children in the mainstream, it appeared, experienced real difficulties at some point in their school life. The conclusion was clear, and formed part of the 1981 Education Act: special education should be part of the responsibility of all teachers.

But how to identify and provide for the teaching of these pupils? This would be a problem still occupying everyone a decade later. Given the complexity of language, and the different kinds of issue raised by the four modalities of listening, speaking, reading, and writing, this was going to be a really hard nut to crack. It appeared there was no linguistic training in place for teachers who were working with children with language disability, even in the special schools. Everyone relied on speech therapists, and they were few and far between. Now mainstream teachers were being asked to deal with language problems, many of which – we knew from the Reading assessment clinic – were highly complicated.

The gap in expertise was noted first, as might be expected, by the children's parents. If your child was in a bad way, linguistically, and the school had no idea how to deal with the problem, then you made a fuss. And in the 1970s there was an organization that was able to make a fuss on your behalf. The Association For All Speech-Impaired Children (AFASIC) had been established in 1968, specifically to focus attention on the needs of the children, their families, and the professionals working with them. Aware of the speech therapy initiative at Reading, AFASIC approached the department and asked if we would establish a parallel course for teachers. I thought a nine-month full-time post-experience course would probably do the job. With our experience in working with therapists and (thanks to the ELT side of the department, which had grown enormously) with teachers, everyone felt this was a logical next step. As a consequence, a Diploma in Remedial Language Studies (DRLS) was duly introduced, with the first group of students arriving in 1979. All were teachers working in school language units or who had special responsibility for language. I directed the course until 1984, with the help of a former teacher-of-the-deaf, Margaret Davison. Margaret then took over for a further two years, until it ended in 1986. The course never had many teachers attending, but in the mid-1980s secondments were drying up, and the full-time requirement was evidently making it difficult for teachers with families to attend, unless they lived near Reading. With university funding also drying up, DRLS could never survive.

But the spirit of the Diploma lived on. In 1982, a three-year dissemination project supported by AFASIC and the Department of Education and Science (DES) explored ways in which the small but growing cadre of linguistically aware teachers could pass their newly acquired skills on to others in their profession. Clearly it required some sort of institutional framework. I could easily imagine a DRLS teacher returning to her school and then, totally isolated, losing enthusiasm. How do you pass on the results of nine months of training to your colleagues? How do you keep yourself up-to-date? I could see three main ways. The field needed annual workshops, at which DRLS practitioners could come together and top up their batteries. It needed a journal, to bring teacher-orientated work together. And it needed an organization, to publicly affirm the professionalism of teachers who were language specialists.

Eventually it all came to pass, though not without a few rows along the way. The DES had to be persuaded that setting up operations of this kind was a good use of their money, and AFASIC were slow to see the point of it all. The journal was first to take off. I made a proposal for it, which Edward Arnold (prophetic as ever) took up: it appeared in 1985, and was called *Child Language Teaching and Therapy* (CLTT). The opening words of my first editorial were 'And about time too' – words I had repeatedly heard from professionals when the news of the journal's appearance became public. And from more than just teaching professionals. Speech therapists too were missing a journal where the focus was exclusively on the crucial questions of language intervention: what to teach, when to teach it, and above all, why? And then it turned out that educational psychologists and paediatricians with an interest in language were keen on it too. The editorial remit of CLTT thus became very broad, but always focused on intervention. I hoped it would become a breeding ground for case studies, as medical journals had been in their early days.

The broader remit affected the proposal for an organization too. I arranged a day conference in June 1985 to discuss the possibilities, chaired by John Lea, the head of Moor House School at Oxted in Surrey. At the end of the day, there was unanimous agreement that we needed a national association – but what was it to be called? A National Association of Teachers of Language-Impaired Children? A bit of a mouthful, NATLIC, but it captured the spirit of the idea well, and it echoed the established phrasing in AFASIC. A steering committee was formed, including many ex-DRLS members, and the first AGM of the new Association took place in the autumn of that year. It was pointed out that the T was too restrictive. A year later, and NATLIC had become NAPLIC. The P stood for

'Professionals'. Everyone was happy, especially me. I became honorary president, and remained so for the next fifteen years.

You might get the impression from all this that I spent my whole life inside classrooms and clinics during the 1970s and 1980s. Well, a fair amount of time, certainly, but not all. I did quite a lot of external examining in those days, and that gets you out and about, especially in June, when final degree exam scripts have to be moderated. That's how I ended up in Dublin with Sister Marie, for instance, as you heard in my Prologue. Examining is a chore: it's a duty, a responsibility, it's part of the academic job. But it does have its good points. You experience some excellent restaurants, catch up with old friends, and get the opportunity to see how other people do things in your subject. The pleasantest experience was undoubtedly a period of examining in Edinburgh, with my host Professor David Abercrombie. That was the only occasion when I found a set of exam scripts waiting for me in a fridge, along with a bottle of fine white wine. David was a member of the Chevaliers du Tastevin, the elite wine-tasting fraternity of Burgundy, and he never missed an opportunity to share his vinolatry with his colleagues.

The 1980s was also a broadcasting decade, and that took me out and about too – though 'inside and down' would be a better way of putting it, for much of the experience was in the basement studios of Broadcasting House. I'd done hardly any radio work in the 1970s – a couple of talks for Radio 3 and that was all. But in 1980 everything changed. The Open University had been established ten years before, and one of the courses (PE 232) was on language development – a thorough exploration of the nature and development of children's language and the way it could be fostered in school. I was the external examiner for a while – and that was an eye-opener, I have to say. At other universities, I was used to hearing excuses from students who felt they had not done justice to themselves in the exams. While many were genuine, some were pushing it a bit. A sleepless night, a row with a girlfriend, or a mild episode of diarrhoea might prompt an anguished or even peremptory request for higher marks. But with the OU I encountered the emperors of excuses. Serious hospitalization, family death, and job redundancy, or a combination of all three, were just some of the reasons which examinees tentatively and politely suggested might be the cause of their possibly not doing quite as well as they might have done, and sorry to have bothered you and hope you didn't mind my writing like this at what must be a very busy time . . . It was humbling, and a real indication of the huge personal efforts people were making to gain these new degrees.

The OU contact led to several radio pieces for their programmes, and my first television programme. This latter was to back up Block 2, 'Patterns of Language', which was largely devoted to grammar, so I called it 'Grammar Rules'. It was recorded in a studio at the top of Alexandra Palace in north London. For years afterwards, it was shown in the early hours of the morning. I got used to people saying they were in bed with me last night. And on later lecturing visits I learned to cope – as I imagine all OU presenters have had to do – with the predictable remark, 'My, you don't look as young as I thought you were!' Television freezes time.

Much more so than radio. Listening to my radio programmes from the 1980s, it is difficult to hear much change in the voice. It's a bit deeper now, and not quite so resonant. I get husky more quickly, and my breath control isn't as good as it was. But it's undeniably the same voice. The first programme, which launched an era, was on Radio 4 in July 1981, called 'How dare you talk to me like that!' It was printed in *The Listener* and repeated by popular demand early in 1982. Why popular demand? Because it was the people who had provided the input. The producer had asked me to go through all the letters of complaint that had been sent in to the BBC during the previous month or so. There were hundreds. I made my survey and produced a 'top ten' of complaints. *Between you and I* was the Number 1 hate. And 'hate' was the operative word. I was amazed at the fury which people unleashed in their letters. People didn't just 'dislike' usages such as split infinitives and intrusive r's. They were 'horrified', 'appalled', 'scandalized', 'disgusted', 'nauseated'. I ended my programme with the thought: if people are using such vituperative language to talk about split infinitives, what language is left for them to use when a pope gets shot? (John Paul II had been hit by four bullets in St Peter's Square a few weeks before.)

The programme hit a nerve. The number of letters (still mainly of complaint) to the BBC increased dramatically. What were they to do with them? Easy: send them to Crystal. And so, for months, the Reading University postman must have thought I was the most popular lecturer on the planet. I got bagful after bagful. Still, never miss an opportunity. A series of thirteen ten-minute talks for Radio 4 followed in 1982, in a series called *Speak Out!* Each one took a usage theme and illustrated it from listener letters. My aim was to bring some balance into the debate. I knew I would never be able to dissuade people with such strong feelings, but I also felt that the people who sent in these emotional letters were a minority, and that there were probably far more listeners out there who were interested in a more reasoned approach. So I adopted an explanatory perspective. As I'd discovered in my Survey days, critics usually think the point they've noticed is a new development, and they use this as evidence for their claim that the language is going down the drain. They are usually nonplussed when they hear that the point isn't new in the language at all.

Did these programmes do any good? I have absolutely no idea. The postbag began to show a few moderate and positive letters. I tried to introduce a balance. 'Why don't you write and tell me some features of language that you actually like?' I asked my listeners; and some did. But they were outnumbered by the continuing missives from the disgusteds of – everywhere. My poor accent was given a regular beating. 'Can we trust anyone who pronounces *one* as "wun"?' asked one listener. She addressed that one to the BBC's director-general. It had to reach the top. And as quickly as possible. It was sent with a first-class stamp.

Some of the letters were truly amazing. One, I recall, from a man who had spent a whole day listening to Radio 4 on the lookout for split infinitives. He had found over a hundred, and his letter tabulated them minute by minute. Another collected intrusive r's, and sent me five pages of them. There were stories here just waiting to be told. And so I told them, or at least a selection of them, in a little Penguin book called *Who Cares About English Usage?*, which came out in 1984. It was a new venture for me, stylistically. I wrote it during a summer holiday in Holyhead, just before deciding to move back there, and thought I'd try out a new style, in the first person, with elliptical sentences, colloquial idioms, lots of examples, and a sprinkling of *Punch* cartoons. It went down well, and I made a mental note to use it again one day.

The *Speak Out!* programmes evidently attracted an enormous audience, and as a result, there were follow-up series. Then in 1984 there was a change of direction. I had been trying to persuade the BBC powers-that-be that there was a lot more to language than complaints about usage, and eventually they took the point, and commissioned a new series called *English Now*. It was a toe-in-the-water move, with just six programmes in the first series; but it worked, and the next year I was given ten programmes, and the following year another ten. The series continued until 1990. I remember all these programmes now particularly for the guests. We took a different theme in each programme – place-names, plain English, children's games, puns, adult literacy, swearing . . . I introduced the topic, often illustrated by material from the BBC Sound Archives (a wonderful Aladdin's cave of recordings), and then I would welcome a guest who had some relevance to the topic of the day. Most were linguists or language specialists of one kind or another – such as Graham Pointon, who was in charge of the BBC Pronunciation Unit at the time. But the most memorable guests were the ones who would not normally be found in an academic language context, such as DJ Simon Bates, talkshow host Jimmy Young, newsreader Richard Baker, wordgame inventor Giles Brandreth, flautist and language enthusiast Fritz Spiegel, and, the most fascinating of all, *Carry On* star Kenneth Williams.

LINGUIST AS INTERVIEWER

One week on *English Now*, the theme was funny voices. I wanted to explore where they came from, what models comedians used, and what they felt about them. I asked for Kenneth Williams. Alan Wilding, my producer, thought there was little chance of getting him. The rumour was that he wasn't well. But he agreed. I prepared a set of questions, and waited in the studio for him to arrive. I mean, this was the *Carry On* star I'd seen in a dozen films. I was as excited as any film fan would be.

The studio door opened, and in shuffled a diminutive figure in an old raincoat. I had to look twice. Yes, it was him. I went over and greeted him enthusiastically, but got barely a nod in return. He sat at his microphone, and I tried to make some conversation to warm my guest up, as I usually did. His replies were monosyllabic. This wasn't normal. I went into the control room and asked Alan what to do. I'd never been in this situation before. Nor had he. 'We'll just have to go for it,' he said. 'Go back in and start the interview.' So I did. The green light went on. I read my introductory script. 'Where do they get their ideas from, these voice-creators? Do they have a model in mind? Kenneth . . .'

It was unbelievable. As soon as he saw the green light, his face lit up. His body movements became animated. He became a different person. He didn't let me finish my question. He just – I can think of no better way of putting it – vocally exploded. Over the next five minutes I was treated to the most glittering display of vocal effects I had ever heard. I could hardly get a word in. Voice transmuted effortlessly into voice – pastiches of Felix Aylmer, Edith Evans, Noel Coward, an unknown newspaper vendor . . . all sources for his characters. It was difficult to suppress my laughter. In the control room, Alan and the studio manager were falling about. It was a phonetic tour de force. And then it was over. The studio light turned to red. And he switched off. He was monosyllabic again. He put on his raincoat and shuffled out, with hardly a farewell.

I must have been one of the last people to interview Kenneth Williams. Our programme was recorded on 25 February 1988. On 15 April he was dead.

By 1990 the series had run to more than thirty programmes and looked as if it would go on indefinitely. Audience ratings were high. But then – as is often the way with radio – some decision-making took place higher up and the series was dropped. I pushed my producer, Alan Wilding, to put the case for a more ambitious series, with half-hour programmes and the opportunity to explore language ideas at greater length. 'It could go well beyond English,' I said. 'We could call it *Language Now*.' He agreed it was a lovely idea, and he did put the case to the controller of Radio 4 – but to no avail. I was therefore not a little miffed when, not long after, Radio 4 did come up with a half-hour series on language. They called it 'Word of Mouth', and it was presented by the writer and broadcaster Frank Delaney – who had been a guest on my series a few years before. Michael Rosen fronts it now, and I've been on it a few times. It does everything I had hoped my series idea would do. I just wish they'd asked me!

Linguists have to get used to taking a back seat, though, when it comes to broadcasting, and learn to cope with the unpredictable vagaries of programming. It's especially noticeable where television is concerned. Programme-makers are happy to milk you as a consultant or researcher, maybe even as a script-writer, but when it comes to presenting a programme, they always want a familiar TV face. I can understand that – but I have never been able to understand the inexplicable changes of heart that you find in radio. I got used to starting a new series, receiving an enthusiastic response from the channel and its listeners, and then being suddenly dropped, usually without any warning. I could never learn why. After Radio 4 dropped me, I was taken up by Radio 5, and began weekly contributions on language to *Five Aside*. That went on for a couple of years and then – they dropped me. Next I made weekly contributions to Hywel Gwynfryn's programme on BBC Wales, and also to the Mal Pope Show. That went on for a few years, and then – they dropped me. I did sixty one-minute talks for National Public Radio in Washington, and then – they dropped me. I began to think I had bad breath or something, until I realized that I was making most of my contributions down the line from a remote BBC studio, so they couldn't even see me, let alone smell me. I was beginning to take it personally until one day, in a pub outside Broadcasting House, I met a group of disaffected programme-makers each of whom had a story to tell which was like mine.

Individual radio projects were a bit more successful. In 1986 I was the consultant for a new series for BBC Schools called *Patterns of Language*, and wrote some of the scripts. That was produced by Al Wolff, and aimed at ages ten to thirteen. A year later, there was another series aimed at older infants, called *Talk to Me*, produced by Paddy Becheley. These were wonderful programmes, I thought, which exploited radio effects splendidly. And everything was at my disposal. When I wanted to illustrate the difference between the News being read correctly and incorrectly, I was able to use the pips and have one of Radio 4's best-known voices, Brian Perkins, read a script in which the language was horribly inappropriate. Having an actor do it just wouldn't have been the same. Another Brian – Redhead – was the presenter of that series. And that I remember especially for the way I ended up having a conversation with him without ever meeting him. How can that be? Our timetables couldn't be made to coincide, so I recorded my side of the script on one day and he did his on another. Then the two tapes were edited together. I had my doubts it would work, but Al had no qualms – and indeed, when it was done you couldn't hear the join. It sounded as if we were face-to-face.

The most ambitious broadcasting project for me in the 1980s was undoubtedly *The Story of English*. This had begun life as a BBC television series, created by Robert McCrum, William Cran, and Robert MacNeil. I'd been one of the consultants, but hadn't taken part in the production. Then the idea came up to make a radio version for the BBC World Service. This was a major enterprise. Could a TV series, especially one which was so brilliantly visual, be turned into radio? All the telerecordings were available for use. I listened to them with the vision off. Very little was directly usable. There were many splendid recordings of pidgins, creoles, regional accents and dialects, and a host of other varieties of English, but they had been carefully chosen to 'work' on television. It was going to be necessary to start from scratch. I couldn't do it alone, and Tom McArthur, the editor of the new periodical *English Today*, came on board. It took us several weeks, but eventually eighteen fifteen-minute programmes went out on the World Service in 1987.

You'll notice that these are all radio stories. What about television? Had anything happened since the OU programme in 1980? The answer is: everything, and nothing. One of my great ambitions was to present a blockbuster television series on language. It was *the* way, I felt, to get this wonderful subject across to millions. And I tried, oh how I tried! I have a filing cabinet full of the corpses of dead television proposals. The first one was in 1982, following the launch of the Radio 4 usage series. I was invited to talk to one of the monthly meetings of BBC journalists at Broadcasting House. Huw Weldon was the convenor, and he was intrigued by the possibility of a television series. It was arranged that I should go over to the BBC 2 offices in Ealing and have a meeting with Sheila Innes, the head of Continuing Education, and various producers. I made my pitch. But nothing happened. It turned out, not that there was no interest in the idea, but that there was too much interest. No one could agree which department a series on language belonged to or which angle to use to present it. Was it history? Current affairs? Continuing education? No one department felt able to 'own' it, and the idea fizzled out.

For a year. Then a producer rang up with an idea for a language series he was proposing to call *Your English*. A flurry of activity on my part, sketch out ideas, draft proposal, send in . . . silence. In 1985, another phone call, for a series to be called *About Language*. Another flurry, sketch, draft, send . . . silence. The same thing would happen virtually every year. If it wasn't the BBC, it would be ITV or Channel 4. Eventually it became wearisome. 'Hello, I'm a TV producer and I've got this absolutely marvellous original idea for a series on language.' 'Really.' 'Yes, and I was hoping that you'd be able to help me put together a proposal for the commissioners. We're in a bit of a hurry, unfortunately . . .' They were always in a hurry. That, I suspect, was part of the problem. But I always responded, because, you never know, the next proposal might be the one that actually gets somewhere. Once, we nearly did get somewhere. In 1990 I heard from a freelance producer, Clive Doig, who had an idea for a series for BBC 2 tentatively called *The Story of Language*. We drew up a detailed proposal. A dinner was arranged in the Groucho Club – a memorable meeting, because there was a power cut and we discussed everything by candlelight. We presented our ideas and were asked to revise them. We revised, presented again, and were asked to revise them. The people we had been talking to at the BBC had in the meantime changed roles, so we had to start all over again talking to new people and receiving new directions. The historical angle was important. No it wasn't. Yes it was. No it wasn't. A proposal for twenty-six episodes of fifty minutes each was revised to be eight, then ten, then five. Eventually, we ran out of steam.

I don't know whether it's the same for everybody, but I find there comes a point, in exploring any new subject, when you run out of steam. My involvement with clinical linguistics is another example. At the start it was like an intellectual jigsaw puzzle, and trying to put all the pieces into place kept me happy for some twenty-five years. I explored the field in as many directions as I could. The original focus on language-disordered children was supplemented by investigations into deafness and deaf-blindness, mental handicap, psychiatry, and adult aphasia. There was a fascinating period exploring different types of sign language for the deaf, especially a project with Elma Craig on one of the popular approaches of the day, the Paget-Gorman Sign System. Both the main teaching professions were being covered, at undergraduate and postgraduate levels. My research programme was available in published form. The MRC project was complete, and its outcome was published in 1987 in the first number of a new journal, *Clinical Linguistics & Phonetics* (whose distinctive '&' was an unsuccessful attempt to avoid the acronym *CLAP*). I hadn't forgotten about the general public, either. My Radio 4 profile motivated a short series in 1983 explaining what happens 'when language breaks down', and there were several articles with similar titles in more down-market periodicals. A programme of public lectures proved very popular, launched by Jonathan Miller, following his hugely successful 1978 television series, *The Body in Question*.

But I was beginning to feel it was time to move on. I had run out of ideas, and was beginning to repeat myself. If LARSP and the other procedures were of permanent value, others would see it and take them forward. If not – well, so it goes. They had helped to form a climate, and that was the most important thing. I always used to tell people that profiling was a way of thinking rather than just a set of procedures. You might dispense with the charts, but never with the descriptive and acquisitional principles which lay beneath them. I could also see that the world of clinical linguistics was getting larger every year, with many linguists now seriously involved, producing new approaches and exploring new domains. The field of pragmatics, for example, hadn't been around when I wrote *Clinical Linguistics*, but it was becoming a major area now, exploring the factors governing the choices patients made as they tried to cope with language. Not only was there a major new journal (CL&P), an International Clinical Linguistics and Phonetics Association was being planned (it would begin in 1991). The jigsaw puzzle was turning out to have more and more pieces in it.

Looking back now, I can see that during the 1980s there were signs that I was beginning to wind things up, as far as my contribution to clinical work was concerned. I collected relevant articles into a book, *Linguistic Encounters with Language Handicap*. That was surely a symptom of mental change. I experienced a rite of passage: in 1983 the College of Speech Therapists made me an Honorary Fellow. Did that make me yesterday's man? The new therapy and teaching journal, and the institution of NAPLIC, both gave me an ongoing role. But the fuel that drives a clinical linguist is a regular encounter with patients in clinics, and the discussion with professional colleagues which arises from it, not editing papers and attending conferences. And for me, routine clinical involvement stopped in 1984. I would later meet the occasional patient, thanks to Hilary's work as a part-time therapist, but the instances were sporadic and the cases were routine. After 1984, I wasn't able to get to clinical meetings, and as a result I began to feel out of touch. When a few years later the need came for a third edition of *An Introduction to Language Pathology*, I felt so much out of touch that it was time to call in the cavalry, in the shape of Rosemary Varley, who brought the book into contact with the modern speech therapy world.

What happened in 1984? An ominous year, according to George Orwell. And so it proved for me.

It all started with a letter.

Chapter 16

Why did you resign?

In the 1960s, Patrick McGoohan, in a series of riveting episodes of *The Prisoner*, enthralled a nation by refusing to explain to his menacing interrogators why he resigned from his job in the secret service. The series became a classic, and forty years on continues to attract devotees, who meet annually at Portmeirion, not far from where I now live in North Wales. The drama lay in the conflict between the intriguing schemes devised by the interrogators and the ingenious stratagems of resistance employed by the Prisoner. 'Why did you resign?' We never did learn why the Prisoner resigned, but it never seemed to matter.

'I was very happy at Reading as the 1980s dawned,' I said in the last chapter. Indeed I was. I had no intention of leaving. I had been head-hunted by other universities to run departments on a couple of occasions, but had not taken up the offers. Too much was going on. New degree and diploma courses. My own clinic. A team of like-minded research colleagues. At home, Hilary was doing some part-time speech therapy in Berkshire. All four kids were now settled in local schools. So when the first letter arrived, in March 1982, I ignored it.

It was from the Vice-Chancellor, sent to every member of staff, drawing their attention to the university's need to reduce its expenditure in the light of grant cuts and a drop in the number of overseas students. Public spending had been reducing since 1978 and was continuing under Mrs Thatcher's government. Earthquaking cuts had been announced in the 1981 budget, and education was one of the areas worst hit. Reading had to lose over a hundred staff if it was to break even by the end of 1984.

A premature retirement and severance scheme had been devised. Leave before 30 September 1984, and you'd do quite well out of it. Older staff had been asked first, but not enough had decided to leave. Now it was the turn of staff under fifty years of age. 'If you would like to explore this further, please telephone to fix an appointment . . .' I didn't.

Another letter arrived in December 1982. The university grant would be cut again next year. Further reductions in teaching, research, administrative, or service staff must be sought. I noted the phrasing: everyone was involved now, not just academics. The tone was getting more urgent. *Please* leave. Even a visiting appointment elsewhere would help! I ignored that one too.

Another letter arrived in December 1983. The special severance scheme was due to finish nine months later. 'May I ask you once again to consider whether this scheme would be appropriate for you?' And please, by the end of January. The tone was desperate. I considered it, and again felt it wasn't for me. Apart from anything else, my MRC research project was just about to take off.

But the consequences of the cuts were beginning to bite. The devil lay in the detail. 'Administrative and service staff.' That meant secretarial help. And if there weren't any secretaries, or not so many, then the academics would have to start doing the routine admin. But there weren't so many academics around, for a few of my faculty colleagues had indeed taken up the offer and left – some to more rewarding posts abroad, others to use their lifetime of research and teaching experience to take up fulfilling employment in restaurants or garden centres. As a result, during the first years of the 1980s, I had watched myself gradually turning from a moderately paid academic into a highly paid clerk.

Not that I was scared of administration, you understand, or tried to avoid it. In the 1970s I had been acting head of department for three years, and I accepted that maybe a quarter of my time had to be devoted to administrative matters. That's how it had been, anyway, when I joined the service in the mid-1960s. Priority 1 was teaching and research within the university, with academic writing the other side of that coin. Priority 2 was teaching outside the university – in my case, either in schools or clinics, or through the media, such as radio. These were areas where I knew I had a contribution to make. And in those days, it was possible to take my turn in ordering books for the library, interviewing new students, representing the department at faculty meetings, working out the teaching timetable, calculating course budgets, getting in touch with external lecturers, and the hundred other tasks which a thriving university department accretes, without the priority roles being adversely affected. It was a busy – a tremendously busy – life, but that was OK – even if, at times, I had to think hard to recall exactly how many children I had.

But by the mid-1980s, this had all changed. As colleagues took 'voluntary early retirement', the administrative load increased on those who were left. The cuts in secretarial assistance meant that academics had to take on unspecialized support activities. A favourite moaning location was in the queue of lecturers waiting to use the single photocopier in the building which housed several social science departments. Had anyone written anything recently? A shaking of heads. My own big project was a language encyclopedia for Cambridge University Press. It had been commissioned in 1983, and a year later I had managed to write about a dozen pages. It wasn't going well. Nor was there any light at the end of the tunnel in the form of leave of absence. The notion of a sabbatical year didn't seem to exist at Reading. I had never had one, and it looked now as if I never would.

I very clearly remember the day I decided that I had had enough. I had spent the whole day working out how to send a cadre of third-year speech-therapy students to their various clinics, scattered in and around Berkshire, and what was the cheapest way of doing so. After a day's research into timetables, fare lists, and clinic times, I was delighted to see that I had saved the university travel budget a few pounds. Then I reflected on the true cost: one day of a professor's salary; one day of that professor not contributing, in some sense, to the sum of human knowledge – unless, of course, you count the potential contribution to some future thesis on student clinic movements. And not just one day. By 1984, about three-quarters of my time had come to be devoted to this kind of thing. The language pathology degree required liaison between departments of linguistics, psychology, and education, and several departments at local hospitals, all to be integrated with the intensive individualized clinical practice regimes for each year of students. The secretarial post which had originally been envisaged to help carry the load had been an early casualty of the cuts. Problem? Not at all. The prof can do it. That's what he's paid for.

I went home and moaned to Hilary – as I had been doing repeatedly for weeks. I spent the evening trying to find some energy to get on with the language encyclopedia; but, like other evenings, there were other things to be done. The demand for new students meant new courses, and new courses meant new lectures to be prepared. On another day, the evening might have had a different direction: answering letters – sent to the university, but processed at home, because there was no available secretarial time for handling staff personal correspondence. There had even been a memo from the head of department banning the use of departmental secretaries for that purpose. Most of these letters would have been turning down requests to speak to a group of teachers here, to give an in-service course there, to attend an academic conference somewhere else. Oh, for the luxury of a nice warm bubble-filled seminar, at which one could lie back and be soothed by the intellectual ripples. (There wouldn't have been time to think up metaphors like that, either, in those days.)

We travelled up to Holyhead for a short Easter break. And, as I had used to do in my younger days, we visited my Uncle John. A routine question about how we were getting on produced a high-quality moan. 'Well,' he said, 'why don't you quit?'

Hilary and I looked at each other, and both spoke at once and at length about how I couldn't possibly do that after all I had tenure and we had a mortgage and four mouths to feed and anyway we were in the middle of developing a new course and I'd built up this other course personally and you can't let your colleagues down and anyway – I remember concluding lamely – I don't know how to be anything else but an academic.

'What does being an academic mean?' he asked.

I told him about the priorities (as per above).

'And right now you can't do much writing, prepare your new courses properly, or do much teaching elsewhere?'

I concurred.

'So in what way are you being an academic?'

I was silent.

'It seems to me,' he went on, 'that you should get out, come up here to live, and start a new life as an academic – some sort of academic consultant, perhaps, like in my own line' (his world was marine engineering).

I said I'd never heard of such a thing and I couldn't see how one could live doing that kind of thing and would the kids want to be moved and anyway where could we live up here with all my books and there just aren't any large houses in Holyhead and it's miles from anywhere and maybe next year or the year after . . .

I can't remember all the arguments I dreamed up. I remember John shaking his head and shrugging his shoulders, as if to say 'I've done my best'. Hilary and I left, mithering on to each other. Our car was parked in the road, and we drove up to the top to turn round. It was a cul-de-sac, and on other occasions I'd always done a three-point turn to get out – but not that day. At the top, we saw a For Sale sign on a large attractive house. I'd hardly ever been to the top of that road before. When I was a child, this road was one children didn't go up much – there were rumours it was inhabited by sea captains and other dragons. I didn't know Holyhead contained such large houses.

Hilary and I looked at each other. It was one of those moments. I think we said 'should we?' or some such. We drove back down to Uncle John's. 'As a matter of interest,' we began, 'do you happen to know how much they're asking for the house at the top of the road?'

The rest is history. We went to see the house, fell in love with it, made an offer, and had it accepted. We returned to Reading, put our house on the market, and sold it within a month. As our buyer left, Hilary turned to me and said, 'Don't you think you'd better tell the Vice-Chancellor?'

Good point. But no problem. After all, the third letter had arrived not so long before, and there was a tempting financial package. Gimme, gimme. I went for it. I told my colleagues what I was doing, and made an appointment to see the VC. I explained my reasons to him, and brought out his letter. His response left me inarticulate. 'Ah, but that letter wasn't meant for you,' he said.

What he meant was that he had had to send the letter to everyone, but there were some departments which were doing very well (that is, bringing in money), and ours was one (with all those foreign students), and he didn't want to freeze posts there. If I left I would have to be replaced, ergo there is no saving for the university, ergo there is no financial package for you if you leave, mate.

Reader, I left him. I spent a fruitless couple of months trying to persuade him that this wasn't fair, but failed. I took legal advice, and was told I probably had a case, but was I prepared to spend what would be a considerable amount of time on it? I wasn't. So I just quit, and moved up to Holyhead during the summer. We'd survive somehow, Hilary and I felt, even without the package. Lucy and Ben came with us. Steven and Susie decided to stay in the south, where the jobs were. Neither wanted to go on to university. Fortunately, the house price differential between Reading and Holyhead meant that we could afford to set them up in flats. We had got a good price for the old schoolhouse, which we had spent a lot of time renovating.

It took a year to disentangle myself from Reading. I had agreed to ease the transition by carrying out some teaching commitments there on a part-time basis, especially on the clinical side. It meant commuting 250 miles from Holyhead three times a term, but at least it kept a bit of a salary coming in while I searched for work in my new capacity as – as what? What should I call myself? I first used the label 'freelance' linguist, but after a short tour of Japan in 1985 I learned a better designation. My hosts refused to introduce me to the audience as 'freelance', on the grounds that such a term better befitted journalists than respected visiting academics. They went into a huddle in the corner. Then one came over: 'We shall call you "independent scholar".' So that's what I became. 'Freelance' was dead. Another phrase I'd gone through.

LINGUIST AS INDEXER

The move from Reading also gave me the opportunity I needed to complete an index. Not one of mine. This was the index to *A Comprehensive Grammar of the English Language*, by Randolph Quirk, Sidney Greenbaum, Geoffrey Leech, and Jan Svartvik (see plate 5.1).

I had always found indexes fascinating, and had always compiled the indexes to my own books. So it was only natural to reflect on the process, and – given my applied state of mind in the early 1980s – to explore whether there were ways in which a linguistic approach could illuminate indexing principles and procedures. In 1984 I wrote an article for *The Indexer*, called 'Linguistics and indexing', and I was going on about this after a meeting of lexicographers in London when Randolph Quirk stopped me short. 'We need an index for the *Grammar*, Dave.' He said it much in the manner of Hal the computer talking to the astronaut in *2001*.

I had never thought of compiling an index for someone else, but this seemed a good opportunity to try. Also, I was really looking forward to this grammar, and doing the index would give me an intimate knowledge of it. And it was likely to be helpful. Indexes always are. They show authors just how inconsistent or repetitive they have been. They cruelly highlight gaps, false starts, and unfinished business. With four authors working on the *Grammar*, and hardly ever getting a chance to meet face-to-face (and email not yet routine), I knew there would be many problems.

I was right. I ended up doing the index twice. A preliminary index of the team's first draft of the *Grammar* brought to light hundreds of small points that needed sorting. Then, when all that was done, I did the final job. I wrote it up afterwards for *The Indexer*. The index itself got a 'highly commended' plaudit from the Library Association's Wheatley Medal committee. It was the beginning of a permanent association with the Society of Indexers. Not long after, I spent an enjoyable three years as their president.

The Linguistics Department at Bangor heard of my arrival in Holyhead, and offered me an honorary affiliation, so that I could keep in touch with the world of academe. And I did keep in touch with it. On the outside I saw the situation continue to deteriorate. Each year old friends and colleagues told me how much worse the situation had become. I could see it for myself – the vast increase in paperwork, the demand to increase student numbers without a corresponding increase in staff and resources, the huge deficits, the continuing rounds of cuts. And then, the subtle signs of British academic decay – the journals being published late, the books announced in publisher catalogues but still not appearing, the new email addresses from former colleagues now in Australia or the USA, and the continual sapping of intellectual energy. 'You were right to get out when you did,' an ex-colleague said to me a year or so after I'd left. I have heard this a thousand times, and still do. The phone rings. 'How are you, Dave?' asks a familiar academic voice. 'Fine thanks, how are you?' 'Ah, well let me tell you . . .' replies the voice, and my ear is then bent for twenty minutes as my friend tells me all about the latest awfulness to hit the academic world.

I was lucky. Very lucky. I now had the opportunity to make progress as a writer, editor, lecturer, and broadcaster – the four domains in which I had found myself working in recent years. I had a wife willing to work as a business partner with me, and she proved to be brilliant at it. In the university world, a scholar needs a registrar, bursar, catering officer, facilities manager, administrative assistant, and others to ensure a smooth life. In the independent world, who should take on those roles – along with all the PR and marketing that comes with having to literally sell yourself, and your knowledge, in a way that was alien to an academic temperament? Enter Hilary, a new career opening up before her. It is conventional, at the beginning of books, for authors to thank people for helping them. Spouses are often mentioned, and I sometimes feel that it is a token acknowledgement. But I say it as a matter of fact: I would never have been able to complete half the books I eventually managed to produce as an academic without her partnership. She is invisibly there, on every title page.

The progress was rapid. Within eighteen months I was able to finish my 1983 commission, which appeared in 1987 as *The Cambridge Encyclopedia of Language* (which I always call CEL /sel/, for short). A few years later, its sequel appeared, *The Cambridge Encyclopedia of the English Language* (known as CEEL /si:l/). One of the commonest questions I get asked is: How did these encyclopedias come about, and how long did it take to write them? Surprisingly – unlike most books, anyway – it is a very tricky question to answer.

One thing most people don't know is that there almost wasn't a CEL. The original idea for such a book came about like this. In 1980 a young relative, still at school, was thinking about what subjects to study at university. He was interested in languages, so he asked me for advice. Was there an interesting book on linguistics and languages which he could read – something which would be intelligible, encyclopedic – with pictures in it, maybe? The pictures seemed to be the critical thing, as far as he was concerned.

I looked along my shelves, and couldn't see anything. At the same time, while looking, I found splendid illustrated guides to all kinds of other subjects – on mythology, for example, with plenty of accessible text and a liberal use of illustrations. Yigael Yadin's marvellously illustrated *The Art of Warfare in Biblical Lands*, where each page was a beautiful balance of text and picture. But on language, nothing. 'Why not?' I thought. I remembered a lovely book that had been compiled for the MacDonald Illustrated Library in 1967, edited by Sir Gerald Barry, with the help of Bronowski, Huxley, and others – *Communication and Language*. That was almost four hundred pages, and full of pictures; but they took communication in its broadest sense, including sections on theatre, music, drama, the press, film, and so on. There was very little on language in the linguistics sense.

So I put together a one-page proposal, and based my argument on two main points, which I now quote:

> I am struck by (a) a massive modern interest in the subject of language, communication, usage, etc., illustrated at popular level by such TV programmes as *Call My Bluff* and *Blankety Blank*, and radio series like *Speak Out*, and (b) the trend in publishing towards illustrated guides, of the Octopus Books, Mitchell Beazley type, the sort of thing that makes excellent Xmas presents. It ought to be possible to bring these two points together.
>
> Language is ideally suited for visual and popular treatment. This might sound odd at first, as people often think of language as an essentially oral/aural medium – speech – which by its nature isn't visual. The fallacy is to think of language as divorced from the people who use it. Rather, language reflects the society, the people who use it. It has no existence apart from them. To photograph language, you photograph the people and places in which it is used, their products and conflicts, their ways of studying language. You also, of course, include the more obviously visual side of language – written language and its derivative codes.

Coincidentally, my brother-in-law Martin worked for Octopus, one of the leading popular-guides publishers, so I sent this in to him, for an opinion. Not a chance, he said. Far too academic. Sorry. I then sent it to Edward Arnold, who I was sure would see the point. No question, they said. Far too popular. Sorry. I decided the time wasn't right, and put the proposal into a bottom drawer, joining several other mouldering proposals, and got on with something else. *CEL* was moribund. But I didn't forget about it.

Fast forward now to early 1983, when I found myself in a meeting about linguistics journals with Penny Carter of Cambridge University Press. *The Journal of Child Language* was doing very well. Might there be others? We talked about a possible educational linguistic journal, and a clinical one. I floated the idea for a journal called *Language Today* – on analogy with *History Today*. (It eventually appeared as *English Today*.) Only at the end did the conversation turn to other possible projects. I mentioned one or two of the things I had lurking in the bottom drawer, and the idea of the language encyclopedia came up. It turned out that various people in CUP had been thinking along similar lines, and she asked me to send in the material I had. I cleaned off the dust.

I was asked to develop the one-page proposal, and it became a twelve-page prospectus. We had a long meeting in which we discussed the best way to handle it. Should it be a single-authored work, or an edited book with several contributors? The arguments in favour of the former were individual creativity and stylistic consistency; the arguments against were the dangers of personal bias and the difficulties in covering such a vast field. We agreed on a middle road: I would write the book, but would have available an international advisory board who would read all the material. *CEL* was finally commissioned in June 1983.

Penny Carter described it as 'one of the most interesting and exciting projects' she'd been involved with. That reaction was crucial, for me. I was well aware that such a proposal would only succeed if it had an enthusiastic press behind it, for the page design and picture research would make major demands on their personnel. It would, in a very real sense, be a collaboration between author and designer.

I decided to use the double-page spread as the chief means of organizing information. I felt it should be possible to treat a topic succinctly, and illustrate it well, within a single opening. Readers should be given the impression that, when they open the book, they can see a topic laid out accessibly before them. So there would be no sentence run-ons as you turn the page. Each verso would present a fresh topic, or a fresh subdivision of a topic. But working with double-page spreads and illustrations is a pain. The temptation is to write too much text and leave too little space for the picture. I had a terrible habit of leaving only a postage-stamp size for the picture. The designer, Roger Walker, trained it out of me, but it took a while. I paid for it dearly, by having to delete chunks of text from my drafts. And there is nothing worse than having to lose text you have slaved over.

The way the collaboration worked was like this. Roger gave me a grid, which I set up on my word processor (available at last!) – so many characters per line, so many lines per column, two main columns and one sidebar per page, and so on. A main chapter heading would use up five lines of text from my column; a sub-heading would use three lines. A certain number of lines would be taken up by the picture(s). The remainder is the amount of text you are permitted to write – usually around a thousand words per page.

It was never possible to get a perfect match on first draft, because the letter-spacing on a word processor is not the same as that on a printed page – so there were always extra lines to be added or taken away, to ensure that the exposition came to an end as close to the bottom of the page as possible. Some of the design sessions were like horse-trading. Can I have two extra lines of text if you crop that picture a bit more? Please!!

I planned a writing schedule with the Press, and started on the job in the autumn of 1983. My proposal had said it would take 'one or two years'. Six months later, as you know, I'd written less than a dozen pages. If I stayed in the full-time university world, there would be no encyclopedia, and not much else either, it seemed to me. It was time to choose. But in a way I had no choice. The encyclopedia had become one of those projects which fill the mind. Supported by the enthusiasm of the people at CUP, I was more convinced than ever that such a book would meet a real need. I wanted to immerse myself in it – and once we'd moved house, I could. By the autumn of 1984 I was working seriously on the project, spending about half my time on it. I carried on in this way through 1985, and by mid-1986 the writing was very largely done – though many changes had to be made as proofs came through, and design drafts had to be rethought. The book eventually came out in November 1987 (see plate 11.1).

It did very well, and after a few years the Press was beginning to think that perhaps a follow-up book would do just as well. *The Cambridge Encyclopedia of the English Language* wasn't my idea: it was the inspiration of Adrian du Plessis, the director of Cambridge Reference. He suggested it in 1989, and as soon as he had done so it seemed an obvious project. Moreover, there had been a change of mood at the Press about encyclopedia-type projects which made the project even more attractive. Full colour was on the table – and a more expensive jacket (see plate 10.3).

Rewind a decade. When CUP took on CEL they had done so with enthusiasm – but also with caution. As nobody had published such a book before, there was a concern to keep the costs well under control. The price of pictures was phenomenal, for example. To use just one *Snoopy* cartoon or a single frame from a movie would cost about £100 each.

When I proposed to use a picture of Yoda from *Star Wars*, the price went way above the Press's budget. I had to make a special case. I was told that one of the Syndics (the Press's academic committee) enquired, a mite cynically, 'Is this the first time the Press has published a picture of a little green man?' I wasn't present at the meeting. If I had been, I would have referred him to Gawain and the Green Knight. But fortunately I was allowed my picture, and Yoda is there now, illustrating unusual word order in the English clause (*Full of the force I am*).

The caution was chiefly shown in the colour treatment – or rather, the lack of it. I wanted the book to be in full colour – not just to motivate young people to read it, but also because of the expressive possibilities. Maps, for example, can really only be done in four colours. But full colour was felt to be excessive, and we settled for the limited use of a second colour, red. It did present problems – not least by having to explain in a caption, from time to time, what the colours were in a picture which depended on them for its effect. There's a picture of television subtitling in a game show, for example, in which the contrast is totally dependent on colour: yellow for the game show host, green for the competitor. It's spelled out painfully in the caption.

But CEL had done so well that the market for an English-language equivalent seemed assured, and the Press was confident that a full-colour book would be viable. And once you have colour at your disposal, throughout a book, you would be a fool not to make as much use of it as possible. That is why CEEL has so many more illustrations than the first edition of CEL, and why there are so many full-page illustrations. Black-and-white reproductions often fail to convey the relevant information, especially in historical texts. I remember going through my whole undergraduate career wondering what a page of the *Anglo-Saxon Chronicle* really looked like.

So I was keen to get going on CEEL, and worked up a prospectus and some sample spreads in early 1990. Then other encyclopedias got in the way, as a later chapter will explain, and it didn't prove possible to get on with CEEL until the middle of 1992. These editorial projects meant that CEEL could be only a half-time commitment, more or less, and it took me a good two years before the book was complete.

The book was written 'left-to-right'. I started on page 1 and worked through until the end. At the same time, the spreads, as they were completed, were sent to the press for typesetting, so that the pictures could be sized and the text trimmed as we went along. We had learned from the CEL experience that this was likely to be a more efficient production process – and so it proved to be. But from an authorial point of view, it was trickier.

It meant that the content of each page, and the sequence of pages, had to be worked out very precisely in advance. There would be no opportunity to revise the earlier pages at a later stage. It was an unusual experience – to be writing page 150, for instance, while page 1 was in proof and being indexed – and it was a challenge for the in-house production controller to keep up with where everything was. But it worked – though I have to admit that Part VI, the final section of *CEEL*, is shorter than it was supposed to be. I just ran out of pages.

Then the wheel turned full circle. In 1997 appeared the second edition of *CEL*. And what is the main difference between the two editions? The use of colour. The appearance of colourful *CEEL* had immediately made the second-colour *CEL* seem dull, by comparison. It had been almost a decade since the first edition, and the subject had moved on. So when the decision was made to have a new edition, I was at last offered the full colour I had originally hoped for. All the pictures had to be researched again, of course, but the result was most rewarding. At last the maps look right. And you can see the subtitle contrast between the words of the game show host and those of the competitor straight away. Those early green ideas – to adapt that linguistic catch-phrase again – are now most colourful, and no longer sleeping furiously.

CEL and *CEEL* together have helped us pay the mortgage. But we didn't know that in 1984, when I made the decision to go freelance – sorry, independent. It was going to be a risk, undoubtedly. There's nothing quite so unnerving as *not* having a salary cheque come through the post at the end of a month, when you've been used to one for the past twenty years. And once you decide to earn a living as a writer, there is a delay before you get a return – and of course there may never be a return. So it was important to find ways of earning a living. I had to cost out my time now. Projects which didn't pay, such as book reviewing or editing the *Journal of Child Language*, would have to stop. I waved a wistful farewell to the child language research world with a Penguin book, *Listen to Your Child*, in 1986. Child language. Another phrase.

Some people, when they leave the academic mainstream, earn a living by writing novels or plays or poetry. I'd tried my hand at that and been found wanting. I was already a failed radio playwright, a failed television playwright, and a failed crime novelist. These experiments had arisen in 1983. I had needed something to get me away from the administrative grind which was becoming the day-to-day norm in the university. Even linguistics could be uninspiring after a not-so-nice day in the office. So whenever I had a spare moment I turned to fiction. I wrote a radio play and sent it in to a Radio 4 competition. It didn't get anywhere, but I'd very much enjoyed the experience of writing it, so I tried television next. I learned how to set out a script, worked up a story, and sent one in. No thanks. I tried a different channel. No thanks. I tried with a second play. No thanks. It was dawning on me that maybe this was not my métier. But it was still fun trying. Maybe a brilliant future lay in other genres? A meeting with one of the publishers at Edward Arnold, whose spare-time work involved vetting crime novels, led to a dare: she bet I couldn't write one. She lost her bet. I did. But then she won it, for when she read my draft she thought it was awful. She was right. I was no good at character description or atmosphere setting – both pretty important elements of a crime novel, it has to be said. I should have remembered that from my earlier attempt at being a novelist.

I was running out of creative genres. Perhaps I should go back to my roots. I had, after all, written an acclaimed (albeit by undergraduates) play, and been recognized (albeit by Montfort missionaries) as a precocious teenage short-story writer. And I had been an infants school poet. Maybe there were genes there just gagging to be activated? I did eventually manage two slim volumes of devotional poetry. No money in poetry, though. The short-story energy I directed into an ambitious scheme to foster language awareness in children through fiction. It was called DIAL, 'Developing Ideas About Language', and it introduced the world to Wiggle the Wizard and his associates. My, what larks he got up to, as he tangled with sounds and letters and words and grammar! Harry Potter, eat your forthcoming heart out! If my scheme had gone ahead, I might well have retired to the Bahamas then and there. And it nearly did. Edward Arnold took it up, then decided it wasn't marketable. Macmillan took it up, then decided it wasn't marketable. Looking back now, I can see that it was all too soon. Language awareness in schools was not yet at the right temperature. The language-conscious National Curriculum was still several years away.

That first year out without a salary was tough. We got through it thanks to a combination of factors. Bangor asked me to do some part-time lecturing. My earlier books for Penguin, Edward Arnold, and André Deutsch were bringing in some royalties. There were new editions of *What is Linguistics?* (see plate 10.1), the Penguin *Linguistics*, and the *Dictionary of Linguistics*. And the regular broadcasting helped. The new child therapy journal had begun, and that brought a small editor's honorarium. So did a consultancy for the new magazine *English Today*, which Tom McArthur was editing. Blackwell, having noted the extraordinary proliferation of linguistic journals during the previous decade, was thinking of a new abstracting journal for linguistics. Psychology had its abstracting periodicals – why not linguistics? I put together a proposal for what became *Linguistics Abstracts*, and that carried an honorarium too. Uncle John had been right. Once people heard that there was a linguist available for consultancy-type work, they were in touch. As a result, it became a curiously mixed year. One week it might be a review of a proposal for some publisher. The next a forensic linguistic examination of a piece of evidence on behalf of a solicitor or the police. The next an index. By the end of the year, Hilary pasted a piece of paper across my phone. It said simply: 'Say NO'.

Every little helped, as they say. But an 'every big' would help more, we thought. And that turned up, quite unexpectedly, in the middle of 1986.

Chapter 17
The encyclopedia game

I had expected to be a full-time, albeit independent, linguist when I left Reading. The editing, writing, lecturing, and broadcasting were all pointing me in the same direction: tell the world all about language, and its study, and its applications. I still thought of myself as mainly an applied linguist, but the language encyclopedia and *Linguistics Abstracts* were keeping my feet firmly on 'pure' ground. Still, pure or applied, it was going to be linguistics for me. And then a letter arrived.

It was from Jeremy Mynott, managing director of Cambridge University Press. In 1986 CUP had decided to enter into a joint venture with the Edinburgh firm of W. & R. Chambers to produce a range of fresh titles, including a single-volume general encyclopedia. Chambers had a long and illustrious history of reference publishing. Their original encyclopedia had been published in 520 parts in the mid-nineteenth century, but the firm hadn't produced a new edition for some time, and had limited contacts outside the UK. CUP had no tradition of encyclopedia or dictionary publishing, but a worldwide marketing and sales operation. It seemed to be a good marriage. And now they were looking for a general editor.

Had I seen the advertisement? I hadn't. Might I be interested? I might. 'But I don't know anything about general encyclopedia editing,' I said to Jeremy over the phone a couple of days later. 'Nor does anyone else,' he replied. 'But,' I persisted, 'what qualifications do you need to have to be an encyclopedia editor?' There was a silence at the other end of the phone. Then: 'I'm not entirely sure . . . but it does help if you've written an encyclopedia.'

Jeremy and I met for lunch with Bill Henderson, the managing director of Chambers, and I began to see what was involved. An editor needed to have two chief qualities, and I seemed to have both of them. First, the ability to manage large quantities of data coming in from diverse sources. I knew I could do that. Any linguist would be able to do that. Second, have wide-ranging interests, or at least a curiosity about everything, or at least an absence of antipathy towards a particular subject. That was especially important. No good having an editor who couldn't stand maths or religion or socialism or alternative medicine or new-age beliefs, or (at a different level) who hated Keynesian economics or Chomskyan politics. Suddenly my ecumenical days in the Reading chaplaincy seemed to have special relevance.

As I travelled back home after our lunch, I had a Pauline moment. Here was someone offering me the chance to study – everything. And offering me the equivalent of half a salary to do it. It was an offer I couldn't refuse. All academics have their chosen profession, but many I suspect at some point look with envious curiosity at colleagues in other disciplines and wonder what it would be like to enter their world. Here was a chance to enter all possible worlds, for it was to be a *general* encyclopedia – the sort of book you would pull down from the shelf to check a point about, well, anything. And the project had solid financial support. There were funds available for computers, secretarial help (wow!), and an assistant editor, as well as to cover all the writing that would have to be done. The book would contain over a million words. There would be a lot of writing and editing. Hilary and I talked it over. This would be a joint venture for us too. We took it on. A general encyclopedia. Another phrase to be going through.

It was the beginning of a new era, though I could never have guessed how life-changing the decision would prove to be. For the next twenty-two years I was going to be intellectually split: half of me would stay being a linguist; the other half would inhabit a world of facts and events, results and records, days and dates, biographies and obituaries. I was going to be geographically split, too, for Chambers was going to look after the entire editorial production of the encyclopedia, and they were in Edinburgh. I found myself up there every few months – not the easiest of trips from Holyhead. Anyone who lives in North Wales soon develops a love–hate affair with Crewe station, depending on whether they make their connections or not; now I had one with Waverley station too. On the plus side, a couple of the meetings took place in August, which was Edinburgh Festival time, and a good excuse for a family break.

'How do you edit an encyclopedia?' It's one of the commonest questions I get asked. The first task was to see what one-volume encyclopedias were already out there. No point in rediscovering the wheel. A new encyclopedia had to be different and distinctive. So I spent an unmerry Christmas reading through the books already being produced by Macmillan, Hutchinson, and Columbia. It did not make good reading. The Columbia was wholly American: lots of details about the battles of the American Civil War; nothing at all on the English ones. And none of the books was truly international. I looked for information about China, where most things seem to have originated. There was next to nothing. Huge chunks of the world were represented only by their country and city entries. And above all, concepts were missing. If you were interested in the notions which drove such fields as politics, economics, and sociology – let alone linguistics – you would get little help from these works. An encyclopedia associated with CUP, it seemed to me, should be strong on internationalism and important abstract notions. It ought to be possible to write short and accessible entries on difficult topics, rather than just leave them out. Would it be possible to cover genetic engineering or special relativity or ergonomics in a couple of hundred well-chosen words? I knew it could be done for linguistics, so why not in other subjects?

I worked out a subject scheme, dividing life, the universe, and everything up into around a hundred subject areas. Each area had to be covered for topics, people, and places. For people and places, I had a head start. The joint venture with Chambers gave me access to the latest edition of the *Chambers Biographical Dictionary* and the new *Chambers World Gazetteer*. All I had to do there was make a selection, and get it checked for up-to-dateness and representativeness with my contributors. Problem: I didn't have any contributors. How on earth to find them? In a few cases, it would be obvious. Space exploration? There was sure to be someone in NASA who knew something about that. Birds and bees? The Natural History Museum. But medicine? Economics? Transport? The Middle East? And who on earth to ask about sport?

This was where the enormous breadth of CUP's publishing list proved of value. I asked their commissioning editors who was who, in the different subject areas. More to the point, I asked them who they thought would be able to write well at this level. Not surprisingly, they suggested I look to museums rather than universities wherever possible. Experience proved them right. Curators spend their lives trying to make their collections intelligible to the general public. Academics only sometimes. And bingo! It turned out that CUP had already contracted Roger Lincoln from the Natural History Museum in London to write something. I was on to him like a flash. He invited me up to the museum, and before I knew it I had all my natural history entries covered by a team from there. That was a major step forward, for natural history was, I soon discovered, the largest section in a work like this. There are just so many darned species.

Why was the museum so willing to collaborate? Roger explained: the museum needed as much good press as it could get. Like universities, they had been hit by funding cuts, and the Thatcher government had introduced admission fees. The museum needed to maintain a high public profile, and a collaboration with a prestigious encyclopedia project – Cambridge University Press, after all – was a good way of doing it. The Science Museum in London proved similarly helpful, providing a team to cover another large field, from combustion engines to tuning forks. And, surprisingly, so did NASA. I rang them up one day and introduced myself. They put me through to their PR unit. It transpired that they were in the same boat: for Thatcher, read Reagan. Some of their projects (such as the space station) were under threat. They wanted to keep their public profile high. The *Challenger* space shuttle disaster had been a major setback in January 1986. A call from an encyclopedia editor a year later might not be much, but it was a small step forward for them. And a giant leap for me. Geoffrey Briggs, the director of NASA's solar system exploration programme, wrote my entries.

And kept them up-to-date. The final proofs were just going to press, in the summer of 1989, when the phone rang. It was Geoff, highly excited. *Voyager* 2 was just passing Neptune, the first spacecraft to observe the planet. New stuff was coming in daily. Could I hold the entry on Neptune? I could. And a few days later, in came a revised version incorporating the latest data on the planet. The *Encyclopedia* duly appeared three months later, and for just a fragment of time, in that tiny respect, I knew my book was ahead of the rest of the reference world. That's the sort of thing that makes encyclopedia editing worth while.

Mind you, if you had to choose a year *not* to be editing the final draft of an encyclopedia, it would have to be 1989. All encyclopedia editors want is a quiet life, ideally no change, or as little as possible. Deaths are a pain, because you have to add an extra line or two to an entry on an already full page (or, in the case of a Robert Maxwell, several lines). Nobel prizes are a pain, because the reason for the prize can't usually be explained briefly. But revolutions! Nobody wants revolutions. Especially not just before final-proof date.

It became funny after a while. The drop-dead deadline (so-called because if an editor asks for extra time after that point, he knows what the response will be) cannot be missed. Too much hangs on it. The window booked at the printers; the announcement in the catalogue; the marketing campaign; the distribution to bookshops. Nothing short of an event of worldwide significance can alter it. But one thing is absolutely certain with encyclopedia publishing: a month, or a week, or a few days before this deadline, that event will take place. Our final deadline was always in October or November. I got so used to something catastrophic happening during the late summer that I asked for the deadline for later editions to be changed to May.

Here is the evidence, from my diary entries of the time. My deadline for the first edition of the *Encyclopedia* is 15 November 1989. On 9 November the East Germans open the Berlin Wall. I manage to postpone the deadline for a fortnight, to see what happens. Just as I think that's it, the Communist Party leadership resigns in Czechoslovakia. I just manage to get it in. The last line in the entry on Czech history reads: 'Continued strong protest movement culminated in the fall from power of the Communist Party in 1989.' That went in the day before the book began to print.

A year later I am in an identical position, as the deadline for the first updated reprint approaches – the end of October 1990. So what happens? On 3 October, the two Germanies unite. That means 700 consequential changes have to be made, as all contemporary references to East and West Germany are now out of date. It isn't something that can be done automatically, by search and replace, as several of the references are historical and have to stay. There is no alternative. Some mug (aka editor) is going to have to go through and change each one by hand. The Press puts the deadline back to the last day of November. And then, on 28 November, Mrs Thatcher resigns. I took that very personally.

A year later, and I am in an even worse position. The second updated reprint now, with a deadline of the end of October 1991. On 19 August there is a coup in the Soviet Union. I prepare for the worst. A few days later, the status quo is restored, and I breathe a sigh of relief. But my sigh is premature. In September the independence of the Baltic States is recognized. In October the KGB is abolished. The Press agrees to postpone until the end of November. On 4 November, almost all Soviet Union Ministries are abolished. The Soviet Union is fragmenting. I see over a thousand references to the USSR falling around me like autumn leaves. For a brief moment, there is optimism: on 14 November, agreement is announced that the USSR will be replaced by a Union of Sovereign States – editorially a superb decision, as USSR to USS will mean a change of only one letter. But a week is a long time in encyclopedia editing. On 25 November, seven republics refuse to initial the treaty. The Press, reluctantly, but sensing a moment of history, agrees to postpone the deadline to the end of December. Perhaps USSR will stay?

I try to find out, and telephone the Soviet embassy in London to ask what they intend to call the USSR, and could I have it in English and in Russian, please? They ask me if I want a visa. I repeat the question. They tell me that it is the Western press which has published the new name (USS), not the Soviets, and that I should phone the Novosti Press Agency. Novosti does not know what the name will be either, but suggest that if I *must* go into print perhaps *ex-USSR* will do? The Novosti spokesman cannot help with the Russian spelling, as he does not speak Russian, and in any case the agency is closing at the end of the month. He gives me the number of the Society for Cultural Relations with the USSR. They are not answering the phone. I have a brainwave: I will phone the Foreign and Commonwealth Office. They will know. They advise me to continue using USSR; there will definitely be no change of name before Christmas. A week later, the Commonwealth of Independent States is proposed, and on 20 December, Soviet embassies all over the world are told to strike the name 'Soviet Union' from their records. My drop-dead deadline is 1 January. It cannot be postponed any further. I have a busy Christmas eliminating a thousand references to the USSR. But then a quandary: dare I write an entry informing the readership of the reprinted *Encyclopedia* (due out mid-1992) that there exists an entity called the Commonwealth of Independent States (CIS)? Dare I write such an entry under 'C'? I dare. In such a manner do encyclopedia editors impose structure on the world.

LINGUIST AS SPYMASTER

Conspiracy theorists might view the CIS story differently. You will recall that there were spies at Cambridge: the 'Cambridge Four' were Kim Philby, Donald Maclean, Guy Burgess, and Anthony Blunt. Some people think there was a Cambridge 'five' or even more. But nobody, as far as I know, has ever suggested that there was a plant at Cambridge University Press.

There must have been. How else can the facts be explained? My theory is this. The Russians are in a turmoil after the events of November 1991. They do not know what to call the new country. This new name CIS has been proposed, but not everyone likes it. Then in January there is a call from their man in Cambridge. 'I have seen the proofs of the next edition of *The Cambridge Encyclopedia*,' he says, 'and they contain an entry on the Commonwealth of Independent States!' He goes on: 'They would not have put this in if they did not know something that we do not know.' The Russians see the wisdom of this remark, and immediately authorize the formal use of the designation.

Nobody ever discovered the CUP plant. Nor has anyone found the message which would provide the evidence supporting this account. But it will be found one day. And in the meantime I humbly accept the view of those who say that I am personally responsible for the final dissolution of the Soviet Union.

Humility is important, if you are going to edit encylopedias. You mustn't let things go to your head, as they easily could. After all, you edit God. But humility is guaranteed by the typos and other glitches that swarm about your eyes. Some you catch. Was Beethoven handicapped by deadness? Was there an American Civil Wart? We caught those. But an infuriating few will always get through into the published edition. There is nothing more humbling than to read an entry that you have sweated blood over, and see a spelling eror or a mi-splaced hyphen. Crystal's Law again. All this was before the days of spelling checkers, of course. But even today, these checkers won't always help. *Wart* is a perfectly respectable English word, and no spelling checker is intelligent enough to know that there was never a civil one.

The first edition of *The Cambridge Encyclopedia* came out in 1990. It sold well, got excellent reviews, and picked up a reference publishing award. CUP decided to go for a *Concise* edition in 1992. Then a *Paperback* edition and a *Factfinder* in 1993. Then a *Biographical Encyclopedia* in 1994. Then a *Biographical Dictionary* in 1996. Each went into further editions (see plate 10.5). It was like a family of new-born birds in a nest, each one squawking for individual attention. My team had rapidly grown. In addition to Hilary, we had data inputters, another assistant editor, and a technical officer. How to handle all the data? The computational side was primitive in the extreme when we began: the first edition was composed on an Olivetti M24, with a disk size of 128 kilobytes. When it was full, we had to send the whole machine away to get extra storage space. And once, on the way back, they dropped it (at Crewe station). It cost us a two-month delay. Fortunately, the computers soon got bigger, and the data management system (a splendid package called Inmagic) more sophisticated. More editors came along as the projects increased. We had to build an extension at the back of the house for them. At its peak in the 2000s there were twelve people working in our home. We were a veritable encyclopedia factory, at the top of a house at the top of a cul-de-sac in Holyhead. All rather Johnsonian, I thought.

It was hard work. To meet the deadlines, on more than one occasion Hilary and I would work through the night. Once, when there was a postal strike, the motorcyclist was scheduled to arrive to take the final proofs to the printers at nine in the morning, and we finished putting in the last corrections at half past eight. The tiredness from such a marathon lasts for days. I call it encyclopedia lag.

Everyone was interested in this home-based business in Holyhead. Even the milkman would enquire how the encyclopedia was going. The tabloids took an interest – though, it has to be said, not so much to enquire about the intellectual problems involved in encyclopedia editing as to find out whether the tough regime was affecting our marriage. So did the Holyhead Rotary Club. Indeed, they thought they were on to a good thing. There was a Rotary quiz, and they figured that if I was coopted on to the team, they were bound to win. But I was a disaster. What they had not taken into account is that encyclopedia editors train themselves not to remember anything. While you are editing entry P you focus entirely on that entry. After all, one day this entry could be the sole reason for someone looking in the encyclopedia, so it has to be as perfect as you can make it. For a moment of time, you remember everything that is in that entry. Then you move on to entry Q, and forget entry P. You put it out of your mind. It could interfere with your editing style otherwise. So a typical quiz dialogue went like this, after asking a question:

Quizmaster: Do you know the answer?
DC: Yes.
Quizmaster: Well, are you going to tell it to me?
DC: No.
Quizmaster: Why not?
DC: I can't remember it.
Quizmaster: So you don't know the answer, then.
DC: I do. After all, I've edited the answer. It's in my encyclopedia. Can I look it up?
Quizmaster: !

That's the best definition of an encyclopedia editor. Someone who knows where to look things up.

A rather more august occasion was an invitation in 1992 to give one of the Friday evening discourses at the Royal Institution (RI) in London on the subject of editing encyclopedias. That was a unique occasion, for two reasons. It was the only time outside of a broadcasting studio where I had to give a talk in which seconds counted; and it was the only time I've ever been locked up for lecturing.

The time-constraint tradition was started by Michael Faraday. The lecture had to last exactly one hour, no more, no less. You start as the clock strikes nine and you must finish as it strikes ten. Thanks to my broadcasting work, I could handle that. I have never overrun a lecture time. If you want me to talk for thirty-nine minutes, or forty-seven, that is what you will get. It's a rebuff to the audience, and an insult to following speakers, if you ramble on out of control. So I finished on the last stroke of the clock, as required, and got approving nods from the audience cognoscenti.

The other thing that made the occasion unique was being locked up before the lecture began. I had joined my RI hosts for dinner beforehand. With five minutes to go, I was disconcerted to find a burly sergeant-at-arms behind me. He took me by the shoulder and led me into a side room near the famous steeply tiered lecture theatre (the one often seen on television, especially when the RI has its Christmas Lectures). He then withdrew and locked me in. With just half a minute to go before nine o'clock, the door was unlocked, I was taken by the shoulder again and led to the closed double-doors into the lecture theatre. As the clock struck its first stroke, he opened the doors, and I was thrust into the room. Another great tradition. It seems that when these discourses first began, a lecturer who had been invited to speak took fright when he entered the theatre and saw the elite scientists of London on all sides of him. He turned and fled. Since then, visiting lecturers have been closely guarded.

Did my background in linguistics help at all, during the encyclopedia years? Yes, in several ways. This was very much a text-based encyclopedia family. Illustrations were few. Most of the work, accordingly, was a close examination of the entries submitted by the various contributors to ensure they made sense and were stylistically appropriate. I didn't want a bland entry style, with all subjects treated in the same way. I wanted the entries to reflect the style associated with the area to which they belonged. Natural history entries had to reflect the elliptical style typical of museum captions. This entry for *rook*, for example:

> A crow native to Europe, Asia and N Africa; black with pale bare patch on face; inhabits open country; omnivorous; forms dense nesting colonies in trees (*rookeries*). *Corvus frugilegus*.

By contrast, an entry in, say, art history would be more leisurely and vivid, as in this sentence from the entry on Jan van Goyen:

> Church towers, castles, and windmills punctuate his small, carefully painted scenes, based on pen-and-ink drawings made while travelling.

And the entry on limericks was a limerick:

> The limerick, it would appear,
> Is a verse form we owe Edward Lear:
> Two long and two short
> Lines rhymed, as was taught,
> And a fifth just to bring up the rear.

Thanks to Damien Grant, for that one.

All the child language considerations, used in my *Databank* days, came back into play. I found myself restructuring sentences to make them easier to process. Finding alternative phrasings. Substituting easier words for jargon. Everything had to be checked with the contributor, of course. Change the language, however subtly, and you change the thought. And often I would enter into a sequence which went something like this:

- The chemistry contributor would send in an entry which I couldn't understand – all about solutes and solvents, for instance.
- I would revise it into intelligible English, without really knowing what a solute or a solvent was.
- I would get a letter back from the contributor, complimenting me on my good English but regretting my bad chemistry. He would tweak my version.
- I still couldn't understand it, so back went the entry with my tweaks.
- He would return it with his tweaks.

Eventually we were both satisfied. The process might take a month or more. Today, email exchanges would make it all happen in a day. Not so then. That is one reason why the first edition of *The Cambridge Encyclopedia* took three years to prepare.

You may have noticed that *Chambers* has dropped out of the title. The books in the end did not use – as originally planned – the combined description of *Chambers/Cambridge*. That's because the joint venture had collapsed in 1989, when Chambers was taken over by the French publishing company Groupe de la Cité, which also owned Larousse. With a new source of encyclopedic material now available to them, a relationship with Cambridge was no longer critical. There was an amicable divorce. I was fortunately able to continue working with my in-house development editor at Chambers, Min Lee, but the final design, printing, and marketing of the book became solely CUP's baby.

The marketing slogan which introduced the encyclopedias to the world was 'like no other'. Nor were the venues. The CUP marketing team took the encyclopedias on a huge roadshow in 1994. I talked about them in some very strange places – next to a sherry barrel in Harvey's Wine Museum in Bristol, under an aeroplane wing in a museum in Manchester, in front of a locomotive at a transport museum in Birmingham, surrounded by some stunning art from the Burrell Collection in Glasgow – and, of course, at the Press's own bookshop in Cambridge, where with all the stock around it was like talking in a palace of encyclopedias.

The divorce had a major consequence for me. The post-nuptial agreement was a curious one. Both sides were allowed to have access to the database which I was compiling in Holyhead. Cambridge would produce the *Encyclopedia*, but Chambers would be allowed also to produce reference works from the database, as long as the content was at least one-third different from the Cambridge product. And conversely. If Cambridge wanted to produce other reference works from the database, the content would need to differ by at least a third from anything Chambers might by then have produced. It sounded like a simple idea, but how to put it into practice? The only person who knew the database intimately was me. I suddenly found myself, unexpectedly, in quite a powerful position. If Cambridge wanted to use the database, they would have to go through me. And if Chambers wanted to use the database, they would have to go through me. And that is what happened. For the next few years, I found myself both a general editor for Cambridge and a non-executive director on the Chambers board, advising on the possible uses of the database for them.

Surprisingly, there was no immediate conflict of interest. Chambers didn't want to compete with the big encyclopedia; rather, they wanted me to look at ways of developing encyclopedic dictionaries based on various Larousse publications. Plans were made for new and more specific projects – an encyclopedia of the environment, a Celtic encyclopedia, an encyclopedia of Europe. They liked the idea of small books derived from the database, such as *Nineties Knowledge*. And I started a new series, called *Making Sense of English in . . . Alternative Medicine, Money Matters, the Law, Religion, Sex* . . . Cambridge weren't interested in that level of publishing. And when the intentions of the two firms did start to overlap, it proved easy to maintain the 'third different' principle. That is why the later CUP book is called the *Cambridge Biographical Encyclopedia*, and not . . . *Dictionary* – to keep it clearly different from the *Chambers Biographical Dictionary*. I added thematic essays, timelines, photographs, and a large ready-reference section to make up that 'third' of difference. Fifteen years on, and looking at such pairs of works as the two biographical books, or the Cambridge and

Chambers *Factfinders*, it is possible to see (in the manner of a comparative philologist) that the books derive from some common source. The overlap in content, it has to be said, did confuse some readers, who naturally thought that one firm had stolen from the other. But as time went by, the differences became greater, with fresh editorial hands taking the books in new directions. It's history now, anyway. As of 2008, that common source no longer exists – but more of that later.

The publication of the *Encyclopedia* had one other unexpected, dramatic, and altogether delightful consequence. When you write books, with an unusual name like mine, you quite often get letters from people who say they have the same surname and wonder if we are related. As we probably aren't, I usually write back expressing polite but doubtful interest, and then hear no more. But the letter that arrived on 31 January 1991 felt different. It was from a legal chambers in Gray's Inn, London.

> Dear Professor Crystal
> My family (Licia my wife, and our two children Ben and Sara) and I think that the Cambridge Encyclopedia is absolutely marvellous!
> I believe that you and I may be related.
> With kind regards,
> Michael Crystal

I sent an unusually long letter back, giving an outline of my background, and told him my father's name. By return I received a fax along with a copy of a page from the 1991 *Who's Who*. There was my entry, and alongside mine, Michael's. Both entries solemnly said 's[on] of Samuel Cyril Crystal'. It transpired that Michael – evidently a late developer – had got into *Who's Who* a few years after me, when he became a QC, and had noticed my entry alongside his. For my part, having already performed that rite of passage and never having become a serial reader of biographies, I was totally unaware of his entry. I must say I had never thought of that worthy book as a means of making relationships. A marketing opportunity missed, surely?

We arranged to meet at the RAC Club in Pall Mall in early March, and during lunch there was a point where I was accumulating relatives at an average rate of one every five minutes (see plate 7.5). Michael, it transpired, had a brother Jonathan. Both of them were barristers. They had a half-brother, Zvi, a businessman who lived in the USA. This was where I learned that Cyril had another brother, Hubert, as well as Boris. Boris and Cyril had been the two doctors in Leeds. Then there were the other children – my (half-)cousins – three of Boris's and one of Hubert's. And their children. I was beginning to lose track of the names. And then I discovered that the family was Jewish.

I wasn't entirely surprised. I had been to Israel a couple of times, as guest of various English-teaching associations, and I had been struck by the fact that an awful lot of the men there looked a bit like me. My host on one occasion had actually said to me directly, 'David Crystal – that's a Jewish name, surely?' As a good Irish Catholic lad, I had denied it hotly. It seems that was premature.

I left that lunch with a minor identity crisis. I had roots in Ireland, I felt at home in Liverpool, and I was living in Wales. So now I wasn't just a Welsh Scouse Irish Catholic git, I was a Welsh Scouse Irish Catholic Jewish git. I was even more extra territorial (see p. 22) than I thought I was.

Michael and Licia were delightful, and we arranged to keep in touch. We agreed that whatever rifts had occurred in our parents' generation, and whether we would get on or not, our children's generation had a right to get to know each other. And so it proved to be. A few weeks later we visited them at their house in Rosslyn Hill in Hampstead, and during the course of 1991 the children all met each other: our Ben (Ben 1), aged 14, and theirs (Ben 2), aged 11, our Lucy (at this point aged 17) and their Sara, aged 9 – later, our Steve and Sue. The two Bens and Sara, being more of an age, became good friends.

There was some unfinished business. Early on I discussed the 'father situation' with Michael and Licia. A bridge had to be built, they agreed, but it would have to be done carefully. We decided to let the children pave the way. We arranged for Ben 1 to visit Ben 2 in London, and during the visit he would meet Cyril. It was late 1991. The timing seemed right. Hilary's father, Ken, had died in October, and Ben felt the loss keenly. Now a second grandfather was on the horizon.

But the meeting didn't happen. Ben found the prospect too daunting. Perhaps it was too soon after Ken's death. Or perhaps he was simply manifesting the same state of mind that I had experienced some twenty years before. It was, upon reflection, quite a responsibility for a fourteen-year-old. I wrote to Michael and we postponed things for a few weeks.

The next try, though, was a great success, and for an unexpected reason. We decided that Hilary and Ben should make the first move, so they travelled to London together, and stayed with Michael and Licia. Then Cyril and Ray joined them all for a meal in the local Chinese restaurant. Cyril sat next to Hilary and spent the entire meal talking to her, telling her about himself. She had a real problem trying to remember everything so that she could tell me later. And then – the bonus. Ray took a shine to

Hilary. And when my turn came, and I met Cyril and Ray a few weeks later, Ray greeted Hilary as if she was a long-lost daughter, and I basked in the warmth. We were no longer a threat.

We met several times after that (see plate 7.4). On one occasion, we arrived to find Cyril playing draughts with Ben 2. After their game was over, he invited me to take him on. I can't recall who won, or even if we finished the game. I do remember thinking: 'I'm playing with my dad.' Forty-five years later than it should have been, but still . . .

The following year was Ben's bar-mitzvah, and we were invited. There was a lunch at the Savoy in London. We walked in to find our places on the seating list, looking out for the name Crystal, and had a profound culture shock. The name was all over the room. I had never been at an event where anyone else had been called Crystal. Now virtually everyone was. We met uncles, aunts, cousins . . . We heard story after story. The older relatives remembered me very well as a baby, and also my mother, with whom, it seems, they had been good friends. An aunt even had photographs of me with both my parents. My attention was caught by one of them. It was the same photograph as the one in my mother's photograph album – only it wasn't torn down the middle (see plate 7.2). There was Cyril, in his army uniform. A khaki uniform. A tiny piece of the jigsaw of memory suddenly fell into place (p. 39).

In no time it seemed as if my new family had always been there. We visited Leeds, where Boris still lived, and Berkhamsted, where Hubert lived. Members of their family interacted with members of mine. One of Boris's children, Diana, bore a striking physical resemblance to Lucy – they could have been sisters. We found many shared interests with Michael and Licia – the arts, in particular – and now meet them regularly. They have a place near Stratford, and we often stay there, taking in a tranche of plays together at the RSC each summer. We sent everyone a copy of our Christmas letter, adding Happy Hanukkah, as required.

A final footnote. Cyril – I found it difficult referring to him as anything else – fell ill in 1999 and died later that year, at the age of 86. We all gathered for the funeral, at the Jewish cemetery near Crews Hill in Hertfordshire. After it was over, we were walking back towards the cars when Ray took me on one side. 'I am glad we met you,' she said simply.

My mother died three months later, unaware of all this activity. We had decided to respect the barrier she had placed around herself. I think if we had told her of our family discoveries she would have been very upset, perhaps even thought of it as a betrayal. It was awkward, especially for the children, finding ourselves living in two worlds that could not interact, but we had no choice. When Michael and Licia visited us in Holyhead, some years afterwards, and we introduced them to my mother's sister, Audrey, she felt we had done the right thing.

Cyril had written a short memoir for his grandchildren, telling them about his childhood and what he knew about his family history (but containing no reference to his first marriage). Boris was more of a genealogist by temperament, and had several photographs reaching back two generations. It appeared that his grandfather had fled from Lithuania with his family in the 1880s, during the time of the pogroms, and eventually settled in New Tredegar, in South Wales. His father, William, stayed there, and the Welsh accent was still very noticeable in Cyril and his brothers when I met them.

The family home in Lithuania was in the town of Vilkomir, present-day Ukmerge. So, when I had the chance to visit Lithuania for the first time, in 2005 – a lecture tour for the British Council – we built in time for a visit. Ukmerge is about an hour's drive north-east of Vilnius, the capital. And we were in the best of hands, thanks to another coincidence.

One day I received a parcel in Holyhead from Professor Dovid Katz, professor of Yiddish Studies at the University of Vilnius (see plate 8.1). It was a copy of his huge encyclopedia of Jewish Lithuania. He was a linguist by training, and he knew of my work and hoped we could meet. This might not be too difficult, he thought, as he lived just down the road. Just down the road? It was true. He lived in Dwygyfylchi ('doo-ee-guh-vul-khee') – just along the North Wales coast – about forty-five minutes' drive from Holyhead.

I couldn't work it out. What was a professor from Vilnius doing in Dwygyfylchi? We met soon afterwards. It transpired that he spent six months in Vilnius during term times, and the rest of the time in North Wales. He had visited the area some years before, and had fallen in love with it. He had a small cottage in the delightfully named Fairy Glen Road, on the way up to the Snake Pass. It was filled to the roof with old Yiddish and Hebrew books.

Dovid was fascinated to hear my story, and filled me in on the Lithuanian political and cultural background; and when he learned that we were to visit Vilnius, he insisted on taking us out to Ukmerge. Moreover, he arranged for us to have the best of guides – one of the two survivors of the holocaust which took place in the town in the 1940s (see plate 8.2). A native of the town, if anyone would know of Crystal family roots in Ukmerge, he would. And if he didn't, he would know who to ask.

We spent a whole day in Ukmerge. We first visited the memorial to the killing fields, where the Jewish residents of the time had been lined up and shot. Then we walked around the town centre. No one came rushing up, arms outstretched, calling 'David, after all this time . . .' It was just like any other east European town. Our guide pointed out all the places he knew, and we photographed most of it. But he had never heard of our surname.

We decided to visit the local library, to see if there were any records. Another coincidence. We arrived just as the senior citizens' club of the town were about to put on an annual show – a folk-musical about a traditional Lithuanian wedding ceremony. The entire senior population of Ukmerge seemed to be there, either as actors or as audience. One man caught my special attention – the accordion player. He was the image of Cyril. We asked someone what his name was. Nothing like ours.

And indeed, no one had heard of the name Crystal. We had tea with the librarian and her colleagues, and they had never heard of it either. They promised to do some research, and if they found something they would let us know. Dovid also made some enquiries, when we got back to Vilnius. There are good records of the area going back several generations. Interest in Jewish roots from all over the world – there had been a huge exodus from Lithuania over the years, especially to the USA – had led to the growth of quite a lucrative local industry of genealogical researchers. One of them made some preliminary enquiries. No sign of a Crystal, or a Kristol, or a Christel, or . . . We began to wonder whether this was one of those names which changed at the border. Perhaps on arrival in the UK, the original name was 'translated' into an English equivalent by the immigration authorities – a common practice with 'unpronounceable' foreign names. If it is original, it would be a professional name – a 'crystal-maker' or jeweller. We do not know. And in the meantime, research continues.

Chapter 18
Schizoid man

In an episode of *The Prisoner*, someone impersonates the Patrick McGoohan character as part of a plot to make him reveal why he resigned. Suddenly there are two of them, look-alikes on the outside, very different within. I felt like that, during the encyclopedia years. In the morning I would be editor-man; in the afternoon linguist-man. That was the tricky bit: keeping the linguistic side of me going, so that it wouldn't be crushed by the weight of general encyclopedic data, coming in daily from (eventually) more than three hundred contributors, or by the minutiae of daily updating. We had a boast in the office: die in the morning and (if you were famous enough) your death would be in our database in the afternoon. If you were thoughtless enough to die in the evening, of course, you would have to wait until the next day. The issue was rather academic while the books were appearing only in hard copy; but when the encyclopedia database went online in the 2000s, it became a real imperative.

There was a period when the encyclopedia side won. The first half of the 1990s. Instead of 50/50, the balance was more 80/20. The discipline of writing *The Cambridge Encyclopedia of the English Language* took up most of the 20. But apart from this, my writing was bitty and sporadic: short articles on this or that for periodicals such as *English Today*, new editions of old books, contributions to anthologies, reviews for *Child Language Teaching and Therapy*, books with A-to-Z entries – anything, really, as long as it didn't require several weeks of continuous thought on a single theme. *CEEL* also fell into that category, actually: its double-page spreads allowed a short period of concentrated work on a particular topic, then it could be left for a while until there was an opportunity to deal with the next one. But the kind of popular introduction to a subject that I'd set my heart on writing, and which I'd begun to do in the mid-1980s with the Penguin books *Listen to Your Child* and *The English Language*, was no longer possible. Having built up a strong working relationship with Penguin, I was sad to see it lapse, but there simply wasn't time. My commissioning editor at Penguin tried taking me out to lunch and suggesting new ideas, but I couldn't take them up. And eventually, the lunches stopped.

The relationship with Chambers stopped too. Despite three years of plotting new ways of exploiting and expanding the database, none of the major projects had been commissioned. The chairman, John Clement, wrote me a regretful letter. The firm was now moving more in the direction of English and bilingual dictionaries. There was going to be less emphasis on reference publishing. They had been translating and adapting 'compact reference' titles from French sources, but they hadn't done as well as had been hoped. (I wasn't surprised: translating from French into English, without a huge amount of rewriting, doesn't produce a readable book. Too many differences of temperament. Better always to start from scratch.) Chambers' associates in America had decided that British reference titles wouldn't sell there without further adaptation. Chambers wanted short-term results, but my involvement presupposed a commitment that was medium-to-long term. The conclusion was unavoidable. 'Chambers Publishing' became another phrase gone through.

I made a big mistake, during those years, though I didn't realize it at the time. I then decided to put all my intellectual eggs into one basket. CUP had published one language encyclopedia and were processing the next. The big general encyclopedia had come out and other editions and versions were in the pipeline. I was writing articles for most issues of *English Today*, a CUP journal. My CV was beginning to look like a CUP marketing brochure. And the Press had plans, big plans. The reference group established by Jeremy Mynott had become a major force, under the direction of Adrian du Plessis. CUP were, it seems, committed to developing their trade reference publishing – a controversial move, it must have been, for an academic publisher – and had great ideas. It had begun to churn out high-quality subject-specific encyclopedias like a factory – on Russia, China, the Middle East . . . It was thought there could be more, using as a core the data that we had already collected. If all this went ahead, I reflected, it would leave me even less time for other things. Correction. It would leave me no time at all. Was it the moment to give up everything else and become, in effect, Cambridge's man? Hilary and I discussed the options. It was interesting work, it would secure a steady income. But it would mean not taking on any other writing, at least for a while. And it would mean withdrawing from journal editing. We decided we would take the Cambridge road. 'My boys,' says Belarius to his sons, in the last scene of *Cymbeline*, 'There was our error.'

Because, just a couple of years later, CUP went in a new direction which left little room for the Holyhead operation and me. As with Chambers, economics was at the heart of it. A new accounting procedure was put in place. Decisions about reference books would in future no longer be made within a separate cost-centre with its own internal accounting mechanisms. The Holyhead operation was just such a cost-centre: £88,000 worth of annual costs, to be precise. Under the new deal, individual encyclopedia titles each had to be financially viable. In other words, they had to sell. And they weren't selling. The first editions had done quite well, but later editions not so much. Encyclopedias, it seems, are not like cars. People buy one, and then think that's it: no need to buy a later replacement edition. Moreover, the emergence of electronic multimedia reference works was also hitting sales: an encyclopedia on a tiny CD was looking more attractive than a bulky print edition. It certainly wasn't going to be possible to keep Holyhead going on the basis of the general encyclopedia titles alone. Reference titles with a more specialized, academic orientation, tying in with student courses or professional needs, were much more likely to survive, in this new dispensation, than those which were attempting to reach the so-called 'general lay reader'. But my team at Holyhead weren't geared to producing specialized books. Nor, for that matter, would I be capable of editing them.

We tried to see a way out of this dilemma as soon as it was spotted. At a meeting in Cambridge towards the end of 1995 we thought we could see ways of keeping the Holyhead operation intact. Perhaps there could be an edition aimed at the schools market? Perhaps I could develop a range of subject-specific encyclopedias? Perhaps we could do our own multimedia edition? After all, if we couldn't beat 'em, we could always join 'em. If these ideas worked, we might be able to keep Holyhead afloat after all.

I followed them all up. I went through the entire database and pulled out the entries which would suit a senior and junior school market. The Press designed some sample spreads. There was an immediate problem: for schools, not only did the typesetting have to be more spacious and friendly, the entries had to be rewritten to suit the lower educational level. I added anecdotes, more examples, and pictures, and new entries to suit the demands of the school syllabus. As a result, everything got bigger, and more expensive. Ultimately the idea just didn't work. The book would need to include around eight thousand entries, but that would take up over a thousand pages and not leave much change from £50. Hardly a viable schools project!

What about subject-specific encylopedias, then? I explored two. One was the Press's idea: *The Cambridge Encyclopedia of Child Development*, a book which would present the subject in an accessible way for parents, and bring together specialists from psychology, linguistics, paediatrics, and other relevant disciplines. It was a novel approach to the subject, and the idea was warmly received by the professionals I approached. I had no shortage of offers for writing and section-editing. But as the idea evolved, so did the doubts. Would parents actually buy such an ambitious book? A book along these lines with a student or professional market in mind would surely be a better proposition? That alternative also fitted better into the more academic mindset which was the Press's growing view of reference works. But such a book would need professionals in charge, not a general-knowledge editor like me.

The other proposal was an ambitious, brilliant, beautiful Catherine-wheel of an idea – a follow-up to the two language encyclopedias, *CEL* and *CEEL*. The acronym this time would be *CECOM* – *The Cambridge Encyclopedia of Communication*. The book would again be aimed at a general readership, and would cover everything in the semiotic world – sound, vision, touch, smell, taste, the verbal, visual and performing arts, technology, animal communication, and more. I was thrilled by the idea, and spent several weeks putting together a detailed proposal. Kevin Taylor, who had become my in-house commissioning editor, was enthusiastic, and that seems to have been the initial reaction of everyone who read it. In a summary of responses, the proposal was described as breathtakingly apt and imaginative. But then the sales and marketing heavies were brought in. *Communication* was a much more diffuse subject than *Language* or *English Language*, they thought. It didn't have the same kind of disciplinary support as could be found in departments of linguistics or ELT. There were a few centres of communication studies around – indeed, my daughter Lucy was studying in one at the time – but nothing substantial. Nor did the notion of 'communication' travel well: there were big differences in the syllabuses of a US course and a British one (much more on journalism in the former, for example). Also, the Press was concentrating on the academic end of the reference market now, not at the lower end of the general trade market. So the idea died. It briefly surfaced five years later, like a Loch Ness Monster head, but then sank without trace, and was never seen again.

That left the idea of an electronic publishing venture. I met with a software group, produced a sample of entries, and suggested the kind of searches which an electronic product might allow. We made a CD, and I presented it at an informal meeting of the Press managing body. There was considerable interest – curiosity, even, for the idea of an electronic encyclopedia was new to most. Perhaps I shouldn't have been surprised when one of the older members of what is, after all, the oldest press in the world, came up to me afterwards, asked to see the CD, and enquired where exactly one placed the needle! But despite the interest the general conclusion was: 'This isn't for us.' So the idea was dropped.

By mid-1996 it was clear that none of the hoped-for initiatives was going to save Holyhead. The Press had agreed to a policy of minimal updating of the database, incorporating just the bare daily current affairs – though even that level, some felt, could not be justified in the new economic and intellectual climate. The questions showed the way people were thinking. Could the Holyhead team be usefully and fully employed? Might there be another way of keeping it going? Perhaps the electronic route was the way forward after all, but with a specialist multimedia publisher sharing in the investment, and thus allowing both print and electronic editions to exist side-by-side? It was becoming clear that Cambridge wanted out. So when one morning I received the message which said that they would now try to find a purchaser for the database and its support staff, I was not entirely surprised. It was still a blow, though. Hilary and I discussed the financial implications with some anxiety. Anticipating a Cambridge way of life, I had already withdrawn from my two journals. I had stopped writing Penguin books. I had turned down consultancies, especially those where there might have been a conflict of interest with CUP. How were these sources of income to be replaced? It would take time to build up new relationships.

We felt very low for a while, but after making our feelings known, and a couple more meetings with the Press, the situation improved. They took my point about the sudden change in our circumstances, and offered me a three-year transitional consultancy, during which I would advise on a range of topics in linguistics and ELT. They were also very keen to continue their relationship with me as an author. There were bound to be new ideas to write about, they thought. And they promised to make every effort to find a high-quality purchaser for the office in Holyhead. If both these initiatives went ahead, I reflected, I would stay schizoid for a while. They did. And I did. I'll tell the story of what happened to the database in the next chapter.

The authorial relationship went ahead well; but it took a while. 'There were bound to be new ideas . . .?' I don't think any of us recognized at the time just how much of an understatement this was. When I look back at the 1990s, I see it as a revolutionary decade, as far as language is concerned. Three major developments took place which meant that language, languages, and their study would never be the same again. It was the decade in which English came to be firmly established as a global language, and recognized as such. It was the decade when it was realized that half the languages of the world were in danger of extinction. And it was the decade in which a new medium, electronically mediated communication, became a part of everyday life, offering radically different opportunities for language use than had been available using the traditional media of speech and writing. It all happened so quickly. At the beginning of the decade there was no World Wide Web (1991); by the end of the decade there was Google.

The three CUP books which came out between 1997 and 2001, *English as a Global Language*, *Language Death*, and *Language and the Internet*, are sometimes called a trilogy, because of the way they addressed these three trends in a complementary way. I see them that way myself, now, and acquiesced with that rhetoric in the 2004 synthesis I called *The Language Revolution*. But they weren't planned that way. The idea for the first of these books came out of the blue. In early 1996 I received a phone call from Mauro Mujica, the chair of an organization called US English. He wanted his membership to read an account of the factors which had led to English achieving its world presence. Would I write it? I was dubious. The history of US English was not one which a linguist would readily sympathize with. I strongly supported a multilingual ethic in language use, in which people were able to acquire powerful languages (such as English) but not at the cost of losing their traditional linguistic identity. US English wanted to make English the official language of the United States, and the obvious risk was that multilingual education would suffer as a result. I personally didn't feel that English needed to be given that sort of status, whether in the US or UK. If there was any support urgently needed, it was for the minority languages that were forming an increasingly important part of both countries. US English saw things differently: linguistic diversity was perceived to be a threat to national unity and mutual intelligibility.

So there wasn't a meeting of minds, when I talked to Mauro. But I am a believer in communication – that ecumenical temperament again – and felt that, if I were to write such a book, a linguistic perspective might do some good in influencing the organization to adopt a more balanced approach. And I had a pragmatic reason, for Mauro was prepared to offer a fee for the work, and I knew where that could go. There was a good cause in Holyhead in desperate need of funds. Not me, I hasten to add. But something I'd helped to set up.

Holyhead had been having a tough time in the 1980s. In 1988 it turned up bottom of the pile in a national economic survey – 'the most depressed town in Britain', it was called. Immediately a task force was set up to do something about it. It was called Holyhead Opportunities Trust, and I became one of the trustees. It meant regular meetings to work out ways of regenerating the town, in association with the main funding agencies. Regenerating the physical condition of the town was relatively easy. But how do you regenerate the spirit of a community? I knew of only one way: the arts.

LINGUIST AS PLANT

When you have wide-ranging interests in language, it can sometimes be difficult to know how to identify yourself. What am I? In various contexts I am, or have been, an intonologist, a clinical linguist, a grammarian, a stylistician, a popularizer, a Shakespearean . . . The labels go on and on – and not all can be repeated in polite company. But beneath them all, I am, very definitely, a plant – though not in the Welsh sense identified in Chapter 2.

I discovered this as a member of the team comprising the Holyhead Opportunities Trust. The company that had been entrusted with the organization of the project selected a group of local volunteers to act as a team of trustees, and then made us all complete a Belbin self-perception personality inventory (named after US psychologist Meredith Belbin). The idea was to establish the strengths and weaknesses of every member of the team, and they chose Belbin because that particular approach examines team roles. It doesn't look for a single 'personality' but rather builds up a profile based on the patterns of behaviour that people display within teams.

There were eight roles recognized when I did the test. I could have been:

- an implementer – turning the team's ideas into practical actions
- a shaper – challenging others and overcoming obstacles
- a completer/finisher – attending to detail and meeting deadlines
- a co-ordinator – facilitating interaction and decision-making
- a teamworker – listening, collaborating, and exercising tact
- a resource investigator – exploring new ideas and adding enthusiasm
- a plant – planting ideas, solving problems, and thinking out of the box
- a monitor/evaluator – thinking strategically and making good judgements.

It turned out that I was primarily a plant, and definitely not a co-ordinator or teamworker. That explained why people got to know me so quickly when I attended linguistics association meetings as a young man: I was always raising fresh (though not always implementable) points. It also explained why I didn't like co-authoring and why I hated committee meetings so much, especially when I had to chair them.

There was only one problem. The notes said that in a good team there ought to be people who fulfilled each of the roles. It was inefficient to have more than one of each. In particular, it was most unwise for a team to have two plants in it. I wondered if that included marriage. Hilary turned out to be a plant as well. But, as she never ceases to remind me, she has had to learn to become a completer/finisher, otherwise nothing would ever get posted.

A fine old building had been part of the Holyhead skyline for the best part of a century, the Bon Sauveur Convent School. It was a silhouette known to shipping in the Second World War. But in the 1980s the school closed and the building, in poor physical condition, was pulled down. Just the chapel, a fine modern romanesque building, was left standing. I put together a proposal to turn it into a community arts centre. It was accepted, funding was found, and the chapel, now called the Ucheldre Centre ('i – khel – druh'), was opened in 1991. (The name *uchel – dref* means 'high town' in Welsh. The Centre is indeed at the top of the town. You can see it clearly as you approach Holyhead along the A55.) I became chair of its management committee, and we began our journey dawn a long and never-ending fund-raising road. By 1996 we had exhausted all local funding sources. I had used up all my contacts – including Cambridge University Press. In 1992 they had agreed to let me hold an Encyclopediathon. We would read the whole of the *Encyclopedia* aloud in one day and the readers would get themselves sponsored. Three hundred people came together. I started them off at *Aachen* and finished them off ten hours and 1.5 million words later at *zygote*. In between, people read at the Centre and in some unusual places – aboard the cruise liner QE2, in a Hawk jet above Anglesey. The Marquesses of Bath and Anglesey read entries on their ancestors. Some of my encyclopedia contributors chipped in, including Geoffrey Briggs. If NASA had had a shuttle up that day, the book would have been read in space. The event raised a tidy sum, and kept us going for a year or so. But by 1996 we were at our wits' end. There had been an unexpected cut in local authority funding. The Centre was in serious danger of closing. We needed £25,000 to survive that year. Where was it to come from? Then Mauro Mujica called.

It seemed like the answer to a prayer. I said I would write his book if he would support the Centre. 'How much?' he asked. I shut my eyes and said £50,000, not expecting him to agree for one moment. But he did. And that saved the Centre, for a couple of years later we had access to other sources of public funding which kept us going. And, as I write, the Ucheldre Centre is still there, though – as with all arts centres – struggling to survive again in a political climate in which the government cannot see further than the end of its Olympic nose.

I received some criticism from people who felt that I should not even have been talking to US English, but I took some comfort from the fact that its funds were now helping to support a bilingual art centre. Whether the perspective I adopted in *English as a Global Language* had any influence within US English, I do not know. But I later had several opportunities to talk to Mauro in which I pressed him to work towards a more balanced multilingual ethic. On the arts front, he was unexpectedly genuine in his interest, even taking the time to visit Holyhead and see the Centre for himself.

In the meantime, Kevin Taylor at CUP had expressed interest in publishing *English as a Global Language*, albeit with some adaptation for the more general market. I was keen, because it had dawned on me that there was a popular mythology about. I had heard it even in the British Council. In a parallel development, I had been asked to join the Council's Board. At the time, the Board had a large membership, with people representing all the domains in which the Council had an interest or connections, such as literature, film, business, politics, the BBC, the Foreign and Commonwealth Office – and the English language. I was brought in to field questions to do with this last domain. And during the lunch break at one of these meetings I was sitting in the Council canteen when I overheard a conversation at the next table. 'So why has English become a global language?' someone asked. The reply sent shivers down my spine. 'Because it's a much simpler language than any other.' 'More logical, too,' opined a third. There were nods all round. That convinced me of the need to get the book out there. It wasn't just US English that needed some linguistic home truths.

The book had a controversial reception when it finally appeared. Because I was by then planning to write separately on language diversity and endangerment, I kept the 'other languages' side of the argument to the bare minimum. As a result, I was picked on by some who felt the rhetoric of the book supported the idea of English becoming a global language. As far as I was concerned, my affirmation about the global status of English was no more than a simple statement of fact. I had assumed that my general background in linguistics, and the attention I had already paid to linguistic diversity in my other writing, especially in the *Encyclopedia of Language*, would be enough to indicate to people what my mindset was about the relationship between English and other languages. But when others have got their own agendas, no assumption is safe, and I found myself having to spend too much time defending a position that I had actually thought to be uncontentious. It was only for a while. *Language Death* appeared soon after and put English in its place.

Like most linguists, I had become increasingly aware of the risks facing the world's languages during the 1990s. The Quebec Linguistics Congress in 1992 had highlighted the situation, and UNESCO had responded by compiling a Red Book of endangered languages. In 1995 Nicholas Ostler had set up a Foundation for Endangered Languages in the UK, and there were similar initiatives elsewhere. The news was spreading. I had never thought of myself as a spokesperson in this area, but in 1997 I was asked to write a paper on 'Vanishing languages' for the Library of Congress periodical, *Civilization*. It was a new field for me, and I struggled to write the piece. I looked for a general introduction to the subject to help me write it – but there wasn't one. That's odd, I thought. This is a major development. Why isn't there an accessible book on it? *Language Death* was conceived at that moment (see plate 10.2).

It took longer than I was expecting. I had to do a lot of documentary research. No field linguist myself (unless you count working on Welsh in Bangor), I had to stand on the shoulders of those who had been doing the really hard work, and catching up on all of that took time. But there was a second reason for the delay. One day I got a phone call. It was from a theatre director, Gregory Doran. He had read my piece in *Civilization* and was interested in the dramatic potential of the subject. The notion of language endangerment, he felt, was perfect for exploration on stage. It was an emotional, urgent, and personal issue, raising all kinds of issues to do with identity, conflict, and loyalty. Might we meet? He was directing a play in March at Theatr Cymru in Mold, just an hour or so away from Holyhead. He could come over.

So he paid us a visit, and over lunch we talked about it. The focus, I felt, should be on the 'last speaker' of a language. This was surely the most poignant of all situations. I recalled some words from a short story by Australian writer David Malouf, 'The only speaker of his tongue', and could not express it better:

> When I think of my tongue being no longer alive in the mouths of men, a chill goes over me that is deeper than my own death, since it is

> the gathered death of all my kind. It is black night descending once and forever on all that world of forests, lakes, snow peaks, great birds' wings; on little fishing sloops, on foxes nosing their way into a coop, on the piles of logs that make bonfires, and the heels of young girls leaping over them, on sewing-needles, milk pails, axes, on gingerbread moulds made out of good birchwood, on fiddles, school slates, spinning-tops – my breath catches, my heart jumps. O the holy dread of it! Of having under your tongue the first and last words of all those generations down there in your blood, down there in the earth, for whom these syllables were the magic once for calling the whole of creation to come striding, swaying, singing towards them.

Surely, if there was to be a play, it would have to focus on that theme. How would a last speaker feel? Malouf's story was about a linguist visiting such a person. What if the linguist wanted to record the language for posterity, but the last speaker did not want him to? How would that be resolved?

Greg and I talked about who might write it. He couldn't think of a playwright with a particular interest in language death, apart from Harold Pinter, who had addressed the issue in a twenty-minute one-act play called *Mountain Language* a few years before. He would ask around, but didn't think he'd find anyone who knew what the issues were. It was the classic conundrum: the playwrights didn't know the subject; the linguists weren't playwrights. 'But David is,' Hilary pointed out. It was true – a failed playwright extraordinaire. But it was enough to make Greg suggest I had a go. And as soon as he was out of the door, I was at my machine, and a draft of *Living On* was on his desk a week later.

I got it back, with detailed comments and a general observation. Evidently all I had done was turn one of my lectures into dialogue form. It just wasn't imaginatively theatrical enough. Try again. The second version was much better. 'Now we're cooking on gas,' said Greg, 'it's astonishingly well done' – an accolade which kept me staying with the play as time went by. His thought was that, once it was thoroughly revised, he would workshop it at a regional theatre with which he was connected. But it never happened. Before he could take it further, he became associate director at the RSC in Stratford, and Shakespeare took over his life. I remember feeling quite aggrieved. Shakespeare had had a good run already. What about the rest of us?

Greg suggested I send the play around to some theatres, and so I did. But the reaction was the same everywhere: lovely play, dwarling, but not for us. Language death evidently wasn't mainstream theatre. And smaller theatres had a problem with the staging, which was quite demanding –

given that a whole dying culture had to be represented. Still, the play did eventually get some readings in due course in various parts of the world, and I found a director, Robert Wolstenholme, who gave it a thorough critique. It received a fully rehearsed reading in London in 2007 during an endangered languages week at the School of Oriental and African Studies, with Joseph Marcell as the last speaker (see plate 12.2). Son Ben, now a professional actor, played the visiting linguist – which was appropriate, as I had used him as a model when I was creating that part. Maybe one day it'll get a full staged production.

Endangered languages continued to be the focus of public attention as the millennium turned. Hilary and I travelled to Lund in Sweden to help launch The European Year of Languages in 2001, and to Strasbourg later that year for the European Day of Languages, on 26 September. The issue was beginning to attract the media in a way I hadn't seen before. I found myself writing for a completely new range of magazines, such as *Prospect* and even British Airways' *High Life*. Every couple of months there were interviews with television and radio documentaries, and film-makers started to show interest, notably Janus Billeskov Jansen in Denmark and Michael Havas in Prague (see plate 12.1). Janus's excellent *In Languages We Live* appeared in 2005. A four-part series on English as a global language, called *Beyond Babel*, which included a moving sequence on endangered languages, was made by Ron Blythe for Infonation, a film-making unit within the Foreign Office.

Politically, things seemed to be moving too. In 2003 UNESCO convened in Paris an international meeting of experts on endangered languages out of which came a statement affirming the importance of linguistic diversity and identifying priorities with respect to endangered languages. In a keynote speech I took as my theme the urgent need to promote public awareness of the issue. Everyone was aware of the dangers facing the plants and animals of the world; but few knew about the even greater dangers facing languages. Only a few per cent of the biosphere was in serious danger: over 50 per cent of languages were. I worked out that, on average, there must be a language dying out somewhere in the world every fortnight – a phrase which caught the imagination, for it was reproduced repeatedly over subsequent years. How could we get the message across to the wider, fund-raising, vote-carrying, politician-influencing public. I had two hobby-horses: we needed to harness the arts to tell our story – every one of them, literary, visual, and performance – and we needed places to tell our story – galleries, museums, exhibition centres of any kind. And thereby hangs a tale.

The tale starts in 1997, just after I joined the British Council Board, where there was a great deal of discussion going on about how to do something special for the millennium. The idea emerged that a language 'something' would be an excellent initiative – an actual building where people could go and explore the languages of the world and reflect on the nature of language in all its forms, spoken, written, signed, electronic. As I had just published the second edition of *The Cambridge Encyclopedia of Language*, this was right up my street. We conferred, and came up with the 'World of Language'. Roger Bowers developed the idea from within the Council; I looked after the content planning. We spent some time exploring possible sites in London – and eventually found the perfect spot, a derelict building just opposite Shakespeare's Globe on the South Bank. We went round the Globe, at the time in its final stages of construction and contemplating an uncertain future (see plate 15.2). A collaboration would be highly mutually beneficial. Meetings were held, brochures printed, a CD created. The British Council took care of the bill. Roger costed everything: the government support needed to get the project launched was relatively small, some £25 million. Political interest was growing. Everything was looking good. Then the government had a better idea. It was called the Millennium Dome.

The funds which were sucked into that misconceived project would have supported twenty Worlds of Language. Grant opportunities for other projects disappeared. We tried to salvage the concept, but to no avail. And as the millennium approached, the idea simply dropped off the radar – at least, in the UK. But I couldn't leave the idea alone. There just had to be a World of Language. Go to any major city in the world, and you can indulge your interest in natural history or painting or science, or transport, or war, or a hundred other things by visiting a museum or gallery. Why not language? So everywhere I went I would talk about this idea. Every now and then I would see a spark of enthusiasm which would turn into a specific proposal – I wasn't the only one trying to get such an idea off the ground, and I met several kindred spirits – but it always died for lack of funding. It seemed an impossible ideal, and I was beginning to run out of steam. Then in 2004 I arrived in Barcelona to give a keynote paper as part of the great Forum of Cultures which was being held in that city that year.

The Barcelona-based organization Lingapax had planned a conference around the theme of diversity, sustainability, and peace. I called my paper 'Creating a world of languages', and went through a series of awareness-raising points. As usual, I bemoaned the absence of a World of Language. But when I said, 'We should be fighting for one, in each country,' something different happened. Pasqual Maragall, the president of Catalunya, was in the audience, and out of the corner of my eye I saw him turn to the man sitting next to him and start talking animatedly (see plate 9.2). Afterwards he came up and said it was an interesting idea. And this time, the speaker meant it. For within two years the project called Linguamón was set up with a director, Antoni Mir, a budget, and a possible building in Can Ricart, in the northern part of the city. It was to be called the Casa de las Llengües ('House of Languages'). I ended up chairing its scientific advisory committee, which has since held several planning meetings, anticipating completion in 2010 (see plate 12.3). It was a great moment, and a great start to what will one day, I hope, be an expected museological presence in the cities of the world.

Annual meetings of the advisory committee in Barcelona continued a travel pattern which had become an increasing part of our lives over the previous ten years. There were several pluses which came from joining the British Council Board. One was to see the workings of that amazing institution from inside, for the first time, and to enjoy the company of the high calibre of personnel it employed. Another was to see there was a real opportunity to make a difference: I was on the Board at a time when the Council was having to take seriously the implications of English becoming a global language. No longer was it possible to think of the English language as something Britain 'owned'. In fact, the British spoke a minority dialect of world English. Four times as many people spoke English in the USA; six times as many in India. The English language being taught and examined through the Council offices around the world was in need of a rethink. There needed to be more flexibility, more dialect inclusiveness, more tolerance of diversity in regional accents (no longer only Received Pronunciation). Some of these issues raised controversial questions of principle over identity and standards, as well as methodological issues to do with staffing and examinations. It certainly wasn't possible to sit back and be passive on that Board. Issues came at you all the time.

As did requests to travel. After leaving Reading, I found myself able to accept far more requests for foreign visits, and these continued, despite – or maybe because of – the Cambridge encyclopedia projects. Indeed, once the encyclopedias had begun to appear, publicity tours abroad became the expected thing. We toured Australia twice on behalf of Cambridge during the mid-1990s, and Japan and New York too. For the Aussie tour which publicized the second edition of the English Language encyclopedia, CEEL T-shirts became collectors' items (see plate 11.4). Lucy and Ben came along with us to Japan, and had their first experience of Disneyland and sushi. In New York, a CUP visit brought to light the fact that their offices were at the time located in an edifice called the Crystal Building (see plate 11.3). That was really nice of them, I thought.

I didn't think it was possible to fit any more foreign travel in, but I had to revise my opinion after joining the Council Board. Whereas previously I would judge whether to accept a foreign invitation in terms of its practicability – to fit in with editorial and publishing schedules, in particular – I felt obliged, as a Board member, not to turn down any request that came from a Council source. For example, I joined a group to advise on the development of English teaching throughout Russia, which made it necessary to visit Moscow on several occasions. On our first visit we stayed at the Council's director's apartment. As he opened his front door he turned to us: 'Oh, by the way, we're still being bugged.' That was a conversation-stopper, until Hilary and I decided that, as good linguists, we ought to give our listeners something to liven up their lives. *Goon Show* voices, for a start.

It was part of any deal that Hilary would accompany me. As business partners, as well as spouses, that was only fair: she was the one who looked after all the advance planning, and on these visits she performed all the PR liaison necessary to make a trip run smoothly. And sometimes she found herself in the front line, for several of my talks required a second person to act out dialogues. Once, this role brought her unaccustomed limelight. I was used to being surrounded after a lecture abroad, with people wanting autographs, books signed, and so on. But whenever we go to a university where women have traditionally not held prominent roles, her presence on stage – as an equal to the lecturer – electrifies the audience. After one such performance in Cairo, I was left alone on my corner of the stage, while she was mobbed. That, I reflected, probably did more good than anything I might have said in my talk.

A day later, on that visit, and neither of us could move. Our British Council host had invited us to see some of the lesser known pyramids to the south of Cairo. 'We go down that one,' he said, pointing up to a door halfway up the side of one of them. Up we went, and then discovered that to get down to the centre of the pyramid, which was our host's intention, we had to follow a steep-stepped narrow shaft, just a few feet square. To move along it you had to crouch down almost on all fours and move yourself along, step by step, crablike. When we got to the centre, we were able to stand in the burial chamber and reflect on the thousands of tons of rock above us. Then it was back up again, crablike in reverse now. We staggered back to the car, and to the hotel, woke up next day and realized we could hardly move. Walking along to breakfast was a major enterprise. We approached a step in the lobby. Brain to knees, brain to knees: lift! The knees would not respond. We shuffled sideways up the step. What was even worse was arriving for a lecture later that day. I got myself into the chair next to the podium, while my host introduced me. End of introduction. Applause. Lecturer nowhere to be seen. Having failed to get up off his chair, he was now sitting on the floor, feebly trying to pull himself upright. It took a while to persuade the audience that the disability was not due to drink.

That Egypt trip was part of a tour on behalf of the Council. And visits increased for the international ELT organizations, too, such as the US-based TESOL (Teachers of English to Speakers of Other Languages) and the UK-based IATEFL (International Association of Teachers of English as Foreign Language), whose patron I had become in 1995. I also became a member of the English-language committee of the English-Speaking Union, and did a stint on their Board, and that brought more visits. The ESU is represented in more than fifty countries these days, and has several branches in the UK. Its work to improve international understanding is second to none, especially with the public-speaking and debating competitions for young people. It does your heart good to see these teams of students using the language in such brilliant ways. Only the bad news about deteriorating standards of articulation, expression, and spelling among young people ever gets into the press. The journalists ought to cover the ESU events sometimes to see an alternative picture.

There's nothing unusual in a heavy commitment of foreign travel when you're in linguistics or (especially) the English-language teaching business. It's almost routine to bump into an ELT author at an airport anywhere in the world. There is doubtless a demonstrable correlation between the emergence of global English as a reality and the growth of ELT air miles. But the result of all this, for Hilary and me, was that we found ourselves away from home every couple of months. It wasn't usually for more than a few days, but it did mean a few years of virtually living out of suitcases.

Were we complaining? Not a bit. There was no domestic problem, as Ben and Lucy were at university now. There was no office problem, as now we'd trained our encyclopedia staff they were well able to hold the fort. Portable computers meant that I could get on with some writing when the departure board said 'Delayed'. We moaned about the actual travelling, of course – the jetlag, the security checks, the interminable queues at the Russian embassy for a visa, the way a trip always seemed to coincide with a world trouble-spot. (Nothing new there, I suppose, remembering my early visits to South America.) We sometimes presented security officers with special problems, too. We were supposed to leave Turkey for home on 12 September 2001. It was a time when Ben and I were compiling *Shakespeare's Words*, so I had all the Penguin editions of the plays with me, packed tightly together in a special carry-all. Our laptops and cables went through the X-ray machine without any problem; but when the security man saw the book bag he couldn't work out what it was. A solid mass of – bomb, perhaps? 'Open, please,' said the guard. I obeyed. He saw the books. 'What eez thees?' I stood tall and used my best 'my man' voice. 'These', I said, 'are the collected works of William Shakespeare.' It meant nothing to him. 'Open, please.' We had to take the books out one by one and flip through the pages, to prove they contained nothing dangerous. Because the books had been well used, and the glue wasn't strong, pages began to fly about the airport terminal. Realizing he had opened a can of words, the guard let us through.

So, complaints? On the contrary. We have enjoyed every one of those visits – as we still do. We have made so many friends around the world, and seen so many marvellous places (see plates 9.4–9.13). That's the beauty of it. When you visit a new place as a tourist, it takes you a while to sort out your ideas about what to go and see, and then when you get there you can find the place is closed because it is some feastday or they are renovating. When you visit a new place as a guest, the locals know exactly where you need to go and know how to avoid all the problems. As a result Hilary and I see more in a couple of days than we would ever have managed if we had visited on our own. In 2008 we visited Colombia, for example – on behalf of both the British Council and the Hay Festival, which was holding its annual bash in Cartagena. We were told a visit to the Museo del Oro (Gold Museum) in Bogotá was a must; but our hosts knew it was closed for refurbishment. No problem: a few phone calls and a private visit was arranged, accompanied by a gun-toting guard who kept looking suspiciously at my beard. Perhaps I reminded him of Guevara.

The beard is a never-ending source of fascination, to young and old alike. It is one of the commonest questions I get asked at sixth-form days, once the audience has run out of sensible questions. 'Why did you grow your beard?' I have never revealed the answer until now – mainly because it is such a boring reason. Quite simply, I caught chicken-pox in 1972, and couldn't shave for weeks. Then, realizing the time it saved in the morning, I decided to keep it. It's a trade-mark now, it seems. There was, I believe, a DC-beard look-alike competition on YouTube a while back. And in Colombia, it gave me a new nickname. Queuing for the funicular railway down from the pilgrimage mountain of Monserrate, a little girl of about four stared at me with big eyes. Then she said to her mother: 'E Papa Noel!!!' The news travelled like wildfire among the other children. It was, without doubt, in their eyes a miracle.

Thanks to these visits, we have seen virtually everything we specially wanted to see. Film locations are always high on our agenda. A visit to

Munich allowed us to visit the Schleissheim and Nymphenburg palaces, where they filmed much of *Last Year at Marienbad* (see plate 13.3). And we have been on Brigitte Timmermann's *Third Man* tours in Vienna three times: 'In the footsteps of Harry Lime' (see plate 13.2). It's always different, and in 2007 there was a long-awaited moment: they opened the sewers! I finally stood exactly where Harry Lime stood as the police searched for him underground. If you choose, you can actually watch this part of the film shown from a projector against the sewer wall. Then in 2001, thanks to a dog-leg movement between Moscow and Bulgaria, we were able to see Ben at work: he had landed a part in the Jon Avnet film *Uprising!*, about the Jewish revolt in Warsaw in 1944, and they were filming in Bratislava, where they had painstakingly and amazingly reconstructed the ghetto. Such moments are precious.

Travelling is wonderful, but it's nice not to have to do it, every now and then. That is why, when Hilary and I are asked these days, 'Where are you going for a holiday this summer?' we answer 'Holyhead'. 'But that's where you live!' comes the surprised reply. Precisely.

Chapter 19
Busyness and business

Cambridge kept its word, and in 1997 sold the encyclopedia database, and all its human and technical accessories, to a Dutch-based IT firm called AND. It was run by a visionary called Hans Abbinck (the 'A' of the AND name), and he wanted what we had – not primarily the encyclopedia content, but the classification system which underpinned it. This was what made Hans see dollar signs.

It's not much use having a database if you can't find your way about in it, and from the very beginning we had been classifying every entry into a set of content categories, using our Inmagic data management system. There was no restriction on the number of categories. The entry on *Winston Churchill*, for example, would be classified not just as 'politician', but also as 'artist', 'journalist', and so on. In this way we were able to answer such questions as: 'Can you find for us all the novelists in your encyclopedia?' Or: 'all the French novelists?' Or: 'all the female French novelists from the twentieth century?' Who sent in these questions? Encyclopedia users. We had offered a Datasearch service to purchasers. People used a form on the back flap of the *Encyclopedia* to ask us to find things for them. All this was before the use of search engines and email became routine, remember.

But Hans could see the future. The first search engines, such as Excite and AltaVista, were already operating in the late 1990s, but they lacked good classification tools. Type an ambiguous word like *depression* into one of these, and you would get a hopeless mixture of results, confusing psychiatric, meteorological, economic, and geological senses. If you were interested in, say, the meteorological sense, you would probably have to plough through pages of psychiatric results before you found any. Hans wanted this sorted, and he thought our approach would provide a solution. That's why he bought us. He wasn't especially interested in the encyclopedia side of things, and for a few years Cambridge continued to publish these, licensing the data from AND.

My first task for the new firm, then, was to apply the encyclopedia taxonomy to the emerging internet, and to devise ways of improving internet searches. This was a perfect task for me, as it combined the editorial and authorial elements that had been kept apart for so long. On the taxonomy side, it meant exploring the internet to find those topics which the encyclopedia had not needed. There were plenty. Believe it or not, *The Cambridge Encyclopedia* was not a hotbed of fast cars, drink, sex, and computer games. All these, and many more commercial categories, had to be added to the taxonomy to make it all-inclusive. The result came to be called the Global Data Model – a system in which topics, people, places, organizations, and products were integrated into a single classificatory framework.

How was this framework to be applied to actual Web pages and other internet material? How could, for example, the different senses of *depression* be distinguished, in such a way that someone using a search engine would find only the hits that belonged to a particular sense? I devised a lexicological approach which I called ALFIE: A Lexical Filter Internet Enquirer. The argument went like this. Anyone writing a Web page on a particular topic has to use words about that topic. If we can predict which words will be used, then we can use that word-set as a filter to find relevant Web pages. A page about *depression* in the psychiatric sense is likely to use such words as *mood*, *emotional*, and *pills*. A page about *depression* in the weather sense is likely to use *cloud*, *rain*, and *wind*. The task was lexicographically simple, but very time-consuming. All words and senses in the language would need to be assigned to a particular encyclopedia category. *Rain* would be assigned to 'Climate'. *Quarterback* to 'American Football'. *BMW* to 'Cars'. *Depression* (sense 1) to 'Psychiatry'. And so on. Once this was done, we would have a powerful tool which could be used to classify any Web page on any topic. If search engines were going to develop as we thought they might (this was still before the public launch of Google), the results we thought might be far-reaching.

So that is what we did. AND gathered together a large team of lexicographers at their offices in Oxford, and I taught them how to use the encyclopedia taxonomy. A taxonomist was appointed in Holyhead too, Jan Thomas, to co-ordinate everything. We all then worked our way through the English dictionary – basically Chambers, with some supplementary words from elsewhere. It took us three years. The editorial work was virtually complete by the end of 1999, and a basic software management tool was built by the AND techies. It worked a treat. Type *depression* into one of the search engines, and up came a request: 'Which sense of *depression* do you require?' You clicked on the one you wanted, the filter then operated, sorting the Web pages, and only those which fitted that category came through to your screen. It was magical. AND was delighted, and promptly initiated patents for the approach in the UK and USA.

Everything was ready to go forward to the next stage, product development, when there was an unexpected glitch. AND went bust. It wasn't alone: at the turn of the millennium, dot.com companies were collapsing everywhere. It seems AND had overextended itself, buying up a variety of companies and starting what it called 'data factories' in India and Ireland, collecting data to put flesh on the Global Data Model. At one base in India, a thousand people were finding all the lawyers in the world, all the hotels, all the street names, all the – everything. The idea wasn't crazy. Hans explained it like this: imagine you are a tourist travelling between Britain and Italy. As you go through the different countries, you need information about routes, garages, cafés, hotels, visitor attractions, and much more, but complete lists are lacking and none of it is integrated. If we collect all this information, plus all the associated data on the populations of towns, their location, their main sights, and so on, we will have an immensely useful resource. His vision was very similar to that which Tim Berners-Lee would later call the Semantic Web. It was true. Such a database would be invaluable. But it would take ages to compile, and it would be costly. Too costly, it seems. For when Hilary and I were in Hamburg in early 2001 we got a mobile phone call from Oxford. We took it in a doorway on a street overlooking the harbour. Its message was simple: AND was in a bad way, and likely to go into liquidation.

We looked at each other in disbelief. How could it possibly be, given the way people had been planning so optimistically? But, a few days later, it turned out to be true. Hilary was in the office one morning, in the extension at the back of our house, with the team beavering away updating the database and evolving the taxonomy. I was out, lecturing somewhere. She got a phone call from Oxford. She was to tell everyone to go home, immediately. It was one of those awful moments. When I got back to Holyhead, the office looked like the electronic equivalent of the *Marie Celeste*. We tried to take it in: five years of ALFIE, wasted; fifteen years of encyclopedia content, finished; and five jobs gone – in a recession-hit town where any new jobs were hard to come by, let alone in the specialist world of IT. We felt numb, then angry, then philosophical, then angry again. What would happen to Anne, Esther, Tony, and Jan, who had spent several years of their lives helping us bring these projects to completion? We shook our heads. Surely there was a way of not letting this happen?

Thanks to Ian Saunders, a way was found (see plate 16.1). Ian had been appointed by AND the previous year to breathe new life into ALFIE product development. But it was too late. When it was clear that AND was going under, he tried to organize a management buyout, but that also was too late. He came from a background in sales and marketing, and knew the business world well. I, by contrast, had no idea what a 'management buyout' was, except as a lexical entry in a dictionary. We had all been highly impressed by Ian on his first visit to Holyhead. He was the only AND manager to have visited us for some years, and he immediately grasped what we were up to. So when he visited us again, after the bad news broke, and suggested that he and I form a new company and make a bid for the assets, both intellectual and physical, we were delighted with the idea.

It was the beginning of a new world for me – a world of assets, leveraging, accounts, sales pipelines, investment strategies, business angels, and exit strategies. To begin with, I met a species I had never met before: a liquidator. Oh, my brothers and sisters, never play poker with a liquidator! His job was to get as much as he could for the assets. Ours was to get them for as little as possible. We began by offering him nothing. After all, we argued, the assets were now worth nothing, as the database was not being updated, and the taxonomy without me in charge could not be progressed. In any case, we didn't have any money. We looked the liquidator in the eyes. His face didn't even twitch. He reminded us of our patents pending and told us to go away and do a bit better. We had a think and offered a pittance. Was that a thin smile? No, a curling of the lip was all. After several toings and froings like this, we eventually agreed a figure, secured the assets, completed the legalities, arranged a bank loan, and got the Holyhead operation up and running again. It took us three months. I became chairman of the new company: we called it Crystal Reference Systems. It had two divisions: one side, Crystal Reference, would look after the development of encyclopedia content, as in CUP days; the other side, Crystal Semantics, would look after taxonomy product development, as in AND days. It made sense, and we looked forward to a rewarding (in every sense of the word) life.

It didn't quite work out that way. We had only a small bank loan. We needed investment to get the taxonomy product off the ground. That was where the big opportunity lay. We were now calling it a 'sense engine', which we felt better captured its purpose, but we needed to appoint technical staff to develop the software required to make it work. It was going to take time before we were in a position to bring a product to market. How were we going to keep everyone employed in the meantime? We looked around for investment. I learned the term 'business angels', and went to Cardiff to meet some. People looking less like my vision of angels I had never seen! I had five minutes in the dragon's den (as UK television would later call it), following a presentation from someone else about a new kind of orange-juice machine, to introduce our proposed product. Think about it. Five minutes to introduce the notion of a sense engine, with its semantic and taxonomic underpinnings, to an audience that was used to investing its cash in products of a much more obvious and concrete kind. If we had called our enterprise a juice engine, we might have got somewhere. We got nowhere.

We needed to get some contracts quickly to keep the existing editorial staff employed, and there was only one place where that might happen – the encyclopedia world. Could we persuade a company to give us enough of an advance to keep us going for a while? I approached Cambridge. A fourth edition of the big *Encyclopedia* had come out in 2000. They were interested in a fifth, but sales were not enough to justify the kind of large advance we were wanting. So I had to look elsewhere. I was already in touch with Penguin. After the CUP relationship ended in 1995, I offered to pick up with Penguin where I had left off in the 1980s, and they were still interested. We had a lunch, out of which came (as it always does) several possible topics. One of them caught their attention – a book on word games. It was the first book I would produce in a long association with Martin Toseland, who joined Penguin in 1997. *Language Play* appeared in 1998. And that was followed by new editions of earlier Penguins and a joint book with Hilary, *Words on Words*, a collection of quotations about language (see plate 5.2). That was a lovely project – a marvellous licence to read anything other than linguistics for a whole year – and it was well received, winning a Wheatley Medal from the Society of Indexers.

I had kept Martin informed of the developments in Crystal Reference, and he in turn had made his manager, Nigel Wilcockson, aware of what was happening. So when it emerged that there was an encyclopedia family available, they made a bid. It was enough to keep our operation going for the next few months – the breathing-space we needed. And *The New Penguin Encyclopedia* duly appeared in 2002. It was different in many ways from the *Cambridge*. There was no Ready Reference section, no end-of-entry cross-references, and the selection of entries differed, to meet the more broad-based interests of a Penguin readership. But the core material was the same. And, with an in-house editorial team of our own, we were able to offer Penguin a complete package, including copy-editing and proof-reading. In the case of the *Penguin Factfinder*, we even took over the design ourselves – Hilary, by this time, having become an extremely competent Quark-designer. The books were sent in, ready-to-wear, on disk. And that is how things continued, on the reference side, for five years. We published fifteen reference books for Penguin, including several 'pocket' editions. And it might have gone on, but for the growth of Wikipedia and other online reference sources, which ate away at the hardback encyclopedia market. Penguin stopped publishing the encyclopedia range in 2008.

It was the income from the encyclopedias that got us started. But we desperately needed venture capital – another new phrase – to take the semantics side forward. I met a stream of venture capitalists – VCs (an abbreviation which previously had had only one meaning for me, 'vice-chancellor') – and learned a Great Financial Truth: borrowing large sums of money is easier than borrowing small sums. 'Can we have £750,000, please?' Ian asked one VC. 'My dear boy,' he replied, 'that would be my fee!' But our business plan didn't warrant an investment of millions, and so most VCs weren't interested. Their ROI (another new term – 'return on investment') wouldn't be enough.

Ian looked after the business encounters. I think he felt it wise, after hearing my reaction to one VC who asked me what my exit strategy was. 'Usually, I just get up and leave,' I said. The VC thought that was very funny, and laughed a lot – but he never came up with an offer. I got a tutorial from Ian afterwards on the various ways in which a loan could be paid back. Slowly, I began to understand the language.

It was living in an economically deprived area of Wales that eventually kept us going. Setting up a business in Holyhead turned out to be a good thing. We were providing employment for several people, and that made us eligible for a Welsh Assembly grant. Finance Wales invested in us. It was 'expensive money' – another phrase I had to learn to live with – but it did the job. We were able to appoint our software developers and a marketing man. The semantics side could finally go forward. But in which direction? It was amazing just how many possibilities there were.

With all the linguistic input it had received, the sense engine had become immensely powerful. It could be used for all kinds of purposes. The lexical sets which defined the encyclopedia categories could be applied not only to search-engine assistance (as in the *depression* example), but also to automatic document classification: if you were a lawyer, for example, with large numbers of files containing widely different content, and you wanted them sorted, the sense engine could do that in no time. The sets could also be applied to e-commerce searching – finding your way around the categories of an online retail store. The typical problem here was that, if you didn't enter exactly the right search term, the store would say they didn't have the goods. I remember once typing *mobile phone* into a retail site. Up popped a message: 'We have no mobile phones. Try again.' I typed in *cellphone*. Same result. I tried each phrase with hyphens, without hyphens, with spaces, without spaces, in singular and plural, and got nowhere. Eventually I discovered that the only search term their stupid software would accept was *cellular phones*. How many sales were being lost in this way? A sense-engine approach would avoid that problem, as the list of keywords would include all the likely words and spellings any customer would think of.

There were other applications too. One which particularly enthused me was the forensic potential of the approach. Hilary and I had attended a conference on internet security in Brussels in 2001, where it became clear that very little time had been devoted to the sophisticated linguistic analysis of internet content. Was it possible, I wondered, to spot terrorists, fraudsters, or paedophiles from the lexical content of the messages they used? I decided to explore the possibilities in the context of child protection in chatrooms. A prototype called 'Chatsafe' was the result. The software monitored a conversation as it developed, and if one party began to use 'dangerous' vocabulary it made a note, eventually alerting everyone to the problem. It proved impossible to get it past a prototype stage, however. To do that it needed thorough testing – and how was I going to get hold of real paedophile conversations? A child protection agency had provided some samples on the Web, so I was able to use those. But anything more would require top-level backing, such as from the Home Office. I had already heard of one university researcher being arrested for downloading sensitive material from the internet, even though he had cleared his project with the authorities internally. I didn't want to be a second.

Lastly, but by no means leastly, there was the application of the sense engine to contextual advertising. Here the problem requiring solution can best be illustrated by an example. CNN once carried a report of a street stabbing in Chicago. The ads down the side of the screen said: 'Buy your knives here', 'Get top-quality knives on eBay', and so on. It was plain what had happened. The silly software had found the word *knife* turning up a few times in the report and thought that the page was about cutlery. A sense-engine approach would never make such a stupid error. It would analyse all the words on the page, and deduce that the page was actually about crime and safety. It would then ask for appropriate ads from the agency supplying them. Some misplacements are truly awful – like the German page which advertised tours around Auschwitz. The ads down the side were from an energy company advertising cheaper gas.

We spent some time, and not a little travelling energy, wondering in which direction to go. One trip took us to Silicon Valley, where we tried to interest Yahoo! and other companies in what we had to offer. There was interest but little action: the big search companies had already invested heavily in their existing technology, and weren't motivated to go for something new – even though the new approach might produce better results. In the end, we decided to go down the contextual advertising route. We went over to the Adtech show in New York. Our stand showed off the way the sense engine could produce better relevance in the ad arena. It was a singularly uncomfortable experience for me. Next to us was a stand for some other product. In front was a man dressed as Spiderman and a woman dressed as Supergirl. They were cavorting around trying to get people interested. Not feeling super in any way, I stood at the back of our stand, thinking 'This is not my pool.' And indeed, in an interview for an ad magazine, the line the questioner took was precisely that: 'What is a bearded academic doing in a place like this?' I was beginning to wonder.

There were now eight people working in our house, and the extension at the back wasn't coping. We had to find new premises. A suite of offices above the NatWest bank in the centre of Holyhead became available, so we moved down there (see plate 16.2). For Hilary and me, it was a bit of a shock. For the first time in almost twenty years we had to go out to work. It was schizoid man and woman now, with a vengeance. We would go down to the office in the morning to work on the encyclopedias and the sense engine, and return home in the evening to spend some time on our personal projects, such as my language writing or the Ucheldre Centre developments. On the plus side, at least we had our home back. It no longer resembled a factory, with people coming and going all day long.

But the new arrangement was not to last. Despite all our best efforts, our limited staff and resources were not allowing us to make the most of the sense-engine technology. A few small contracts had come in, but we were not covering our costs. Our VC probes finally bore fruit when Tim Partington came on board; we were grateful for his support, which kept us going for a couple of years. But we needed major investment and expertise to really take things to market. We put the news out that we were ready for 'acquisition' (another term which hurt my brain, for it had collocated only with 'child' and 'language' before), and were pleasantly surprised to find that we were really rather desirable. Several suitors came to our door from the USA and Europe. In the end we chose to 'exit' with Ad Pepper Media, a European-based e-advertising network. We needed someone who was interested in both the reference and semantic sides of our business, and Ad Pepper's CEO had a background in publishing, so this seemed like a promising direction. In 2006, Crystal Reference Systems became a subsidiary of Ad Pepper. I switched roles from being chairman of a company to being a director of research and development – much more to my taste. I definitely did not like being a businessman.

The new regime focused our minds wonderfully. We were now to work all out on the contextual advertising solution – what I later came to call 'semantic targeting'. Other applications would remain very much on the back-burner – in fact, not cooking at all. The classification system immediately expanded to nearly three thousand categories, to take into account the commercial realities that drive advertising. Out went notions such as 'literature' and 'physics'. In came sellable products such as 'refrigerators' and 'holidays in Bermuda'. The sense engine was given a new name: iSense. I suddenly found myself a linguist again – and this time, unexpectedly, a comparative linguist as well as an applied one.

The comparative aspect emerged because Ad Pepper wanted iSense to be available in all the countries where the company was represented (see plate 16.3). So the whole lexical system needed to be translated. By that time it consisted of around a quarter of a million words and phrases, so this was no small task. Also, it wasn't a straightforward translation – more a cultural localization. Think of all the words which identify the category of alcoholic drinks, for example. Some will be brand names of particular beers and liqueurs, and many of them simply don't travel. The drinks on sale in a Italian bar are not the same as those on sale in an English one – or a French, Spanish, German, or Swedish one. Anyone 'translating' the English lexical set for alcoholic drinks into Italian, then, has got to omit the UK-specific names and replace them by Italy-specific ones. All kinds of interesting problems of equivalence crop up when you do this sort of thing – especially when it comes to dealing with sensitive areas.

Sensitivity was an issue which raised interesting linguistic questions. Advertisers don't just want their ads to appear on a particular Web page. They are also concerned that their ads *don't* appear on pages they don't approve of. For instance, if you are advertising children's clothing, you certainly wouldn't want your ads to appear on a porn site. But how do you stop this happening? The answer is simple: you turn the sense engine into a screening device to warn advertisers when they are approaching an unpalatable page. I called this application Sitescreen. Of course, before it could begin to work, an appropriate lexical analysis had to be made of all the kinds of sites considered to be sensitive, such as smoking, gambling, drugs, pornography, weapons, and extreme views. I spent a mind-boggling, soul-destroying few weeks doing a lexical analysis of all these sites, to find out what words they used. I think Hilary began to worry for my moral state of mind during those days. She would come into the office and see me staring intently at an adult website. 'But I'm not looking at her body,' I insisted, 'only at the words they are using to describe her body!' I *think* she believed me.

The Ad Pepper relationship had one unfortunate consequence. Although the semantics side of my company was taking off, the reference side was not. As sales of paper encyclopedias around the world dropped and Penguin decided to withdraw from the fray, the content database began to make an increasing loss. We launched it online, under the name of Find Out, but there weren't funds to develop it. I had always wanted to update all my specialist areas (such as medicine and law) every three years, but this would cost more than we could afford – and Ad Pepper certainly weren't interested in a research commitment of that order. Nor could we compete with the Wiki phenomenon. Even though we operated a rigorous system of quality control, and maintained a daily updating service for current affairs, this wasn't enough. People don't seem so interested in quality these days. In the end, Ad Pepper decided to cut their losses, and closed the encyclopedia division down. Out went my little team on to the streets again – but this time, there would be no return. It was a crying shame – a stunning database, the result of twenty-two years' hard labour from many people, and now gathering dust on an electronic shelf. But that's business, I'm told.

However, the new deal with Ad Pepper had a fortunate consequence too. It freed me up to do more linguistics. I became part-time, in my new role as director of R&D, and I very much appreciated the flexibility that this arrangement offered, because, while all the sense-engine drama was going on, I had been exploring some fascinating but very time-consuming applied linguistic and literary worlds. I must say that, as I've got older, I've been expecting to find myself continually revisiting old topics, and encountering fewer and fewer novel domains. The opposite has proved to be the case. There seems to be no end to the number of new areas of application for linguistics, or new contexts in which some kind of popularization is needed. I think the internet has had a lot to do with it. The internet is so vast now, and so multi-faceted, that it is effectively saying to linguists: remember all the books that have ever been written on spoken and written language? Well, write them all again now, but with an internet perspective. Even a tiny area of novel technology, such as text messaging, can prompt a new project, as I discovered myself when I investigated the field for my *Txtng: the Gr8 Db8* in 2008. There are dozens more awaiting exploration. What's going on, linguistically, in podcasting and blogging, on YouTube and FaceBook, on iPhones . . .? I don't know.

The internet is one of the reasons why there are so many new applied areas for language study. It is opening up huge areas of enquiry for language analysis – spam filters, plagiarism, privacy issues, simplified spelling . . . Very little has yet been done. For example, there is a huge potential application for forensic linguistics, as the Chatsafe initiative illustrated. I've kept in touch with the forensic field over the years – indeed, have become president of one of its associations (a role which, apart from anything else, immediately barred me from jury service) – and still do the occasional piece of linguistic investigation. Thankfully, I've never found myself in court as an expert witness – the time it takes can be horrendous – but the preliminary analysis of an issue, such as a possibly forged statement or a question of telephone voice identity, is always a fascinating exercise.

The internet perspective also applies to language awareness in schools, and the general problem of literacy. I've kept in touch with this field too, and have contributed to it from time to time, through such books as *Rediscover Grammar* and *Making Sense of Grammar*. I also did my time in literacy campaigning. These campaigns became big news in the 1990s, as the new National Curriculum began to bite. There was – and still is – widespread concern at low literacy levels, especially in some deprived parts of the country. For several years I was chair of the National Literacy Association, a network of professionals involved in literacy – teachers, publishers, writers, and others. They felt their role was to raise public awareness of the extent of the problem, and they certainly succeeded. Tony Blair was one person who signed in support of their first major campaign. Benjamin Zephaniah was another. Several of the projects they sponsored resulted in demonstrable gains in literacy levels, notably one in which young pupils from an inner-city London school were given computer Notebooks as part of their literacy tuition. Their scores shot up during the year. How many other computational linguistic applications to literacy are awaiting exploration, I wonder?

Dictionary production is another domain waiting to exploit the electronic world. The internet is now the largest corpus of written language there has ever been, and lexicographers have only recently begun to probe it. My own connection with professional lexicographers (apart from my own occasional forays into the genre) was through Longman, which had established a lexicography advisory panel called Linglex as early as 1979 (see plate 5.3). I was a founder member of it, and am still on it – and I've been struck by the way lexicography has altered during the past thirty years. Once upon a time, dictionaries had few or very artificial examples of word usage. Then they started including real examples, gained from collections of real spoken and written texts. Now they have the internet to explore, with frequency counts to die for. It isn't straightforward. The anonymity of many internet contributions makes it difficult to judge how a usage should be evaluated. But for such areas as language change, the ability of the internet to date-stamp its pages opens up fascinating opportunities for historical linguistic studies.

LINGUIST AS VOICE-COUNSELLOR

Times change as well as language, and that can lead to other new opportunities for linguistic study. As recently as 1980, the BBC was regretting its first appointment of presenters with regional accents. Scots presenter Susan Rae, whom I interviewed for *English Now*, was one of the Radio 4 casualties. Her attractive voice nonetheless attracted hate mail from people who couldn't tolerate hearing anything other than Received Pronunciation coming out of their radio set.

The growth of regional radio broadcasting changed the climate for ever. Local radio stations were stealing the BBC's audience, and they were bathing their listeners' ears in local accents and dialects. As a result, within twenty years regional accents were back. And in 2005 the process was given a blessing. The BBC spent a week celebrating regional linguistic diversity, in a project they called 'Voices' (see plate 13.1).

I was the project consultant. There was a meeting in Birmingham to which came journalists and producers from virtually every regional BBC station, and we hammered out the methodological issues. What sort of people should be interviewed? What sort of topic would they talk about? What other language topics could be explored during the week, in addition to dialects?

I was highly impressed by the commitment and professionalism shown by the regional broadcasters as they collected dialect data that, quite frankly, I'd never heard before – and certainly never heard recorded so clearly. Most people think of dialects in a traditional way, belonging to such areas as the West Country. Today, most of the diversity of British accents is to be heard in the cities, among immigrant groups. The Voices project focused specifically on these new sounds, and pointed the way towards new horizons in dialectology. And also in broadcasting – for by then Susan was back reading the news in her lovely Scots tones.

Voices is still around, in the form of a website where people can hear some of the recordings, read up the results, and continue to contribute their language anecdotes. Go to http://www.bbc.co.uk/voices.

There seems to be no end to the opportunities to be a linguist. Samuel Butler had this to say in his *Notebooks* about 'the choice of subjects':

> Do not hunt for subjects, let them choose you, not you them. Only do that which insists upon being done and runs right up against you, hitting you in the eye until you do it. This calls you and you had better attend to it, and do it as well as you can. But till called in this way, do nothing.

And in his entry on 'My books', he observed:

> I never make them: they grow; they come to me and insist on being written.

That is certainly how it has been with me. I have hardly ever gone out looking for a project. They come in their dozens, knocking at the door – or perhaps a better metaphor these days is calling from the screen. They continue to do so. And they will knock at the door of anyone who chooses to be involved in language study. You don't have to be a highly experienced professional linguist. As many an A-level English language student has found, with just a little bit of training it is possible to do a tiny piece of local research – into school slang, for instance, or shop names – which is fascinating and totally original.

It's difficult to think of a walk of life which doesn't offer an opportunity for linguistic enquiry – and then, you discover, to do linguistic research. I was once asked to do a training course for Sealink employees, to improve their intelligibility over the ship tannoys. Why could I not find linguistic studies of this, to help me prepare? I regularly work with church readers, with the aim of improving their presentation skills. Why can I not find linguistic studies of this, to help me prepare? There are still many intriguing topics awaiting exploration.

Part of the intrigue is that you never know in advance just how extensive a topic is going to be. It hits you in the eye, as Butler says, so you begin to look into it, find it's fascinating, and then it is too late. There is no retreat. The new world may occupy you for a day, or a month – or years. A casual message from Penguin a few years ago seemed harmless enough. As part of the interest surrounding the 250th anniversary of Dr Johnson's *Dictionary* (1755), they wanted to publish an anthology of entries from the work for the Penguin Classics series. That didn't seem too onerous. I would just pick out a few, and there we are! Not so, of course. Every entry had to be read and evaluated. It was a wonderful motivation to read through the whole *Dictionary* – something no normal human being would ever otherwise do. This was different from the usual intensive, get-it-written book. This was a steady, six-pages-a-day discipline. The work has 2,261 folio pages. You work it out.

As ever, one thing led to another. My interest came to the attention of the Johnson Society in Lichfield. Would I become their president for a year? And so I ended up getting to know Samuel Johnson far more intimately than I ever imagined. I visited his house/museum, opened a new Dictionary exhibition room there, and met the Johnson enthusiasts of this world – who are more than you might think. Their annual commemorative dinner in Lichfield town hall is full of eighteenth-century memorabilia, clay pipes and all. The memoir you are now reading first appeared in 2009, the 300th anniversary of Johnson's birth on 18 September. A good omen, they would say.

But that Johnsonian year paled into insignificance beside the John Bradburne project. This literally arose from a knock on the door in the early 1990s. The knock came from Kevin Jones – Casey Jones, as he is known on the popular music circuit. I had been at primary school with Kevin. His parents had owned the house we bought when we returned to Holyhead, and he used to call in for old times' sake. One day he arrived, produced a blue airmail letter from his pocket, and asked me whether I'd ever seen anything like it. It was a letter written entirely in verse, addressed to Casey from John Bradburne. I asked who Bradburne was. A lay Franciscan missionary, who had gone to Mtemwa in Southern Rhodesia (Zimbabwe now) in the 1960s to work with lepers, and who had been killed by the guerrillas when he refused to leave his charges. His cause for sainthood is now being progressed, and Mtemwa these days has become an African Lourdes.

Casey put me in touch with the John Bradburne Memorial Society, and John's niece, Celia Brigstocke. 'If there are any more verses like this, I'd like to see them,' I said. A few days later, a suitcase arrived in Holyhead containing thousands of poems. If they had been placed in a vertical pile, they would have reached my waist. Bradburne, I can now assert with conviction, is the most prolific poet the English language has ever seen. His oeuvre consists of nearly 5,000 poems, some several thousand lines long. His total line-count is over 150,000 lines. Put this in context:

Wordsworth wrote some 54,000 lines of poetry; Shakespeare some 87,000. Of course, quantity isn't everything, and the quality of Bradburne's writing varies from the sublime to doggerel. But I was hooked by his human and playful approach to profound subjects, and found myself in immediate sympathy with his thought. His poems didn't just hit me in the eye; they hit me in the heart. I started to edit them, to make them more publicly available. It was another drip-feed approach, like the Johnson project, but much larger. In fact it took fifteen years to get through them all. I added the last of the collection to the online database in 2008 (www.johnbradburnepoems.com) – but I don't think the editorial job is over yet. Bradburne wrote most of his domestic letters in verse, and doubtless in attics and bottom drawers of his friends and relatives around the world there are poems of his still awaiting discovery.

Probably the most enthralling of all these new developments was the opportunity to work with Shakespeare's Globe. I had seen the Globe when it was almost complete, during my World of Language investigations, and saw a play there as soon as I could. Then in 1997 I was approached by Nick Robins, the editor of its new magazine, *Around the Globe*, to write a piece on Shakespeare's language. It was like renewing an old friendship. I decided to focus on the supposed neologisms that Shakespeare used, calling them 'Williamisms', and wrote an article for each issue. One thing led to another. I gave some lectures for Globe Education, relating to the theme of the current season of plays, and saw virtually every production. By 2003 I was so much part of the furniture that they made me Sam Wanamaker Fellow for a year – an honour named after the man who had inspired the Globe project (and whom I had seen as Iago nearly fifty years before). Then, in 2004, I was asked to provide the transcript for a production of *Romeo and Juliet* in 'original pronunciation' (OP) – a rendition of the text, insofar as far as it is possible to determine it, into the phonological system of the Early Modern English of Shakespeare's time (see plate 15.3). I've told that story in *Pronouncing Shakespeare*, from my first encounter with the wide-eyed and fearful company to my final experience of being hauled up on to the Globe stage after their highly acclaimed performances and getting a kiss from Juliet. 'For an ageing historical linguist,' I concluded, 'that is as good as it gets.' What impressed me more than anything else, though, was the discovery of a new branch of applied language studies that did not really have a name – applied historical linguistics for dramaturgical purposes, perhaps.

It's a dangerous road for a linguist to take, the Shakespearean one. You are conscious at every step of three hundred years of Shakespearean scholarship peering critically at you from the wings. When I started writing for *Around the Globe* I could see that it could build up into a more systematic study on Shakespearean language, but I also knew that it would need a lot of preparation. Once again, it was like fitting pieces into a jigsaw puzzle. *Shakespeare's Words* provided the lexical pieces. Books by Norman Blake and Jonathan Hope in the early 2000s provided the grammar pieces. The OP project provided the phonological pieces. An invitation from Stanley Wells to write an introductory essay for the second edition of Wells and Taylor's *Collected Works* provided the pieces on discourse analysis. And, thanks to the internet, searchable electronic versions of the plays made it possible to survey the orthography in a way that would not have been possible a decade ago. How many exclamation marks are there in the First Folio? 350. Whatever you make of that, it is a fact that enables us to explore Shakespearean language in unprecedented ways. I had turned down an invitation from CUP to write a book on Shakespeare's language in 2000, but when the invitation was renewed in 2005 I felt more confident. *Think on My Words* was the result.

I think one of the major factors accounting for my renewed encounter with Shakespeare was Ben's decision to become an actor. Knowing that actors don't work as much as they'd like, he'd had the sense to do a degree first, and chose (without any pressure from me, I hasten to add) linguistics and English language at Lancaster. How he got the degree I'm not entirely sure, for he seemed to be always in the theatre there; but he did, and as a consequence when later he had some time 'resting' it was possible for us to work together on Shakespeare. *Shakespeare's Words* was his idea, and our first collaboration – a glossary of all the words in the canon that are different in some way from modern English (see plates 14.1–14.3). The development of the associated website (www.shakespeareswords.com) was one of the reasons I valued the extra time in the new Ad Pepper arrangement. 'What's it like working with a son?' I'm often asked. A delight, I answer – except after an argument when it turns out that he's right and I'm not. That's not fair. When we were deciding on the coverage of words in the glossary, I said we didn't need to include *Goths*. Ben disagreed. I said that everyone knew who the Goths were. 'Yes,' interposed Ben, 'people who wear black clothes and eye make-up.' *Goths* went in.

Language explorations, like Dylan Thomas's memories of childhood, 'have no order and no end'. If you are thinking of being a linguist, in my sense, you have to be prepared to jump about from subject to subject in sometimes quite unpredictable ways, as this final chapter has shown. Language inspires the most intimate explorations of human thought and identity, involving heart as well as head. It provides the most exciting opportunities to investigate any domain of society, any culture, any literature, any belief-system. It motivates intriguing connections between traditional divisions, such as art and science, or theory and performance. There is never a shortage of subjects. There never will be, with linguistic study. The slow, steady process of language change will see to that. Whatever language was like yesterday, it will be different tomorrow. That is its fascination and its challenge.

Epilogue

'No species of writing seems more worthy of cultivation than biography,' said Dr Johnson, and 'there has rarely passed a life of which a judicious and faithful narrative would not be useful'. True enough, but one has to ask what it is in a life-story which people find useful. In my case, it is not, I suspect, my tastes in cars, TV soaps, clothes, wine, football teams, or broccoli. Rather, it is the answer to such questions as: How does one get to be a linguist? What is it like, being one? What do linguists actually do? What is the point of spending a life in language? This memoir is an autobiography, but one seen through a linguistic window. It is a look behind the curtains.

I wish linguists had spent more time writing personal memoirs about their field. I have searched and searched, but found hardly any. Danish linguist Otto Jespersen produced one, as did US linguist Yuan Ren Chao; and Elizabeth Lea, the wife of Joseph Wright, wrote a two-volume epic on her dialectologist husband. In 2002 the Philological Society sensed the gap, and published a book of autobiographical vignettes on British linguists. It was a nice idea, and the collection provided a lot of worthwhile detail about the history of linguistic thought in the twentieth century, but on the whole it lacked fire. There is very little hint in those pages of what Johnson called the 'irregular desires and predominant passions . . . which tell not how any man became great, but how he was made happy'. I don't know about irregular desires, but predominant passions there have been a-plenty in *Just a Phrase* . . .

I've tried to answer the expected questions you might ask of a linguist.

But there are unexpected questions too, and an Epilogue provides an appropriate place to acknowledge them. Running A-level 'language days' for schools usually brings them up. After the formal part of the day is over, I always offer a 'linguistics clinic', in which the students can go beyond the topics of the day and ask anything they like. When I started this, I expected that these questions would be all about linguistics. I was wrong.

I remember this happening to someone else. The Puppeteers' Company visited the Ucheldre Centre once, and after the show was over Steve Lee showed the children how the puppets worked. Then he said, 'If you have any questions, anything at all, just ask.' A moppet in the front row raised her hand. 'Why', she asked, 'did the hedgehog cross the road?' Steve had to confess he did not know. 'Do *you* know?' he asked. 'To see his flat mate,' replied the moppet. Thereafter, Steve always qualified his question – 'any question at all, *about puppets*'.

I've felt that way sometimes, but if I had introduced such a restriction I would never have learned what people really want to know. I suppose they fall under the heading of what Johnson called 'caprice, obstinacy, frolick, and folly'. Here are a 'top twenty' of questions, some silly, some sensible, that have come up over the past couple of years.

1 'Where does the name Crystal come from?' There is no record of the name with this or similar spelling (Kristol, etc.) in the records of Vilkomir, Lithuania (p. 233), but that is certainly the name used by my grandfather, William Crystal, born there in 1884, when he arrived in England in 1910. His wife Pauline's maiden name was Goldman. Both names suggest the profession of jeweller. Dovid Katz tells me that Jewish people often altered their family names in those days. It may be that the name was adopted by William to mark a new beginning upon his arrival in England. (Coincidentally, there is also a Christian source for the name, related to Christopher, and seen in such family names as McCrystal.)

2 'How many children do you have?' Five, if I think back to include Timmy. But these days, the question, alas, is more likely to be, 'How many grandchildren?' The answer is (so far) three, as the plate section illustrates (see plates 8.3–8.4): two via Steven (Matthew, George) and one via Lucy (Mateo). I also have fourteen (at the last count) grand-dogs, for Sue (p. 182) has gone in for dogs in a big way, and is now a canine counsellor with a dogblog.

And with one of these (grandchildren, not dogs) has come a new linguistic experience. Mateo is growing up in Amsterdam, and learning English (from his mother), Spanish (from his Venezuelan father), and Dutch (from his friends and teachers in crèche). It is a stunning, natural, unselfconscious tour de force. Millions around the world do the same. My guess is that about a third of the world's children are trilingual. It is another little-explored linguistic topic. But I have discovered the downside: Mateo assumes that I am trilingual as well. There is nothing quite so unnerving as being unable to answer a three-year-old in his mother tongues.

3 'What have you noticed most about getting older?' Once upon a time people would come up to me and say 'You taught me.' These days, the greeting has changed: 'You taught my mother.'

4 'Does linguistics get you the girls?' Well, yes, I suppose, in my case, seeing as I married a speech therapist. I have no data on the question of whether it also gets you the boys.

5 'Have you ever been the answer to a crossword puzzle clue or a quiz question?' Yes. Crossword puzzle: in *The New York Times Magazine*. Quiz question: on *University Challenge*. Having got to know Jeremy Paxman through *Start the Week*, I expressed my astonishment to him afterwards. 'It's downhill all the way now, baby blue,' he replied.

6 'Why did you grow your beard?' See p. 251.

7 'How do you manage to write so much?' It's what I do. (Why do people not ask this question of artists or composers, I wonder?) Factors must include: becoming freelance; good health (nothing serious since the TB episode); ability to type fast (albeit not with all fingers); accumulation of a large personal library, for convenient look-ups; a policy of never throwing anything away; a nose for a fresh topic; and, above all, as mentioned earlier (p. 211), a collaborating wife.

8 'How can you be so often on the radio?' Because I have a studio at home. When we moved to Holyhead, the nearest BBC studio was in Bangor, twenty-five miles away. Five-minute interviews or contributions were impossible, at that distance. So we invested in an ISDN line and a Glensound Reporter's Box, and now I can do short pieces in my pyjamas.

9 'Do you have a blog?' Yes. I started it as an experiment in 2006 to see if language issues could be fruitfully explored through that medium. It's only a reactive blog, though – that is, one which answers questions from correspondents. I'm not a blogaholic, writing about my cornflakes every day.

10 'Have you been the model for any fictitious character?' Having got to know comedy scriptwriters Lawrence Marks and Maurice Gran through events at the Hay Festival, I watched with interest the way

they developed the character of Professor Adonis Cnut, an Oxfordian Quadruple Professor, played by Rik Mayall, in their series *Believe Nothing*. When I met the cast, at one of the recordings, he introduced me as the real Cnut. At least, I think that's what he said.

11 'What do you do when you're not doing linguistics?' Anything non-verbal. Music is a big thing, though when I was a guest on Michael Berkeley's *Private Passions* on Radio 3 I think I must have bored him a bit. But you'd expect linguists, with their penchant for patterning, to be enthused by Michael Nyman, Philip Glass, and Steve Reich, wouldn't you? Also, I spend as much time as I can helping to run the Ucheldre Centre (p. 242), which is as much a contrast with sitting in front of a keyboard as anything could be. The fund-raising side is not so wonderful, but meeting and introducing the various artists and performers is a real delight – though it has its risks. I chaired a talk by P. D. James at the Centre in its early days, in which she reflected on how she liked to find an atmospheric setting for her plots, and cast an approving glance around the high walls and roof of the building (an old chapel) where she was speaking. And also, she went on in a sepulchral tone, 'I like to find people who might be a good model for a murderer.' I wondered why the audience found that remark so funny – until I realized that she was looking judiciously at me.

12 'Anything else?' Yes. 'Name it.' Films. And that usually leads me to obsess about my obsession, which is to look out for real-world situations into which it is possible to insert lines from *The Third Man* without anyone noticing. 'Name it' is an example – the flat-toned, professional response by Major Calloway (Trevor Howard), when Holly Martins (Joseph Cotton) asks him what price he would pay for his services in catching Harry Lime (Orson Welles). I am not alone in such madness, as you will know if you have read John Walsh's cinematically inspired memoir, *Are You Talking to Me?*, subtitled significantly, *A Life Through the Movies*, about how some films do change your life. (Actually, all I am doing is a daily exercise in applied stylistics. Stylistics is the study of how language is used appropriately in all of its situations. I am just keeping linguistically fit.)

13 'Have you ever been an actor?' Lecturing *is* acting, of course, as is learning to speak a foreign language (see Chapter 3). But the questioners are thinking about theatre. The bug gained in school never left me. I joined a local amateur group in Reading in the 1970s, doing pantomime and local drama competitions. Then in the 1990s, Hilary and I joined the Ucheldre Centre repertory company – and Ben too,

before he became a professional. You should have seen my Shylock, darlings. Mwah!

14 'Do you still do any acting?' Some. I used to do a lot of solo shows for various charities – evenings of readings, usually. My *Evening with Dylan Thomas* has travelled the world a bit, as has a reading of the St John Gospel, which ended up as a CD. Hilary, Ben, and I have also done some events together, such as a three-handed version of *Under Milk Wood* for IATEFL (p. 250) at one of their annual conferences.

15 'What was your most out-of-the-ordinary experience?' Being the narrator in Prokofiev's *Peter and the Wolf* with the North Wales Philharmonia.

16 'What was your maddest enterprise?' Starting a small publishing house to publish local interest books, when we returned to Holyhead. We called it Holy Island Press. It never made any money, but it was great fun, and it still produces the occasional book on behalf of the John Bradburne Memorial Society (p. 266).

17 'Do you have any unfulfilled ambitions?' This book has identified a couple. I still hope to see a television blockbuster on language, in all its glory. And I'd love to see a full staged production of *Living On* (p. 245).

18 'Which of your books is your favourite?' Always, the next one. I'm by no means the first to think this. Jean-Paul Sartre, in his memoir *Words*, ruminated: 'My best book is the one I am busy writing; immediately after that comes the one most recently published, but I am getting ready, quietly, to loathe it soon afterwards.' 'Loathe' is a bit strong, but basically I sympathize.

19 'What's your next book about?' I'm never sure, because there are so many topics knocking at the door, and who knows which one will enter first? All I can say is that it will be either about something which I've not written on before, or an attempt at a new genre. I hate having to do second editions and raking over old ground. What intrigues me most, these days, is to take familiar content and process it in new stylistic ways, such as the stream-of-consciousness linguistics I used in my language travelogue *By Hook or By Crook* (see plate 10.4).

20 'Are there any genres you haven't yet tried?', I was asked last year. Just one came to mind. Autobiography.

Index